Bands of America

Da Capo Press Music Reprint Series

Bands
of
America

BY

H. W. Schwartz

DA CAPO PRESS • NEW YORK • 1975

Library of Congress Cataloging in Publication Data

Schwartz, Harry Wayne.
  Bands of America.

  (Da Capo Press music reprint series)
  Reprint of the 1st ed., 1957, published by Doubleday,
Garden City, N.Y.
  Includes index.
  1. Bands (Music)—United States. I. Title.
ML1311.S35 1975   785'.06'70973   74-23385
ISBN 0-306-70672-5

Published by Da Capo Press, Inc.
A Subsidiary of Plenum Publishing Corporation
227 West 17th Street, New York, N.Y. 10011

Bands
of
America

Nineteen ex-Gilmore stars were enrolled in Sousa's second band in 1893.
CULVER SERVICE

Bands
of
America

BY

H. W.
Schwartz

DOUBLEDAY
& COMPANY,
INC.
GARDEN CITY
N.Y.
1957

ACKNOWLEDGMENTS

Much of the material used in this book was secured during the period 1935 to 1941. At that time there were no books on the subject except Sousa's *Marching Along*. Subsequently several books on bands have been published, most important of which are *A History of Military Music in America*, by William Carter White (1944), and *Irish Orpheus*, by Marwood Darlington (1950).

Although a substantial amount of material in these two books was already in my notes, they have been helpful to me, and I wish to make full acknowledgment.

Various libraries, from Boston to San Francisco, have made old newspaper files, magazines, music programs, and illustrations available to me, but mention for special help should be made of the Boston Public Library, the New York Public Library, and the Newberry Library of Chicago.

I would like to make personal mention of Miss Elizabeth Baughman, reference librarian of the Chicago Historical Society, for research assistance on T. P. Brooke; of Mr. John F. Majeski, Jr., editor of *The Music Trades* and of *Musical America*, for research assistance on P. S. Gilmore; and of Mr. Eugene Slick, editor of the *Sousa Band Fraternal Society News*, for making available to me the complete file of this valuable publication.

H. W. Schwartz

San Francisco, Calif.
March 1956

CONTENTS

1 Monsieur Jullien Rings Up the Curtain, 15

2 Patrick S. Gilmore, the "Eager Beaver," 31

3 The "Bigger and Better" Ague Strikes Gilmore, 49

4 Gilmore and the 22nd Regiment Band, 76

5 Gilmore, Madison Square Garden Fight Promoter, 102

6 Gilmore's Most Productive Years, 119

7 Sousa Establishes His Business Band, 143

8 Liberati, Innes and Brooke Start Bands, 168

8

9   Sousa Makes Four Tours of Europe, 188

10   Creatore Starts Italian-Band Vogue, 212

11   Brooke, Innes and Kryl, 224

12   Pryor, Conway and Sweet Launch Bands, 237

13   Sousa World Tour and World War I, 251

14   "Twilight of the Gods," 269

15   The Sousa Saga, 284

16   Epilogue by the Goldman Band, 308

Index, 311

Nineteen ex-Gilmore stars were enrolled in Sousa's second band, Frontispiece

Monsieur Jullien—"a splendid, bold, dazzingly successful humbug," 15

Full sideburns and chin-tuft whiskers made Gilmore appear older, 31

Ned Kendall was the "Paul Bunyan of New England," 37

Boston Brass Band in 1851, 42

The National Peace Jubilee rocked the rafters of the vast coliseum, 49

Two thousand musicians were placed in the hands of J. Thomas Baldwin, 70

The volcanic monster started to erupt on June 17, 1872, 72

Finally, on July 4, all was quiet . . . the World Peace Jubilee had ended, 73

Gilmore devoted his life to the 22nd Regiment Band, 76

Allentown Band (Pa.) had only twenty-five players, 81

Famous Stonewall Brigade Band, Staunton, Va., organized in 1845, 84, 85

Theodore Thomas had presented a long series of concerts at the Central Park Garden, 91

"Jules Levy—the greatest cornet player living," 92

Levy—"the world's greatest cornet player ALL THE TIME," 102

Walter Emerson of Boston, a finished artist, 115

Signor Liberati shared billing with Levy, 116

Signor Carlo Alberto Cappa was eminently well fitted to conduct, 119

Fred Weldon was prominent as bandmaster of the 2nd Regiment of Illinois, 123

The Alexander Band of Wilkes-Barre, 124

Gilmore became a heavy drinker before his death, 137

David W. Reeves became conductor of the 22nd after Gilmore died, 140

E. A. Lefebre, greatest saxophone soloist of all time, 141

Sousa's boyish face was camouflaged by a black beard, 143

"Who booked the band into those god-forsaken little crossroads?," 152, 153

Hardly any event could be properly observed without a band, 168

Innes looked out upon the world unsmilingly, 182

In 1900, Sousa made his first European tour, 188

Six numbers requested by the King were Sousa compositions, 195

"Mark the blackness of his hair ... Mark the close-cropped beard ...," 197

Pryor's cadenza was remarkable for extraordinary agility, 199

Mantia's solo cadenzas were brilliant exhibitions of technique, 201

Clarke could play a chromatic scale of three octaves four times with one breath, 202

From any angle, Giuseppe Creatore was a sad spectacle, 212

All of these Italian bandmasters wore fierce mustaches. Vessella, Philippini, Gallo, Tommasino, 220, 221

Thomas Preston Brooke inherited a fortune, 224

In 1902, Kryl wore his wavy locks close-pruned, 231

This leonine mane was a Kryl trademark, 233

Herman Bellstedt was advertised as "Germany's Greatest Cornet Soloist," 235

After 1910, Pryor abandoned the regulation tour, 237

Mantia joined Pryor's band as assistant conductor, 241

On the podium Pat Conway was every inch a gentleman, 243

Al Sweet and His White Hussars were chautauqua headliners, 245

The Navy granted Sousa special leave to complete the summer tour, 251

Sousa remained clean-shaven, except for the mustache, 266

Liberati's medals jangled on his chest when he bowed, 269

The White Hussars were now black, except for the trousers, 276

Ted Lewis forced Sousa to play syncopated music, 284

This even temper stayed with Sousa to the end, 300

Life span of important bands of America, 308

Bands
of
America

One

Monsieur Jullien—
"a splendid,
bold, dazzlingly
successful humbug."
BETTMANN ARCHIVE

The series of concerts put on in New York and Boston by Monsieur Antoine Jullien in 1853–54 was like an overture to an opera, which might well have been called "The Golden Age of Bands of Music." As the overture, in its developed form, gives a sampling of the musical themes and sets the mood of the opera that follows, so the Jullien concerts foretold Gilmore, Reeves, Cappa, Innes, Sousa, Pryor, Liberati, Creatore, Brooke, Sweet, Conway, Kryl, and many others. Jullien was a prolific creator of novelty in interpreting, conducting, and promoting music, and each of these great bandmasters, consciously or unconsciously, took a page or two from Jullien's book and went on to success and riches.

Gilmore took practically the whole book. Of all these great bandmasters he was the only in-the-flesh disciple who sat at the feet of the great Jullien. When the Monsieur appeared in Boston, Gilmore was director of the Boston Brass Band, and it is a million to one that Gilmore attended these concerts, although there seems to be no documentary evidence that he did. Gilmore was twenty-four years old at the time, and he was fired with ambition to make a great name for himself. Watching and hearing Jullien, he became tremendously impressed with Jullien's success and thoroughly infected with his showmanship methods.

Six years later Gilmore was able to organize his own band. He went to New Orleans and in 1864 staged his first extravaganza, comprised of a chorus of five thousand and a band of five hundred—plus cannons and church bells. In Boston five years later, when he staged the National Peace Jubilee, he doubled this number, using ten thousand voices and one thousand instrumentalists—plus one hundred anvils, two batteries of cannons, and the bigger and better bells of Boston. For the World Peace Jubilee held in 1872 he *redoubled,* using twenty thousand voices for the colossal chorus and two thousand instrumentalists for the behemoth band. Thus Gilmore became Jullien's apostle and showed bandmasters who came after Jullien how to spellbind the populace.

Then there was Reeves, who developed what was probably the greatest marching band of all time. And Missud and Gay, who taught and coached the local bands of Salem and Brockton until they became nationally famous for the excellence of their performance. And Innes, who was trombone soloist with Gilmore before he started his own band and who modeled his programs after the popular style of the "Irish Orpheus." Sousa wore white gloves, directed with a white

baton, wrote marches instead of quadrilles, toured the whole world
for forty years, and grossed an estimated forty million dollars. Liberati,
the dapper cornetist and circus bandmaster, sometimes directed from
horseback. Creatore's directing antics made Jullien look like a wooden
soldier but did not prevent the mad Italian from making great music.
Pryor, after playing ten thousand trombone solos with Sousa, made his
own band a household word through long tours, twenty-five years of
recording with Victor, and the new medium of radio. Brooke, called
"The Popular Music King," toured the great Middle West for
many years. Al Sweet and his White Hussars were favorites of
circus and chautauqua audiences alike. Kryl, the great cornet virtuoso with Sousa, Innes, and other famous bands, directed his own
band behind a hirsute adornment as caricatured as Jullien's mustache
—and besides, he sometimes used anvils with his band.

Such were some of the great bandmasters to come, for whom
Jullien ran up the curtain in 1853.

Jullien was a talented musician, a superb showman, a promoter
and organizer of outstanding ability. He was born in 1812 in France,
where military bands had reached a higher state of development and
where they were held in greater esteem than in most other countries.
He was the son of a bandmaster and he became familiar with bands,
band instruments, and music when a child. He studied at the famous
Paris Conservatory, but he left before graduating and at twenty-four
became leader of his own dance band.

He early knew what he wanted to do—he wanted to entertain
the public and win their applause. When he was twenty-eight he went
to London and became conductor of the summer concerts in the
Drury Lane Theatre, where he led an orchestra of ninety-eight and
a chorus of twenty-four. Soon he was made conductor of the winter
concerts, and finally Monsieur Jullien became all the rage with his
Concerts de Société. He and his handsome mustache and whiskers
were caricatured in *Punch* and he was dubbed "the Mons."

In 1847 he leased the Drury Lane Theatre and began planning a
great series of operas in English. He engaged his famous countryman
Hector Berlioz as conductor and started recruiting his talent. He was
unable to get the grandiose scheme in motion, however, and finally
the whole thing folded.

Undaunted by this failure, he announced in 1849 the *Concert Monstre
et Congrès Musical,* an even bigger undertaking, in which four hundred
instrumentalists, three distinct choruses, and three distinct military

bands were to take part. Three of the six concerts planned were actually presented, but the production was a financial flop and the last three concerts were canceled. H. G. Farmer credits Jullien with giving "the first great public recognition of military bands" in England when he "brought them into his monster concerts." Thus Jullien gave impetus to bands in England even before he performed the same service in America.

In 1852 he completed his opera *Pietro il Grande* and produced it on the most magnificent and costly scale at Covent Garden at his own expense. This project too was a financial failure, and after a short run it closed.

During these years in London, when repeated triumphs were followed by repeated failures, he turned his gaze more and more toward America. It seemed increasingly clear to Jullien that in America lay the solution of his artistic and financial difficulties. He kept hearing about the procession of musicians who went to America from England, Italy, Germany, France, and other European countries—and returned with fabulous tales of success and big bank accounts.

One of the first of these was Ole Bull, the Norwegian virtuoso of the violin, who gave two hundred concerts during 1843–45 and grossed four hundred thousand dollars. How he did it held for Jullien probably more interest than what he did. Ole Bull unquestionably possessed great technical mastery over his instrument, but he rarely played in the classical style; his repertoire was mostly those pieces that allowed him to play with bravura and fire. He was eccentric and spectacular, and he knew what pulled in the dollars at the box office.

Americans shouted enthusiastic approval when he played *Yankee Doodle,* with all the flourish of the bow, doublestops, staccato, and trills usually lavished only on the compositions of the masters. Patriotic fervor and unbounded enthusiasm greeted his playing of the *Grand March to the Memory of George Washington.* The greatest climax to any program, however, was created when he played with the orchestra that war-horse piece called *Polacca Guerriera.* For this tour de force he marshaled all his great powers. He tremoloed, glissandoed, staccatoed, double-stopped, triple-stopped, and worked himself into a veritable lather. His audience worked itself into a frenzy—and his fame mounted like a huge conflagration.

Triple-stopping and even quadruple-stopping were a trademark with Ole Bull. He tried to create the belief that he was able to do this only because of the colossal strength of his bow arm, but the backstage boys said it was because of a slack bow and a bridge that Ole had made more flat than standard bridges.

The prolonged pianissimo at the termination of a piece was another trademark. It hypnotized his listeners into a kind of mass tension that exploded violently the instant Ole dropped his arms and gravely bowed. Everyone could hear the tone fading, fading into nothingness, and continuing to fade and fade and still to fade. Such attenuation of tone, according to the Ole Bull propaganda, was achieved only through extreme sensitivity in drawing the bow across the strings, but the people peeking out from the wings said that while the bow appeared to move across the strings, actually it did not touch the strings at all during the final bars of the music.

The Ole Bull of the piano was Henri Hertz, who arrived from Paris about the time Ole tied up his moneybags and started for home. Hertz stayed in America for six years and is credited with establishing the piano-playing vogue of excessive ornamentation and unending variations, replete with spectacular runs, arpeggios, trills, and just plain arm waving and head bobbing. Henri, like Ole, realized that the rank and file of those who attended his concerts came to *see* him play even more than to hear good music. Many came just to see the spectacle of a thousand candles, which he advertised that he used to light his concerts.

Signor Giuseppe de Begnis, celebrated opera star from the Italian Opera House of London, came to America at this time. Jullien probably knew about him in London, where he made a name for himself by singing the buffo, or comic, roles in Italian opera. He hadn't been in the new land long, however, until he fell in with the local custom of promoting attendance at musical programs by using some special "gimmick." The "gimmick" of Signor Begnis was to advertise that he would sing six hundred words and three hundred bars of music in the short space of four minutes! This convinced a lot of people that they were sure to get their money's worth when they attended his concerts.

The easy pickings afforded these visiting virtuosos were denounced in an editorial that appeared in the Pittsburgh *Evening Chronicle*. This was written in the same year of Jullien's coming to America and may not have influenced Jullien, but undoubtedly similar writings had come to his attention. Instead of feeling the indignation of the writer

Jullien probably was interested in only the part that told of all the money to be made. The editorial said, in part:

A hobby of society at the present day is to be music-mad, and the adulation and toddyism lavished upon every Piano-Forte player of any talent is enough to disgust all sensible people with the instrument forever. From the language of the musical critiques of the Eastern press, one would suppose there was nothing else worth living for in this life but music, and Piano-Forte playing especially. The musical world, following the key-note, look for the advent of each fresher greater Signor Pound-the-keys with a devotion and constancy unparalleled. He makes his advent and the whole town talks . . . . And Signor Pound-the-keys, for having rattled and splurged and hammered and tinkled and growled through three or four musical compositions with long-line names, fills his pockets for one night's work with as many dollars as three-fourths of the community earn in a year, while the moustached gentleman who assists him by quavering, quivering and shouting through three or four songs in as many different European languages . . . pockets one-half as much.

It was the strange team of Jenny Lind and Phineas T. Barnum, the man who persuaded her to come to America, that probably had the greatest effect on Jullien. The great Swedish soprano had hardly returned from America to her native land, with one hundred and thirty thousand dollars net profit for two years of concertizing, when Jullien started making definite arrangements to come to New York. He no doubt had heard Jenny Lind sing, for she made her debut in London in 1847. Jullien assuredly knew about Barnum, for he was internationally known as the great humbug who made a fortune by exhibiting stuffed monkeys, dead mermaids, midgets, and a biological monster of a horse that had a head where his tail should have been and a tail where his head should have been.

Barnum was a promotional wizard, and since he had demonstrated that he could profitably manage a musical attraction in which Jenny Lind received the fabulous fee of one thousand dollars per concert with all expenses paid, Jullien was confident that he could be a great success. He felt that he had all the elements of success within himself: musical talent, showmanship, and promotional ability.

Further confirmation of Jullien's beliefs was supplied by the Germania Society, a group of twenty-five superb instrumentalists who had fled the revolution in Germany and had arrived in New York in 1848. Barnum secured the services of this fine orchestra for his Jenny Lind show. After two or three appearances by the great soprano the balance of the program was taken over by the supporting cast, of which the Germanians were the most important. They played better than any group that up to that time had appeared before the American public. They performed Bach, Handel, Mozart, Beethoven, and even Wagner, some of the numbers being read from manuscript and presented for the first time in America, and a few of them for the first time anywhere. But they had learned and they repeatedly demonstrated that novelties and light numbers included in the otherwise heavy program were necessary to draw the crowds and send them away happy and pleased.

Among the pieces that made such a hit and that would naturally appeal strongly to Jullien was a descriptive fantasia called *Up Broadway*. The music pictured a walk up this famous street, with all its sights and sounds: past Castle Garden, past Barnum's Museum with its blaring band of six players; past a firemen's parade with its brass band, accompanied by the clang! clang! of fire bells; on into Union Square with the discordant music of two bands playing in different keys. Finally a display of fireworks was touched off and the piece closed with the playing of *The Star-Spangled Banner*. It was amusing, thrilling, and understandable, and the "concertgoers" loved every bit of it. Another popular piece was called the *Railroad Gallop*. This was a lively number animated by a miniature locomotive that ran around in a circle on the stage with a streamer of black wool fastened to the smoke stack to give the illusion of black smoke.

That settled it! In the summer of 1853 Jullien arrived in New York, bringing with him over forty picked musicians of tiptop ability, twelve hundred orchestrations of music, and well-formulated plans for spellbinding the populace. He leased the famous Castle Garden, the very spot in which Jenny Lind had launched her successful concert career in America in 1850. Carpenters and painters and decoraters were soon swarming over the old show house to make it suitable for the great Jullien productions.

Meanwhile, "the Mons." was augmenting his orchestra to one hundred players. The forty men he brought with him were superb musicians, some of the greatest in Europe. Among them were Bottesini, known as the "Paganini of the contrabass"; Herr Koenig, great cornet virtuoso and teacher of Matthew Arbuckle; Lavigne on oboe, Reichart on flute, Wuille on clarinet, E. A. Lefebre, virtuoso on alto saxophone and one of the great luminaries later in bands of Gilmore and Sousa; the Mollenhauer brothers, great violinists, later identified with American symphonies; and Hughes, great master of the ophicleide. There are some who claim that Jules Levy, one of the all-time greats among cornet virtuosos, was one of the forty, but if this is true he had not attained his great powers, for he would have been only thirteen years old. There is also evidence that Koenig's famous pupil, Matthew Arbuckle, was in this select group, for he came to America in 1852 or 1853 and a few years later he was a star with Gilmore.

Jullien auditioned and selected the finest musicians available in New York, paying top scale. The great number of musicians who fled from Europe in 1848, following the revolutions in Central Europe, added to those who had been steadily streaming over during the previous decade, afforded a large group of accomplished musicians from which to recruit the kind of performers he had to have. Typical of the kind of talent he could hire was Theodore Thomas, then an immigrant youth of eighteen but already recognized as a musician of unusual ability. Theodore Thomas, who in later years became one of America's greatest conductors of symphony and opera, was chosen as a first violin.

Rehearsals began, and if anyone had had any misgivings about the musical ability of Jullien, these misgivings were quickly replaced with admiration. From behind the handle-bar mustache and the extravagant mannerisms of this fanatical Frenchman stood out a competence and a drive that caused these fine musicians to give to him the best that was in them. He knew exactly what effects he wanted, and he rehearsed and drilled his hundred instrumentalists until they played as a unit and with precision and polish.

As if it were not enough to supervise the remodeling of Castle Garden, audition musicians, and rehearse the orchestra, Jullien was also busy composing the *American Quadrille,* which became such a sensation, as well as waltzes, polkas, and other numbers which were introduced during the early weeks of the engagement.

The announcement that Jullien was composing new polkas and quadrilles carried much more novelty in 1853 than it would today, for both were relatively new forms of music then. The polka was first danced in Prague in 1835 and found its way to Paris in 1840, where it became very popular in the most fashionable society. It did not reach America until 1844. This happened to be the year in which James Knox Polk was elected President, and the punsters had a field day.

The quadrille was equally new in America. French in origin, it became popular as a social dance during the Napoleonic era. It spread slowly, reaching London in 1815, Berlin in 1821, and America somewhat later. It was comprised of five parts which alternated between 6-8 and 2-4 time. Each of the five parts was thirty-two bars in length, but each part often was repeated several times. Jullien was a past master in composing the quadrille, having previously established a reputation with this music form, both in Paris and in London.

While waiting for the opening Jullien also spent considerable time reviewing symphonies and other compositions submitted by native composers. Most orchestra leaders had disdained to place an American work on their programs, but Jullien defied the long-hair critics and performed a number of these American works, much to the satisfaction of the populace and to the benefit of the ticket sales.

Several weeks before the opening, on August 29, Jullien unleashed his promotional campaign. He used all the tricks which Barnum had employed so successfully, plus a few new ones of his own. He plastered the city and surrounding country with posters, garishly printed in black and flaming scarlet. He distributed handbills broadcast and passed out by the thousands pictures of himself, of his soloist Anna Zerr, and of other principals in the cast. To all critics on newspapers and music magazines and to important personages in the music world he sent a huge, flamboyant invitation and admission ticket, printed in scarlet and gold.

In a prominent window on Broadway he put on display "the world's largest ophicleide." He advertised that this gigantic instrument would be used in the concerts and was essential to the stupendous effects he would produce, implying that without such an instrument (which of course nobody else possessed) no performance could equal the ones being prepared. He also put on display "the world's largest bass drum," advertising that it also would be part of the colossal musical spectacles which would be unveiled for concertgoers in the near future.

No doubt the giant ophicleide was physically present in these concerts, but whether or not anyone (including the great Hughes) could produce a tone from it is a moot question. The huge bass drum, however, was played on every program. Many a cannon blast and many a crack of doom were simulated by a tremendous bang on the head of this overgrown drum.

Almost a full column on the front page of every New York newspaper was used daily for the entire week preceding the opening. In big display type the announcement proclaimed: "M. JULLIEN has the honor to announce that his first series of GRAND CONCERTS VOCAL AND INSTRUMENTAL in the United States of America will commence on MONDAY EVENING, Aug. 29, 1853, and be continued EVERY EVENING for ONE MONTH ONLY."

Then the copywriter, unabashed, continued: "Encouraged by his European success, M. JULLIEN has been induced to introduce his musical entertainments to the American public, well assured that such patronage as it may be considered they merit will be liberally awarded. With this in view, he has engaged CASTLE GARDEN. When the improvements now in progress are completed, from both its natural and artificial advantages, Castle Garden will form the most perfect SALLE DE CONCERT IN THE WORLD."

Concerning the orchestra, the ad had this to say: "M. Jullien's Orchestra will be complete in every department and will include many of the most distinguished Professors, selected from the Royal Opera Houses of London, Paris, Vienna, Berlin, St. Petersburg, Brussels, etc.

"The selections of music," according to the ad, "in addition to those of a lighter character, will embrace the grander compositions of the great masters, the gradual introduction of which, with their complete and effective style of performance, cannot fail, it is believed, to contribute to the enhancement of musical taste. . . . The program (which will be changed every evening) will be selected from a Repertoire of TWELVE HUNDRED PIECES and will include a Classical Overture and two Movements of a symphony by one of the great masters, a Grand Operatic Selection, together with Quadrilles, Waltzes, Mazurkas, Polkas, Schottisches, Tarantelles, Galops, etc."

Moving on to the climax which was always a part of Jullien's programing, the following was promised: "In addition to the above general arrangements, M. Jullien will each evening introduce one of his celebrated NATIONAL QUADRILLES, as the English, Irish, Scotch, French, Russian, Chinese, Hungarian, Polish, &c.: and at the beginning of the second week will be produced the AMERICAN QUADRILLE, which will contain all the NATIONAL AIRS and embrace no less than TWENTY SOLOS AND VARIATIONS, for twenty of Jullien's solo performers, and conclude with a TRIUMPHAL FINALE. The American Quadrille has been composed by M. Jullien since his arrival in America, and is now in active preparation.

Several other new Quadrilles, Waltzes, Polkas &c. will also be introduced during the season."

Whew! Such bombastic and sweeping claims sound like the spiel
of a midway barker with a circus. What actually happened? Everything that Jullien promised was carried out—and more. No words
could picture M. Jullien himself, and that was a bonus, an extra.
The opening performance was described in vivid language by an
eyewitness writing for the New York *Courier and Enquirer:*

Exactly in the middle of the vast orchestra was a crimson platform
edged in gold, and upon this was a music stand, formed by a fantastic gilt figure supporting a desk, and behind the stand a carved
arm chair decorated in white and gold, and tapestried with crimson
velvet, a sort of throne for the musical monarch. He steps forward,
and we see those ambrosial whiskers and moustaches which *Punch*
has immortalized; we gaze upon that immaculate waistcoat, that tran-
scendant shirt front, and that unutterable cravat which will be read
about hereafter; the monarch graciously and gracefully accepts the
tumultuous homage of the assembled thousands, grasps his sceptre,
and the violins wail forth the first broken phrase of the overture to
Der Freyschutz. The overture is splendidly performed. . . . The discipline of his orchestra is marvelous. He obtains from fifty strings a
pianissimo which is scarcely audible and he makes one hundred
instruments stop in the midst of a fortissimo which seems to lift the
roof, as if a hundred men dropped dead at the movement of his hand.

Later, even in Boston, where John S. Dwight, editor of the *Journal
of Music,* was the oracle on all things musical, Jullien drew reluctant
praise. "Jullien *can* play the best kind of music," the erudite Dwight
conceded. "If he makes a colossal toy of the orchestra in his quadrilles and polkas, he has also his Mendelssohn and Mozart nights,
in which he proves his love and power of interpreting the finest
works. . . . We were present last week at his Mendelssohn night, and
never before have we so felt the power and beauty of the A minor or
Scotch Symphony."

Among the compositions by native Americans were four symphonies by William Henry Fry, a prominent New York musical person-
age. The names of the four were *Childe Harold, A Day in the Country,
The Breaking Heart,* and *Santa Claus.*

Before and after Jullien arrived in America, Fry was in a heated
controversy with publishers and critics about the relative merits of
native American compositions. Jullien may have smelled good box

office in playing such controversial music, for it was sure to start a lot of comment. He may even have liked the music and considered it of sufficient merit to warrant a place on his programs.

Probably the real reason that Jullien played Fry's symphonies was because they were made to order for a Jullien program. They were descriptive music, especially *Santa Claus,* and that was the kind of music Jullien hardly could obtain enough of. The average patron attending a Jullien concert had to have a story of some kind that went along with the music to keep his attention from wandering, to give the music some meaning. Absolute music, whose appeal is the pure sensations of tone and structure, held no interest for the average concertgoer in Jullien's time.

The *Santa Claus* symphony was the story of Christmas, from the Star of Bethlehem and the Nativity scene down through the ages to the Christmas of our childhood. The music told of Santa Claus and his reindeer, and the patrons could hear the hoofs clatter, the sleigh bells jingle, the snowstorm howl, the whip crack, Santa laugh. To appropriate music the cold starry night turned to warm sunny morning; the mother roused her children, who scampered around the Christmas tree, opened their toys, laughed, and chattered. For the finale the composer introduced "an orchestra of drums . . . to represent the rolling of the celestial spheres . . . towering sonority to crown a long work designed to be of religious and romantic character."

As Jullien no doubt hoped and expected, the playing of *Santa Claus* caused much comment in the newspapers and music journals. One critic, writing in the *Musical World,* belittled the composition and dismissed it with a few curt words. He called it "a kind of extravaganza which moves the audience to laughter, entertaining them seasonably with imitated snow-storms, trotting horses, sleighbells, cracking whips, etc."

In reply composer Fry inserted a protest in the same journal, pointing out that the *Santa Claus* symphony was the longest composition on a single unified theme that had ever been written, and further that any composition that began in heaven, then descended to hell, climbed back to heaven, thence down to earth to portray such a precious thing as the joy of a family on Christmas morning had more merit than any critics had been willing to admit. Jullien had stirred up a hornets' nest, but the buzzing only added to hosannas and anathemas which grew in volume as concert followed concert.

Jullien reached the all-time high of his career the night he put on the *Firemen's Quadrille*. This was the quadrille to end all quadrilles. Historians have neglected to tell us what "Classical Overture and two Movements of a Symphony by one of the great masters" he played on the program that night, or whether Anna Zerr, his soloist, sang *Old Folks at Home* or *Old Dog Tray*. When the concert was over, all the patrons and critics could talk about was the quadrille.

Just before the quadrille was to be played, the audience was warned that something unusual was about to take place. This was more than the casual pronouncement "You ain't seen nothin' yet," which Al Jolson used to shout at his audience. There was something mysterious and ominous about it. After a sufficiently impressive pause Monsieur Jullien arose from his throne of white and crimson and gold, wiped his perspiring brow with his gorgeous silk handkerchief, picked up his baton from the gilded music desk, and with a scarcely perceptible beat the music started quietly and slowly. It was night, the new moon was shining dimly, the leaves in the trees were moved noiselessly by a soft breeze, the inhabitants were sound asleep behind closed doors and black windows; all was peaceful and innocent of harm.

Then a discordant phrase punctuated the music, the tempo became faster, the orchestra increased in volume, the brass began to blare forth, above the tutti screeched the piccolo like an eagle above the battle, the patrons began to move to the edge of their seats and lean forward. Suddenly the audience was galvanized by the loud and persistent clang! clang! clang! of real fire bells. Flames burst from the ceiling. Three companies of New York firemen rushed in with ladders, dragging their hoses behind them. Real water began streaming from the nozzles. False wood panels were splintered with fire axes, glass was broken, firemen shouted commands and warnings. Men in the audience arose from their seats, bewildered. Women screamed and some of them fainted. The orchestra was now playing at a tremendous fortissimo and in the most agitated manner. By this time ushers saw that things were out of hand, and they began running up and down the aisles shouting that it was all a part of the show. Nobody believed them. They looked pleadingly toward the maestro, showing plainly that they thought he should stop the show. Jullien could see that he had gone too far, and he switched the disciplined orchestra quickly into the blaring strains of the *Doxology*. For a moment this reverenced hymn sounded a little as if the Day of Judgment had come, and a new wave of terror spread through the house. Then the fires went out and the firemen began an orderly exit. Those who had not suffered apoplexy started to sing timidly with the orchestra. The volume of singing rapidly increased, and finally relief came and the end of the program came, with the audience standing and singing.

Jullien was "good copy," and the newspaper and magazine scribes took advantage of their opportunities. They were generally agreed that his playing of the classics was superb, for never before had they heard such power and authority in the interpretation of these works. But they ridiculed his mannerisms and his innovations and his striving after overpowering effects. They were flabbergasted when they heard members of the orchestra, some of them playing and some of them singing parts from Auber's opera *La Muette de Portici*, a form of rendition made common by Al Sweet and his Singing Band around 1900 and more recently by Fred Waring and his Pennsylvanians.

In Jullien's time the technique of directing was by no means standardized, and the baton was used by most directors as a simple time beater. Jullien used it to cue in the various sections of the orchestra and to control dynamics, a practice that has become common today. To the critics of those days this seemed superfluous and ostentatious, although there is little doubt that the audience enjoyed it immensely. One writer was particularly sarcastic:

"Other conductors use their batons to direct their orchestras. Not so with M. Jullien. His band is so well drilled at rehearsals that it conducts itself at performances, while he uses his baton to direct the audience. He does everything with that unhappy bit of wood, but to put it to its legitimate purpose of beating time. The music is magnificent, and so is the humbug, as M. Jullien caps its climax by subsiding into his crimson gilded throne, overwhelmed by his exertions, and a used up man."

Many of the new ways of producing, interpreting, and conducting music which Jullien introduced and which so shocked and offended the critics in 1853 have become justified and accepted through usage, especially in the band field. There are some, however, which are still pure bunkum. The one which today seems the most ludicrous had to do with Jullien's playing of Beethoven. Whenever a Beethoven composition appeared in the program, its playing was preceded by a ceremony such as a priest performs before the altar. Jullien would pose solemnly beside his music stand and face the audience. He would then go through a ritual which suggested the washing of hands but which was only the turning back over the cuffs of his black coat the white, lacy, very wide wristbands attached to his shirt sleeves. At a signal from Jullien a caparisoned flunky would come forward, holding in his hands a silver salver. On the tray lay a pair of white kid gloves and a jeweled baton. With deliberate motions Jullien would pick up the gloves and put them on with great care. Then he would pick up the jeweled baton. The flunky would then bow in authentic oriental style and disappear. In an atmosphere of quiet and reverence that was almost stifling, Jullien would then turn slowly and face the orchestra. Standing then in a suppliant pose, with white gloves and jeweled baton lifted heavenward, he would pause for an instant. Finally, the ritual to the great Beethoven completed, he would proceed with the music.

Jullien was called a charlatan, a fop, a trickster, and a dealer in claptrap, but the favorite word was humbug. Anything new is strange and therefore questionable, and Jullien was a great innovator. He had slight respect for tradition as such, and he was bound to offend those who adhered rigidly to classic forms and manners. No one accused him of sloppy performance or of musical incompetence, but many were offended by the wide liberties he took in achieving the spectacular and vivid effects he was always striving for. This feeling is fairly stated by a writer in the *Courier and Enquirer:*

M. Jullien is a humbug. . . . Let us not be misunderstood. M. Jullien is not a pitiful humbug, or a timorous humbug, or worse than all, an unsuccessful humbug; he is a splendid, bold, dazzlingly successful humbug; one who deserves his great success almost as much as if he had not employed the means by which he has achieved it.

With the words "a splendid, bold, dazzlingly successful humbug" ringing in his ears, in June 1854 Jullien gathered up his profits and went back to England, only to lose everything in a few years. In 1856, Covent Garden burned, destroying his entire library of music, including all his original and famous quadrilles and polkas. The following year he lost five to six thousand pounds in an unsuccessful opera venture. Starting again from scratch, he gathered together a small orchestra and began touring the small towns of England. Harassed by his creditors, he was compelled to fly to France. This was all very bitter medicine, and it soon broke him spiritually and mentally. In 1860 the end came for Jullien in the confines of an insane asylum near Paris.

By this time, however, Gilmore had organized his own band and had set forth as Jullien's apostle. During the following three decades Gilmore outdid Jullien and earned for himself immortality as "Father of the American Band." Two days after Gilmore laid down his baton and died on September 24, 1892, Sousa played the first concert with his own band, the beginning of forty years of illustrious band performance. Together, the Gilmore and Sousa bands span practically the entire golden age of bands of music in America.

Two

PATRICK S. GILMORE
THE "EAGER BEAVER"

*Full sideburns and chin-tuft whiskers
made Gilmore appear older
than his twenty-seven years.*

Less than two years after Patrick Gilmore sat under Jullien's spell at the Boston concerts, he was the subject on everyone's tongue in Salem, Massachusetts. Gilmore had been in Salem a little more than a year, but during this time he had become very popular as director of the Salem Brass Band and as an exceptionally talented cornet soloist. Early in December 1856, Gilmore, ever a good promoter of his band concerts, had announced the appearance of Edward (Ned) Kendall as soloist with the Salem band. Kendall was celebrated all over New England as the greatest keyed bugle virtuoso of his day. In addition to playing solos with the band Kendall was to stage a contest with Gilmore in the playing of the *Wood Up Quickstep,* Gilmore on his cornet and Kendall on his keyed bugle.

The concert was held in Mechanic Hall, a drill hall of the Mechanic Light Infantry, and the place was packed. Admission was twenty-five cents, paid at the entrance. Beyond the rows of seats and at the far end of the hall, opposite the entrance, was a low bandstand, occupied by chairs and music stands for about twenty players. Two potbellied stoves, one at each end of the hall, barely took the chill off the cold, damp air, and the spectators sat wrapped in mufflers and coats. Oil lamps, swung from the rafters by long chains, flickered and smoked.

The Salem Brass Band, although made up of civilians, was "attached" to the militia company, playing drills, reviews, and parades. Only the leader drew a salary, the individual players donating their services as a patriotic duty and for the fun of playing. However, they participated in the revenue obtained from engagements outside military functions, and at the end of a good year, after deducting cost of music and incidental expenses, each man might receive as much as ten or twelve dollars.

Directly behind the bandstand the musicians were removing their instruments from cases and flannel bags. After the instruments were out, the players would blow their breath through them to warm them up, or they would cup their hands into double fists and blow warm breath through them to thaw out their fingers. Others were standing around with their horns under their arms and their hands in their pockets. Soon most of them were playing exercises or snatches of melody to limber up their instruments and fingers and to get some circulation in their lips.

Gradually the cacophony died down and a tuning note, played by the cornet, began to be heard. Finally all was quiet behind the bandstand and the men in single file marched to their places. People in the audience stopped their chatter as the last man seated himself on the bandstand, and for a brief moment the only sound in the hall was the sputtering of the oil lamps.

Suddenly, from a small anteroom, out bounded a young man who walked rapidly to the bandstand and mounted the director's podium. He turned quickly to face the audience, smiled, and made a low bow. The audience broke into applause. Standing erect once more, he acknowledged the continued applause by nodding his head and smiling. Full sideburns and chin-tuft whiskers made him appear older than his twenty-seven years, but his every movement and gesture betrayed his bubbling enthusiasm, dynamic energy, and contagious friendliness. No wonder Patrick Gilmore was the talk of Salem and surrounding country.

With a military about-face he stood before his music stand, picked up his baton, extended his arms for an instant, and then gave the down beat to start *The Railroad* overture. This was followed by the *Rover Quickstep*, an original composition by Harvey Dodworth, famous contemporary bandmaster and composer of New York.

Upon the completion of this number and while Gilmore was acknowledging the applause, Kendall arose from a chair in which he had been sitting behind the bandstand, walked to the podium, and stood beside Gilmore. Gilmore announced Kendall as "the world's most famous keyed-bugle soloist," and the audience applauded enthusiastically.

Ned Kendall acknowledged the applause with a gracious, even grave bow. He was twenty years older than Gilmore and stood a head taller. His black mustache and tuft of black whiskers on his lower lip made his face appear severe, but there was an unmistakable kindness in his eyes. Gilmore turned to the band, but over his left shoulder he kept his eyes on Kendall. Kendall put his bugle to his lips, and as he started the first note, Gilmore gave the down beat, following the brisk tempo set by the soloist in *The Wrecker's Daughter*.

The prolonged applause which this solo created called for an encore, and Kendall announced he next would play *Winslow Blues*. This number aroused even greater applause, and from the audience came a shouted request for *Money Musk,* a piece for which Kendall was especially famous. The band was familiar with this popular solo, and when Kendall turned inquiringly to the director, Gilmore nodded and asked the band to turn to this number. The applause which greeted the playing of *Money Musk* continued until the soloist and director had retired to the anteroom at the back of the stand. The concert so far had been a triumph for Kendall.

During the intermission the audience engaged in comments on Kendall's playing. Some of the old-timers opined that, although Kendall undoubtedly was good, they would rather listen to Francis Morse, first leader of the Salem band and an accomplished bugle player. They recalled the thrill Morse always gave his audience when he played *Away with Melancholy,* with variations. He was noted for his sweet, clear tone. Others, who could not go back as far as Francis

Morse, recalled the amazing technique of Jerome Smith, who had succeeded Morse. His forte was *Lily Dale,* and it was the opinion of many in the audience that in his prime Smith could outplay Kendall.

This chatter gradually died down in expectation of the beginning of the second half of the program, during which the long-anticipated contest would be held. It was almost quiet when from the little ante-room came Gilmore and Kendall, talking amiably to each other. Each had his instrument under his arm, Kendall his silver E♭ bugle and Gilmore his silver E♭ cornet. Gilmore mounted the bandstand and placed his cornet on his music stand, while Kendall seated himself in a chair directly below. The opening number was a brisk piece called the *Ogden Polka.* Polite hand clapping greeted the playing of this piece, and it was evident that the audience was impatient for the main event.

Gilmore then announced that he and Ned Kendall would play the *Wood Up Quickstep* with the band, "one of the most difficult of bugle solos, attempted by only the most accomplished performers." First Mr. Kendall would play a passage on his keyed bugle, then, at the repeat sign, Gilmore would play the same passage on his cornet, and so on.

The tension and suspense could be felt by everyone in the audience. Francis Morse had played the *Wood Up Quickstep* once, several years after it had been published in 1835, and he had included it on the program occasionally afterward, but not often. When Jerome Smith first took over the band, he also had performed the number several times, but during the last few years of his tenure, when he was weakened by sickness, he had not felt up to it. It was a solo acclaimed generally as the tour de force in the repertoire of the great performers. And now it was to be played by two great soloists, on a single program!

Gilmore turned to the band, raised his baton, watched Kendall wet his mouthpiece and place it against his lips, and then he came down with his baton to start the music. The first eight bars were in 2–4 time, and Kendall's bugle pealed forth clear and stirring. At the repeat sign Gilmore spun around toward the audience and played the same passage, beating time for the band with a slight up-and-down movement of his cornet. Except that Gilmore's cornet sounded somewhat more brilliant the two passages were identical.

Immediately Kendall launched into the next sixteen bars. This passage was in 6–8 time, and with two beats to the measure in the same tempo, the eighth notes rolled out like triplets. Sharp rests followed by sixteenth notes produced the impression of speed-up, requiring faster execution. At the repeat sign Gilmore turned toward the audience with the precision of a mechanical man and repeated the passage. Confidence and ease of execution marked the playing by Gilmore.

Simultaneously Gilmore gave the beat with his right hand for the next note and dropped his cornet in his left hand, and Kendall began the most difficult part of the solo. This part consisted of a series of sixteenth notes slurred into dotted eighth notes, followed by an eighth rest. Such music required precision tonguing, and the slurred intervals, some of them as much as a whole octave, called for clever lipping. It was superb playing, and the audience were in such ecstasy that they started a ripple of applause. It was cut short, however, by Gilmore's cornet. Giving the band the beat by bobbing his cornet slightly up and down, Gilmore perceptibly increased the tempo. He raced through the passage, each note as clean and true and clear as a bell.

Unperturbed, Kendall accepted the faster tempo and breezed through the next eight bars of broken notes and tricky fingering. Gilmore followed in his sure, clean style. While Gilmore was playing, Kendall fingered the keys of his bugle absently and looked a little tired.

And now came the home stretch of twenty bars. Kendall started forte but contrasted the next phrase piano. On he romped, a forte phrase being followed by a piano phrase. It was a bouncing kind of music and Kendall made the most of it, taking the occasional grace notes smoothly in his stride. On the closing five bars he really "let her out," ending with a ringing tone that was positive and authoritative. But when he had finished he was visibly spent and a little flustered.

Before Kendall had regained his composure, Gilmore was lilting along the home stretch on his cornet, and at a faster and faster pace. With faultless technique and with great brilliancy of tone, he ended in a forte galop that left his listeners breathless. Recovering quickly, the audience broke forth with loud and prolonged applause. Gilmore took Kendall's hand and shook it warmly. Then he propelled Kendall forward to take the applause alone, after which the two of them, hand in hand, bowed their thanks to the enthusiastic audience.

During the prolonged applause Pat turned to Ned and said something. A blank look passed over Ned's face for an instant, then he smiled and nodded. Pat walked to the edge of the bandstand, and motioned to a spectator to hand up an empty chair, which he took and placed in the cornet section. Then he sat down and laid his cornet across his lap. Kendall walked to the music stand, took Gilmore's baton, stretched out his long arms for an instant, and then the final number started. Kendall was directing the band, and Gilmore was playing like an ordinary bandsman, under the baton of the great Ned Kendall.

Here was climax built on climax, a feat of showmanship which was to become the trademark of the fabulous Pat Gilmore. Here was good music coupled with audience participation. Everyone understood the meaning of this generous gesture by Gilmore, and an air of good fellowship and friendliness spread through the hall. When the piece ended, the applause was spontaneous and enthusiastic, and Kendall and Gilmore enjoyed it equally.

After Gilmore and Kendall stepped down from the bandstand, most of the people began filing out, but many friends came forward and milled around the musicians, offering further congratulations by word and handshake. As the last of them turned to leave, they looked back and saw Pat Gilmore and Ned Kendall walking to the small anteroom with their arms across each other's shoulders.

It was pretty generally agreed throughout Salem that Gilmore had outplayed the great Kendall, and there is little doubt of it today, for the *Wood Up Quickstep* is regarded as a relatively easy piece by the average cornet soloist. On the keyed bugle, however, this piece presented difficulties which could be surmounted only by the individual prowess of the player, and Kendall had built his fame on overcoming these difficulties to a degree attained by few if any other bugle players.

Although in Europe the cornet had generally superseded the keyed bugle ten or fifteen years before, in America at this time it was relatively new, and the keyed bugle was still used to a considerable degree. The cornet was superior to the keyed bugle in every way, and the day of the keyed bugle was over. These two instruments were opposite in acoustical principle, the opening of keys on the bugle sharpening the open tones, whereas the use of valves on the cornet flattened the open tones. Other instruments with the "clapper keys," such as the alto, tenor, and bass ophicleides, had also been made obsolete by the rotary and piston valve instruments, variously

Ned Kendall was the "Paul Bunyan of New England."
No feat on the keyed bugle was too difficult for him.

called originally saxhorns, saxtrombas, and ebor cornos but today known as alto and baritone horns, euphoniums, and bass tubas.

Edward (Ned) Kendall has become a legend in the annals of bands. He is the Paul Bunyan of New England. There was no feat on the E♭ keyed bugle too difficult for him. What was absolutely impossible for others was very easy for him. He could play higher and longer and faster and sweeter than any man who ever put the keyed bugle to his lips, so it was said. He traveled rather widely as soloist, and there was hardly an important band in New England before which he hadn't played at least once. As experienced bandsmen listened to Kendall play music which was impossible for them to play, an aura of magic and mysticism grew up about him. Having heard him play what was beyond their own powers, these players put no limits whatsoever on the marvels Ned Kendall could perform, and stories about his exploits grew wilder and wilder. Many of these stories are apocryphal, but there is a basis of fact in most of them.

A story is told of a military parade in Charlestown, Massachusetts, when a band next in line failed to salute Kendall's Boston Brass Band as it passed. This was a courtesy observed at the time, and Kendall considered the other band's failure to salute his band as an unforgivable slight. He told the men in his band: "Just for that, boys, we'll see to it that their band plays nary a note during the rest of the parade. We'll just keep playing all the way." And that is what the Boston Brass Band did. Kendall was noted for his "leather lip," and he played one piece right after another at the top of his lungs and without a rest. He was a powerful player and could drown out a whole band almost unaided.

Another story is told about a visit he made to London. He answered an ad for a bugle player in one of the Guards bands. The leader was a pompous young man right out of music school, and when Kendall applied for the job, the leader was very condescending, saying he doubted if Kendall could qualify but to appear the following morning for rehearsal. The next morning Kendall unobtrusively took a seat in the bugle section, while the leader was rehearsing the solo clarinetist in a passage. The clarinetist was having difficulty in performing the music, and Kendall brazenly asked if he could demonstrate on his bugle how it should be played.

Reluctantly the leader gave assent. He probably thought the Yankee player would cover himself with shame and that the lesson would be good for him. To the leader's surprise Kendall played the difficult part flawlessly. The leader walked down to Kendall's chair and asked him who he was. Kendall replied quietly, "Ned Kendall." "You couldn't, by any chance, be the celebrated American bugle player, Ned Kendall?" the leader asked. "One and the same," said Ned. The cold stares from leader and players immediately turned into a warm welcome, and Kendall was much gratified that his fame had spread even to England, the home of the keyed bugle.

We first hear of Ned Kendall in 1835, when he became leader of the newly formed Boston Brass Band. He was only twenty-seven years old, but even then he had won a reputation for his extraordinary ability as a bugle soloist. He directed the band for four or five

years and made it famous in and around Boston. Many of its achievements were largely owing to the prowess of Kendall. The remainder
of his life was spent as soloist on the keyed bugle. When he played
with the Salem band under Gilmore, he was at or slightly past his
peak. Information about the last five years of his life is vague, but it
is evident that either failing health or John Barleycorn took hold of
him.

We learn something of his decline from an unnamed young minister of the gospel from Boston who took a pastorate in the South.
About two years after Kendall's appearance with Gilmore the minister one day noticed a circus poster advertising that Ned Kendall
would be featured as bugle soloist with the circus band. He hardly
believed the famous Kendall would be reduced to traveling with a
small circus, after the illustrious career he had known in Boston, but
when the circus finally paraded in the little town, there was unquestionably the famous Ned Kendall, though broken in health, shab-
bily dressed, and his person ill-kept.

If there were any doubts in the young pastor's mind that this was
the man he had known a few years before in Boston, these were removed when the band marched down the street playing *The Wrecker's
Daughter,* with Kendall leading on his inimitable keyed bugle. When
Kendall played *Money Musk* with the band, the pastor was dead sure
of his man. Although somewhat lacking in the old vigor and flourish
of Kendall in his prime the playing was such as only Kendall could
have performed.

Three years later Kendall died at his home in Boston after an illness of two years.

Gilmore was what we would today characterize as an "eager
beaver." His rise to the directorship of the Salem Brass Band had
been rapid, but he was richly endowed with native musical talent
and he was fired with ambition to make the most of it. He was a poor
boy, born in Athlone, Ireland, in 1829. His first job was as apprentice to a wholesale merchant. Athlone was a garrison town and there
were always two or three regiments stationed there whose bands paraded through the town in their gay uniforms. Pat early acquired the
band fever, and when sixteen years old he applied to the Athlone
bandmaster Keating for cornet lessons. In three months Pat had
mastered the cornet sufficiently well to fill a vacancy in the town band.
Two years later he joined a regiment headed for Canada, but after
a year in the service he quit and came to Boston.

The only job he could find in Boston was in the Ordway Brothers Music Store as manager of the band instrument department. He promptly organized a minstrel company among the store employees, called the Ordway Eolians, in which he was the featured cornet soloist. The company gave regular shows at the Province House, and Gilmore attracted considerable attention with his cornet solos.

During this time he made certain contacts in nearby Charlestown, and persuaded the militia company there to organize a band and put him in charge of it. He did well with the new band and won sufficient reputation to enable him, in 1852, to land the job of bandmaster of the Boston Brass Band, one of the best in New England at that time.

And so our "eager beaver," only twenty-three years old and in America only four years, landed at the top of the heap.

In the summer of the previous year a Mr. F. Gleason of Boston established the *Gleason's Pictorial Drawing-Room Companion,* the first illustrated weekly magazine ever published in America. In the twelfth issue of this magazine was published an article on the Boston Brass Band, illustrated by a line engraving of the band in their new uniforms and with a new set of instruments. The uniforms consisted of "a blue frock coat, red pants, and a blue infantry cap, with a fountain plume." The instruments are described as a great improvement, being a set of over-the-shoulder instruments, which became quite common later during the Civil War. The picture of the band shows seventeen players.

"Our city," says the writer of the article, "has for a long period of time, been noted for the excellence of its military bands of music, and they have enjoyed a reputation, far and near, for the extraordinary harmony, and correct musical performance they have always exhibited when in public. In only two instances have we ever heard our Boston bands excelled in those points of beauty that appertain to their profession, and these were listening to the governor general's military band, in the plaza of Havana, and the second time, on hearing Dodworth's famed band, of New York City . . . .

"The Boston Brass Band, more familiarly known as Flagg's Brass Band . . . claims priority over all others in this, or any other city of the union, as being the first association of the kind in the country, being first organized in 1835, under Edward Kendall, the far-famed bugle player, as its leader. Joseph Green, the present efficient and popular leader of the American Brass Band, at Providence, R. I., was the next to succeed Mr. Kendall. Its present head is Eben Flagg, who has led the band for some eight years or more, sustaining an excellent reputation, no less for his professional skill than for his manly and sociable qualities. The members of the Boston Brass Band are composed mainly of professors, musical composers, and artists, each one highly accomplished in the use of his particular instrument."

The loose phrase "association of the kind" probably enables the writer to escape libel, but the Boston Brass Band was not the first band to be organized in Boston, for the Boston Brigade Band was several years old in 1826, when it played in the musical exercises held in connection with the double funeral of the two Presidents John Adams and Thomas Jefferson. It was, however, comprised of flutes, clarinets, hautboys, and bassoons, with a couple of trombones and ophicleides, and if the writer of the Gleason article means an all-brass band by the phrase "association of the kind," the Boston Brass Band antedates as a brass band the Boston Brigade Band, for the latter did not become all brass until about 1838.

The Salem Brigade Band, organized in 1806 as a mixed brass and reed band, was reorganized in 1835 and transformed into an all-brass band, making it at least as old as the Boston Brass Band. But in New York the Dodworth Band was equipped entirely with brass instruments in 1834, at the insistence of Allen Dodworth, then director. This band is believed to be the real holder of the title of the first brass band in America.

We do not know what happened to Eben Flagg, so highly praised in the Gleason article in September 1851, but only a few months later Gilmore had his job. Whatever the circumstances surrounding this change, we can be sure that Gilmore's conduct was honorable. Gilmore was always aggressive, to be sure, but he was also one of the kindest, friendliest, and most sympathetic of men. Throughout his active life he made thousands of staunch friends and rarely made an enemy.

Regardless of the statement by the writer of the article in *Gleason's Pictorial Drawing-Room Companion* that the new over-the-shoulder instruments were an improvement, it is doubtful if Gilmore considered them so. This type of instrument had been invented and patented in 1838 by Allen Dodworth. They were manufactured in Vienna and imported to this country for many years by the Dodworth family. They were designed for use by military bands when marching at the head of a column, the sound being directed backward for the benefit

*It is doubtful if Gilmore considered
over-the-shoulder instruments an improvement.
Boston Brass Band in 1851.*

of the marching soldiers. Even the inventor did not recommend them
for concert purposes.

In his instruction book, entitled *Dodworth's Brass Band School,* published in 1853, Allen Dodworth states: "In selecting the instruments,
attention should be paid to the use intended; if for military purposes
only, those with bells behind, over the shoulder, are preferable, as
they throw all the tone to those who are marching to it, but for any
other purpose are not so good . . . . For general purposes, those with
the bell upward, like the Sax Horn, are most convenient, and should
be adopted by all whose business is not exclusively military; care
should be taken to have all the bells one way."

So far as we know, the Boston Brass Band was primarily a concert
band. The picture of the band in the Gleason magazine shows the
band in concert formation. Gilmore, with his bell-front cornet, must
have felt strangely out of place while playing with his new band. No

doubt one of his first objectives was to switch the instruments to sax-horns, cornets, and slide trombones.

During his three-year tenure with the Boston Brass Band, Gilmore entered into business with Joseph M. Russell, a music publisher located at 61 Court Street, the firm being known as Gilmore & Russell. Apparently this association was continued after Gilmore left Boston to take charge of the Salem Brass Band, for in 1859 the firm of Gilmore & Russell was listed in a Boston directory as a dealer in musical instruments.

It was also during Gilmore's directorship of the Boston Brass Band that Jullien came to Boston, in 1854, for a series of concerts, and planted in the mind of the young bandmaster those extravagant and grandiose ideas which were to dominate his musical career ever afterward.

In Salem, Jerome Smith, director of the Salem Brass Band, was looking for a successor. Having taken over the baton from Francis Morse in 1846, he had been quite successful with the band. Recently he had been suffering from some lung trouble, and he knew he would have to give up the post soon. He had become acquainted with Gilmore and his work with the Boston Brass Band, and considered him the best bandmaster in the country. After Smith had held some conferences with officers of the Salem Light Infantry, an offer of "one thousand a year and all he can make" was made to Gilmore. Pat terminated his three years with the Boston band and came to Salem in 1855.

Gilmore took hold of the Salem band with his usual fire and energy. The Gilmore-Kendall contest concert was only one instance of the interesting shows Gilmore put on. The fame of the band spread and it often accepted invitations to play at special events far from home. Three months after the Gilmore-Kendall contest the New England Guards militia company of Charlestown engaged Gilmore and his band to lead them in their parade down Pennsylvania Avenue in Washington in the inauguration exercises for James Buchanan. The Salem band was a standout, so much so that the Washington *Post* made special mention of it, commenting on the excellent playing of the band, the military bearing of the players on the march, and their sober and well-disciplined behavior all during their stay at the capital. Most newsworthy was the sobriety of the bandsmen, for it seemed to be the prerogative of a band to get inebriated after a playing engagement away from home.

The various Boston bands were incensed by this engagement, for they all felt it should have been given to one of them rather than to a band so far away as Salem. Gilmore, however, had made some good friends in Charlestown among the officers when he organized and directed a band there six or seven years before, and he had an inside track when it came to getting the business.

Gilmore had his eye on that part of his contract at Salem which read "and all he can make," and he was always hustling for business. As job after job was taken away from the Boston bands by Gilmore, the Boston musicians were driven to desperation. When Gilmore secured an engagement one time right in the city of Boston, they went berserk. Then planned to wait for the Salem band to embark from the train and start marching toward their engagement. When the band reached a certain spot, the Boston musicians were to break from cover and run toward the Salem band with blood in their eyes. They would fix the lips of those Salem musicians so they wouldn't be able to play for weeks, and they'd batter the instruments so they could never be played again.

Call it Gilmore luck or acumen or what you will, Gilmore got wind of the plan to waylay his band, and he prepared for it as cleverly and thoroughly as he did everything else. He brought along with him a group of the toughest mugs he could find along the waterfront in Salem. As the band marched from the railway station, Gilmore had his "pug uglies" tag along at the rear of the band, with instructions to wait until he blew a whistle. That was the signal for them to come running with brass knuckles and blackjacks and belaying pins.

The Boston boys made the attack as planned. Gilmore blew his whistle and his mob of bodyguards came on the double. The Boston boys were so flabbergasted they even forgot to run until the belaying pins began coming down on their heads, and then they turned and fled. It is said that after the concert Gilmore's band remained sober, as usual, but that his bodyguards got gloriously drunk.

Business among the Boston bands got so bad that finally the Boston Brigade Band followed the old advice: "If you can't beat 'em, join 'em." They put out feelers to see if Gilmore would be interested in directing their band. Gilmore was interested. Further negotiations were carried on, and in 1859 Gilmore resigned from the Salem Brass Band and took over the Boston Brigade Band—and he really took over!

Gilmore's arrangement with the Brigade Band was a new idea.

He was to assume all expenses for music, uniforms, rent, and everything else, but he was to be the sole proprietor of the band and it was to be known as Gilmore's Band. In substance the band was to work for him, he was to finance the undertaking, and he was to collect all the profits.

He had for some time been wanting a band of his own. He was tired of being "attached" to some military company, at the beck and call of the military. With a band of his own, he could book engagements far ahead, and he could make arrangements, not for a concert at a time, but for a whole series of concerts, without fear of interruption by the militia company.

Gilmore proceeded to carry out his part of the agreement. He bought all new uniforms—beautiful gray ones with plenty of braid —for thirty-two men. Then he paid two hundred dollars rental for a good rehearsal hall and fitted it up with comfortable chairs, new music stands, and good lights. He reshuffled the players, put them through their paces, and rehearsed them as they had never been rehearsed before.

He also bought all kinds of the newest music: a big library of everything imaginable—operas, symphonies, overtures, quicksteps, quadrilles, polkas, and songs. He bought all the pieces he believed usable from the catalogs of Russell & Tolman and of Ditson & Co. in Boston, and he got practically the entire list of band music from Dodworth & Co. of New York. From several foreign publishers he bought classic overtures, symphonies, and operas.

It wasn't long before he was offering to furnish practically any kind of music wanted—large band, small band, reed band, brass band, or combined reed and brass band. He had the players and the music for every occasion. He could play a heavy concert or he could send out a small group to play soft dinner music. He had a setup similar to that of the Dodworth family in New York, and was prepared to make a business of furnishing band music to order.

For the first Fourth-of-July celebration after he organized his own band he staged a concert in the Boston Common that was so successful that it became an annual event. During the fall and winter he staged the first of the famous Promenade Concerts in the Boston Music Hall, an English idea new to America. People flocked to these concerts. They liked the informal nature of walking around the hall while the band entertained them with light and popular music.

Everything was coming along as Gilmore had planned. The band was whipped into shape as one of the best in America, and business was pouring in. Finally one day Gilmore received word that he and his band were requested to play at the Republican nominating convention in Chicago. He made his first trip to the metropolis of the West and scored a big hit before the assembled delegates. He made the famous "Wigwam" of the Republicans resound with such stirring music as they had never heard before.

The only cloud in Gilmore's sky was the dread issue of slavery. He returned to Boston with misgivings, but he proceeded as if his successes could go on forever. His promenade concerts that winter were more heavily attended than ever, and his band was kept busy. The following spring the Southern states began seceding, and by April the terrible Civil War had begun. Gilmore turned his band to patriotic uses, leading parades and playing at recruiting rallies, without remuneration. His band was continually in the streets, marching in their gay uniforms with ribbons streaming from their hats.

Every Saturday evening Pat took his band down to Fort Warren, in Boston Harbor, to play a concert and for dress parade. The Boston Light Infantry battalion was stationed there. It was made up of about two hundred and fifty men, most of them students and clerks. They called themselves "The Tigers." They had no band of their own, but they started a glee club, which sang a song written by a member named Henry Halgreen. Music was provided by James Greenleaf, but the tune was really an old camp-meeting song called *Say, Brethren, Will You Meet with Us?* This glee-club song was quite popular, and when Pat heard it, he arranged to have it sung over for him several times, while he made notes. The next Saturday when he returned to Fort Warren with his band, he bowled them over by playing his band arrangement.

Thus was born the famous *John Brown's Body* ("lies a'moldering in the grave"). Gilmore played his band arrangement every time he went to Fort Warren, and the glee club sang the words to the accompaniment of the band. A few months later Julia Ward Howe wrote new words ("Glory, Glory, Hallelujah"), and it came to be known as the *The Battle Hymn of the Republic*.

In October 1861, Gilmore and his entire band enlisted with the Massachusetts 24th Volunteer Regiment. The band changed their gray uniforms for the Union blue. Before the regiment left for the front, the band gave two patriotic farewell concerts. A special stage setting was created simulating a soldiers' camp, and the concerts were called "An Evening in the Camp of the 24th Regiment, New England Guards." A large chorus of soldiers performed with the band. The production was an impressive affair, and brought the war close to the people as nothing else before had been able to do.

About two weeks before Christmas the 24th Regiment left camp and proceeded to New York, where it was met at the foot of Twenty-third Street by the famous Dodworth Band under Harvey Dodworth. Gilmore's Band led the parade along Twenty-third Street to Fifth Avenue, thence down to Fourteenth Street and over to Broadway and the City Hall.

The regiment was assigned to the Burnside expedition and by February was embroiled in bloody fighting in Virginia and North Carolina. Gilmore and his bandsmen took up the usual wartime tasks of bearing stretchers and rescuing the wounded under fire. But occasionally they reassembled and performed as a military band. It is said that on one or more occasions, when the Union and Confederate forces were bivouaced close together, Gilmore and his band played brief concerts. Included in the program was *Dixie's Land,* and when the final note had been played cheers arose, not only from the Union but also from the Confederate lines. This story may be spurious, but it is in the Gilmore character and may well have occurred as related.

In August 1862 an act of Congress discharged all regimental bands from the service, and the Gilmore band arrived back in Boston early in September. Gilmore and his band boys were returned heroes in the eyes of the people of Boston. Pat was asked to play and he readily consented. He put on a concert with the men wearing their service uniforms, which were faded and frayed. This was a stroke of the usual Gilmore showmanship. The audience was deeply impressed and stirred by this unusual concert.

Prospects were anything but bright for Gilmore as he exchanged his Union blue uniform for the gray band uniform. All his rosy future as America's greatest bandmaster had been engulfed in the dark clouds of war. Slight Union victories were followed by reverses at the hands of the brilliant General Lee. Whatever the outcome of the bloody struggle, he decided to go on and do what he could. He announced a new series of promenade concerts, to be held every Wednesday afternoon and Saturday night at the Boston Music Hall. Because so much money was being drained away in the cause of war he lowered his prices. Single admission was fifteen cents, but a book of ten tickets could be bought for one dollar. A lady accompanied by her escort was admitted for twenty-five cents.

Gilmore did his best to cheer and comfort. He carefully planned each program and presented the music most in tune with the war conditions. People found the concerts a godsend. They filled the lower floor with their promenading and packed the balconies, where they sat and listened to relaxing and inspiring music.

Light and happy numbers such as *Old Dan Tucker, Oh! Susanna,* and *Nellie Was a Lady* were intermixed with sacred songs such as *Nearer, My God, to Thee, Abide with Me,* and *Ave Maria,* the last a newly published composition by Gounod. Favorite patriotic numbers were *The Battle Hymn of the Republic, The Star-Spangled Banner* and *Columbia, the Gem of the Ocean.* A brand new song, hot from the pen of Stephen Foster, immediately became popular as a timely war song: *We Are Coming, Father Abraham, 300,000 More.*

And at the ticket window "greenbacks" began to appear, the initial issue of the new wartime currency.

Three

THE "BIGGER AND BETTER"
AGUE
STRIKES GILMORE

For five days the National Peace Jubilee rocked the rafters of the vast coliseum.
CULVER SERVICE

In 1863, Governor Andrew of Massachusetts asked Patrick Gilmore to reorganize the state militia bands. This assignment indirectly resulted in planting a grandiose idea in Gilmore's mind that was to occupy his thoughts for the next eight or nine years, challenge his abilities to the utmost, and lead to undying if questionable fame.

This grandiose idea happened to be concerned with music because Gilmore happened to be a bandmaster. It sprang from the "bigger and better" complex, which was a strong motivating influence among

Americans generally during this age. If Gilmore had happened to be interested in sports, he likely would have organized the Olympic games on a grand scale in New Orleans and Boston. If he had been a farmer, his big extravaganza probably would have been an international livestock fair.

Not until he had given full rein to the Big Idea that was working in his brain, in the Grand National Concert in New Orleans in 1864, in the National Peace Jubilee in Boston in 1869, and in the World Peace Jubilee in Boston in 1872, could he turn his attention to the more constructive and artistic labors of raising the standard of military band music. This work he undertook in 1873 when he began building the 22nd Regiment Band into the finest musical organization of its kind in the world.

Gilmore instantly accepted the assignment from Governor Andrew and turned all his energies to this new task in the war effort. In record time he formed twenty bands and sent them to join the Union forces. In New York another famous bandmaster and warm personal friend of Gilmore was engaged in a similar undertaking. Harvey Dodworth, leader of the celebrated Dodworth Band and of the 13th Regiment Band, furnished fifty bandmasters and over five hundred bandsmen for the Northern forces.

Gilmore's services in this type of patriotic duty were cut short when he chose to accompany two of his bands to New Orleans. General Nathaniel Banks, commander of the Department of the Gulf, was quick to feel the magnetism and spirit of Gilmore, and asked him to remain in New Orleans and take charge of all bands under his command.

In addition to routine duties Gilmore organized a special band and put on a series of his famous promenade concerts in New Orleans, to which leading Confederate families of the city were invited. At first squeamish about attending, these proud Southerners soon learned that Gilmore had a way of making everyone feel welcome and at ease. *Dixie's Land* and *Bonny Blue Flag,* rallying songs of the Confederate forces, were regularly programed along with *The Battle Hymn of the Republic* and *Just before the Battle, Mother,* and Gilmore soon made many friends among the Confederate families.

On March 4, 1864, Michael Hahn was to be inaugurated as governor of "freed and restored Louisiana," and General Banks asked Gilmore to provide music worthy of the occasion. Such an assignment was to Gilmore right down his alley. He obtained permission from the public schools to form a great chorus of five thousand children. These he coached and drilled with skill and thoroughness. Then he formed a massed band of five hundred instrumentalists from the bands under his supervision and added a large number of drum and bugle players for special effects.

Knowing the instrumentation of the typical Civil War band, one can imagine what Gilmore's massed band sounded like. The standard complement in a band was seventeen players, made up of four cornets, three altos, three baritones, two basses, three snare drums, and two bass drums. To have five hundred players, Gilmore would have had to muster thirty of his bands. This would have brought into action the following:

Cornets	120
Altos	90
Baritones	90
Basses	60
Snare Drums	90
Bass Drums	60
Total Players	510

The ceremonies were held in Lafayette Square, which was jammed with spectators. The Grand National Concert started with *The Star-Spangled Banner,* followed by *America* and *The Union Forever.* The five thousand children of New Orleans sang with unbounded enthusiasm, each child waving a tiny American flag held in the hand. The huge band played spiritedly. One hundred and twenty cornets screamed above the brass chorus of ninety altos, or "peck horns," ninety baritones, and sixty basses. Ninety snare drums rattled like musketry, and sixty bass drums boomed like artillery.

The final number and the climax of the program was *Hail, Columbia.* Gilmore worked his magic on the great band and on the immense chorus of child voices, and the thousands of listeners were caught in this magic spell. Piling effect on effect, during the final thirty-six beats of the music Gilmore fired by electric buttons from the podium thirty-six cannons, each tremendous boom in time as he directed the music in *maestoso* tempo. As the cannons began booming, the bells from the churches and cathedrals of the city began pealing wildly. The combined effect was breath-taking and awe-inspiring. Frenzied and prolonged applause greeted the fiery bandmaster as he bowed and bowed to the huge audience.

As an expression of appreciation for the splendid services Gilmore had rendered, a testimonial banquet was held at the famous St. Charles Hotel, attended by one hundred of the leading citizens of New Orleans and by important civil and military officials. General Banks thanked Gilmore on behalf of the government and the people of New Orleans, and presented him with a beautifully inscribed silver goblet, filled to the brim with gold coins. Governor Hahn dispatched a letter to President Lincoln extolling Gilmore as "a true gentleman and a musician of the highest ability" who had done "great good to the cause of the Union by his faithful and patriotic service."

During his stay in New Orleans, Gilmore intuitively sensed the end of the war. General Grant had already won important Union victories, when he captured Fort Henry on the Tennessee River and Fort Donelson on the Cumberland. He had held the Confederates at Shiloh and defeated them at Corinth. Victory had been won at Gettysburg. Lincoln's Emancipation Proclamation had freed over three million slaves.

With an uncanny insight into the future and into the minds and feelings of the populace he sat down and wrote the words and music of *When Johnny Comes Marching Home.* It was published in 1864 by H. Tolman & Co., Boston, under the pseudonym Louis Lambert. There has been some doubt as to the real composer, but Sigmund Spaeth, well known "tune detective," gives Gilmore full credit for the composition and calls it a "great, galloping tune in 6–8 time." It was second in popularity during late Civil War times only to *John Brown's Body,* which Gilmore had a hand in launching three years before.

Gilmore was right. The tune had hardly been published when Johnny came marching home. It rapidly was adopted as a favorite marching song of the soldiers and the joyful thanksgiving song of the people at home. Copies sold by the tens of thousands. Its popularity spread through the South as well as through the North, for it gave expression to the wishes and prayers of millions of people, irrespective of their political feelings. Although there were over half a million Johnnies who would never march home, even in these bereaved homes the happy, rollicking tune was a release from the horrors of war. Long after Gilmore ceased to collect royalties from the song it continued in popularity, for it is timeless in its appeal. In every war there is the strong longing for peace and the return of loved ones.

When the war was over, Gilmore again returned to Boston, again reorganized his band, and again gave concerts in the Music Hall and the Boston Theatre. Not much is known about Gilmore during the next few years, but we can be pretty sure that he was not a happy man. His concerts were well attended and he was making money, but there was no challenge in this sort of routine. It was old stuff to Gilmore and this was something he could not endure for long.

Gilmore's discontent at the time was caused partly by his nature and partly by the age in which he was living. By nature Gilmore was dynamic and bursting with energy, and he was happy only when his mental and physical resources were being adequately used up in some big project, as they had been in the Grand National Concert at New Orleans. On the other hand, the twenty years of living in America had made him a man of the age, full of adventure, big hopes, and grand schemes. To Gilmore, as to most other Americans in 1865, the previous two decades had been an age of superlatives— the biggest, the best, the first.

And "culture"—what about culture during these twenty years? There was lots of it! French, Italian, and German opera, including some late Wagner, plus the symphonic classics, could be heard in Boston, New York, Philadelphia, Cincinnati, New Orleans, Chicago, and San Francisco, and sometimes in smaller cities. The musical giant Theodore Thomas had appeared on the scene, and little Adelina Patti was beginning to replace Jenny Lind on the concert stage. In metropolitan theaters one could witness plays by Shakespeare, or melodrama such as *Ten Nights in a Barroom, Uncle Tom's Cabin,* or *East Lynne.* The Negro minstrel was popular but had to compete with "bloomer girl shows" and with "blonde shows," which a few years later would develop into burlesque. In New York alone there were fourteen amusement houses with a combined seating capacity of nearly seventeen thousand.

Songs and hymns and sentimental music came off the press in large quantities. Probably the best of the songs came from the pen of Stephen Foster. Among those most widely remembered today were *My Old Kentucky Home, Jeanie with the Light Brown Hair,* and *Old Black Joe.* Other song writers of the era brought out such perennial favorites as *Listen to the Mocking Bird, Darling Nelly Gray* ("they have taken her away"), and *Jingle Bells* ("jingle all the way"). Heard for the first time were such romantic and sentimental music as Suppé's *Poet and Peasant Overture,* Rubinstein's *Melody in F,* and Mendelssohn's *Wedding March.* They have taken their places among the most played-to-death pieces of music on record. Especially numerous were the sacred hymns, many of which are well known today. Three of these all-time favorites were *Nearer, My God, to Thee, Abide with Me* and *Holy, Holy, Holy! Lord God Almighty.*

Ever a bandmaster to give the people what they liked to hear, Gilmore placed most if not all of this new and popular music on his programs in Boston.

Gilmore saw 1865 pass, with peace at Appomattox, Lincoln assassinated in Washington, and the newly formed white-hooded Ku Klux Klan creating terror among the carpetbaggers and Negro voters of the South. He filled some of his idle time with testing and inspecting band instruments at the Gilmore, Graves and Co. factory, in which he had purchased an interest in 1864. But there was peace—relatively, at least.

The year 1866 also passed, with new and strange organizations springing up everywhere: The Grand Army of the Republic, Christian Science Church, Y.W.C.A., National Labor Union, and Society for the Prevention of Cruelty to Animals. The name of his band instrument factory was changed to Gilmore & Co., the Graves interests apparently having been bought out. But there was peace in the land, Gilmore kept telling himself.

Clashes between President Johnson and Congress over reconstruction policies in the South began early in 1867, and became so violent that they led to impeachment proceedings. Many heated words passed between pros and cons over purchase of Alaska from Russia at two cents per acre. Tired of running a band instrument factory by himself, Gilmore took into the business E. G. Wright, an experienced manufacturer, and the firm name was changed to Wright, Gilmore & Co. A few months later Gilmore could stand no more, and he sold out his interests to Wright. This was supposed to be a time of peace, but Gilmore's mind was in turmoil.

During the year 1867 Gilmore emerged from darkness into a great light, when he received his celebrated vision of the National Peace Jubilee. He was like the Buddha, returning from seven years of ascetic life in the desert to bring his great spiritual message to the people; or like Muhammad, returning from seclusion in the Arabian oases after fifteen years, with the new teachings of Islam. As Gilmore later wrote in his 758-page book, *History of the National Peace Jubilee and Great Musical Festival,* published at his own expense in 1871:

A vast structure rose before me, filled with the loyal of the land, through whose arches a chorus of ten thousand voices and the harmony of a thousand instruments rolled their sea of sound, accompanied by the chiming of bells and the booming of cannon, all pouring forth their praises and gratifications in loud hosannas with all the majesty and grandeur of which music seemed capable.

Gilmore professed to have seen a vision, but there were others who believed he was simply having another attack of the "bigger and better" ague. The attack in New Orleans had been a five-thousand-unit attack, but this one was more violent, being an attack of ten thousand units. The fever of imagination brought on by this attack was also twice as hot and consuming.

His wife Ellen was happy to see Stephen, as she called him, come back to "normal," his eyes feverishly blazing with grand ideas, his talk bubbling with vast plans and his step bounding with action. She encouraged him to expatiate on his plans, and the details of the vision began to enlarge.

A great and bloody war had been fought, he said, half a million young lives had been slaughtered, millions of slaves had been freed, and the Union saved. After the great holocaust peace had been officially declared, but there was no peace. The fighting continued under many different disguises. What was needed was a stupendous celebration and festival of great music to enable the people to realize fully that peace ruled throughout the land.

He would construct a gigantic coliseum, such as he had seen in his vision, and it would seat fifty thousand people. The greatest singers and musicians of America would produce celestial music such as had never been heard before. All the most important people of the land would attend: the President of the United States and his Cabinet, the Supreme Court and leaders of Congress, the military heads of the Army, Navy, and Marine Corps; ambassadors, governors of all the states, and leading citizens in various walks of life. The message of peace and joy, which he had been anointed to bring, would pervade the great assembly and would be carried home to every citizen throughout America.

The more he talked and thought about the great idea, the more vast and elaborate it became. He decided to put it down in a prospectus, and he accordingly prepared and had printed a long, detailed, and enthusiastic outline of the entire project. With printed copies under his arm he started out to win disciples and influence contributors of money.

For several years Gilmore had been casting his eyes toward New York, for this city had begun to forge ahead of Boston. He now thought this was the opportune time to make a change, and what could bring him before the people more forcibly and dramatically than the staging of the National Peace Jubilee? But one of the first contacts he made in New York was with Thomas Boese, president of the Board of Education, and Mr. Boese flatly refused to allow twenty thousand school children to take part in the proposed program. Furthermore Gilmore was not well known in New York, and after canvassing the city for several days he gave up and returned to Boston.

He then recalled the recent formation of the Grand Army of the Republic, which had headquarters in Washington. With the support of such an organization behind the project the success of the Jubilee would be assured, he felt. Besides there was a good chance that he could obtain support of the government and stage the Jubilee in connection with the inauguration of General Grant, who just had been elected President. The trip to Washington, however, was a failure. Again he returned to Boston. The conclusion began to grow on him that the Jubilee would have to be staged in Boston or not at all. Accordingly he set about organizing the Boston forces of music behind the project.

Early in 1868 he made a list of the most important musical leaders in Boston, the men who would give the Jubilee the greatest prestige, the widest acceptance, and the biggest following. At the top of the list were Eben Tourjée, Julius Eichberg, Dr. Upham, Carl Zerrahn, and John S. Dwight. Gilmore's dynamic personality and contagious enthusiasm swept them over to his side, one after the other—all except Dwight.

Eben Tourjée was director of the New England Conservatory, established only the year before. His appointment as head of this important institution was sufficient recognition of his high place in music circles and of his sound musical abilities. Gilmore succeeded in getting Tourjée to agree to assemble and rehearse the main chorus of ten thousand adult voices.

Julius Eichberg was director of the Boston Conservatory, also established in 1867. For eleven years before coming to America in 1857 he had been professor of music in the Geneva Conservatory. He was a violinist and composer, a music educator and conductor. As supervisor of music in the Boston public schools, he was just the man to create a chorus of twenty thousand school children that would sing popular songs during a one-time appearance on the program. Under Gilmore's spell Eichberg agreed.

Dr. Upham was chairman of the Committee on Public School Music in Boston. Eichberg probably tipped off Gilmore that before anything could be done about creating a chorus of twenty thousand school children, the consent and co-operation of Dr. Upham would have to be forthcoming. Gilmore called on this eminent gentleman, pointed out what a stimulus the Jubilee appearance would be for all the school children in Boston and how the Jubilee would create favorable comment by Boston taxpayers concerning music instruction in the public schools. He also emphasized that the children's chorus would be strictly a school affair since he wished Eichberg to take over the whole project. Dr. Upham consented.

Carl Zerrahn was one of the most widely known and highly respected musicians in New England. He had come to America in 1848 as flutist with the celebrated Germania Society and had traveled with the orchestra until it was disbanded in 1854. Since then he had been conductor of the Handel and Haydn Society, prominent choral group of Boston, and was conductor of choral groups in Worcester and Salem. From 1855 to 1863 he had been conductor of various orchestras of symphonic caliber which had gone under the name of Boston Philharmonic. He also had been connected with public-school music. With his wide acquaintance among musicians and his proved ability as choral director and orchestra conductor Zerrahn was the man for gathering the thousand-piece orchestra together and for polishing the performance of both chorus and orchestra. After an hour under Gilmore's spell Zerrahn acquiesced.

"Four times at bat and four home runs," ejaculated Gilmore, using the language of baseball, which already had become the nation's most popular game. Full of victory and confidence, he tackled John S. Dwight, editor of *The Journal of Music*. Although this music magazine had hardly more than one thousand readers, these readers were key people throughout the country in all phases of serious music. Dwight had launched the *Journal* in 1852 and had been editor for sixteen years, establishing himself as a kind of oracle on all things musical. Musicians sought his advice and courted his favor, and it was important to secure his support of any worth-while music venture.

But Gilmore struck out! Dwight failed to see any solid music value in the grandiose Peace Jubilee plans. He doubted that music—the kind of music Dwight stood for—would receive any benefit; in fact he felt this circus presentation would result in irremediable damage to the cause of good music.

Failing to reach Dwight through a strict music appeal, Gilmore poured on the evangelistic talk about his vision, his being anointed to carry on the work, its being a project of the Prince of Peace and unquestionably having God's distinct and special blessing. Dwight had once been a Unitarian minister of the gospel, but he was not impressed. Years before, he had frowned on Jullien, and now he was frowning on Jullien's disciple. Dwight stood for good classical music, performed with taste and dignity, and he would not be swerved from his singleness of purpose.

Gilmore felt the loss, but he was not one to brood. He believed he had sufficient musical backing without Dwight, and he turned with enthusiasm toward finding guarantors who would put up the money to finance the great project. Among the first men he approached was Oliver Ditson, head of Oliver Ditson & Co., probably at that time the biggest and wealthiest music-publishing house in the United States. It didn't require much of Gilmore's eloquence to convince Ditson that the Jubilee would be good for the music-publishing business, and he quickly subscribed one thousand dollars. Ditson also owned *The Journal of Music,* having bought out Dwight's interest in 1858 but having retained Dwight as editor. It is possible that Gilmore tried to persuade Ditson to bring a little pressure to bear on the stubborn Dwight, but if he did he was unsuccessful. Dwight continued his opposition.

Also high on Gilmore's list of possible contributors was Henry Mason, of Mason & Hamlin Organ Co., makers of reed organs and at the time reaping a bonanza on the "Cabinet organ." This instrument was a development of the firm, and the name Cabinet had been registered as a trademark in 1861. It was a relatively small reed organ with everything inclosed in a single cabinet, and became probably the most popular keyboard instrument in American homes before the advent of the piano. Mason was easily won over to the view that the Jubilee would be good for business, and he subscribed one thousand dollars.

A couple of hotel operators subscribed a like amount, and there were a number of smaller contributions from musical instrument manufacturers, music publishers, and the rank and file of merchants and businessmen. Gilmore was optimistic. He felt assured that raising the money would be easy, and so he went to the newspapers and broke the story. It appeared during the next day and the following day or two in all its fabulous novelty and fantastic detail.

The effect was sudden—and disastrous! The Bostonian populace were not stirred to enthusiastic applause and activity, as Gilmore had envisioned. They were stunned, veritably paralyzed! Julius Eichberg, Eben Tourjée, and Carl Zerrahn they knew. They seemed a part of reality, still. But a coliseum to seat fifty thousand! A coliseum five hundred feet long and three hundred feet wide! A chorus of ten thousand adult singers, recruited from the Atlantic Ocean to the Mississippi River! An orchestra of one thousand instrumentalists from all over the United States! The President and his Cabinet, the Supreme Court and the Congress! Pat Gilmore must be stark and raving crazy!

Even the men whom Gilmore had recruited to help him put the Jubilee across now began to wonder if they had not succumbed to the personal witchery of the persuasive Irishman and had agreed to something which was too preposterous and bizarre to accept in saner moments, exorcised from his spell. Money sources dried up. Active opposition arose. The manner in which Gilmore won out in the face of such a situation is more of a testimony to his genius than the original conception of the Jubilee.

He methodically retraced his tracks and one by one recharged his followers with his original enthusiasm. He made them see again the bright vision he had unveiled to them in the beginning. He renewed their faith that this great and good undertaking could and would be accomplished. He was the prime and inexhaustible source of energy, inspiration, and conviction that was needed to drive them all along toward achievement.

He went further. He saw that the conservative and hardheaded Bostonians and New Englanders needed something more tangible than his own persuasive eloquence and contagious enthusiasm. He organized the National Peace Jubilee Association to take over the management of the whole affair, and he inveigled leading citizens of Boston to accept offices in this association. Most important, he prevailed upon Eben Jordan, the John D. Rockefeller of Boston, to become treasurer of the association and handle all financial matters. This step registered with the staid and stolid Bostonians, and public opinion began to be favorable. If hardheaded businessmen like Eben Jordan thought enough of the great scheme to devote their time and money to it, that was good enough for most people. The tide turned and was to gain great momentum during the few weeks before the Jubilee was to take place.

The old and aristocratic families of Back Bay Boston raised a howl about using the Boston Common for the unsightly coliseum and the cheap street fair that was to accompany it. In order to pacify this segment of the opposition a compromise was made and the site changed to St. James Park.

As the coliseum began to take shape early in May, a rumor was circulated that the structure was unsafe. Gossips gave out "on good authority" that it was structurally weak and that the balconies would collapse, killing hundreds of people. To allow twenty thousand children to become trapped in such a treacherous building was openly to court wholesale murder among the children of Boston. Gilmore gave the *coup de grâce* to this bugaboo by placing the children's chorus on the program the last day, "after the building had been thoroughly tested and proved." This silenced the rumor and took Dr. Upham off the spot.

Eichberg proceeded confidently with the children's chorus of twenty thousand voices. This was not such an undertaking as might be imagined. Annually since 1858, when Carl Zerrahn assembled a child chorus of twelve hundred voices in the Music Hall, the children of the Boston public schools had been assembled in large demonstration choruses. Most children in grade schools could sing in unison or two-part harmony the standard repertoire of such songs as the *Anvil Chorus, Angels Ever Bright and Fair, See, the Conquering Hero Comes* and such patriotic songs as *My Country, 'Tis of Thee* and *The Star-Spangled Banner.*

Eichberg's problem, therefore, was not an artistic problem so much as one of logistics: how to transfer hundreds of groups of young singers from a multitude of locations over the city to a huge auditorium in St. James Park, in the proper sequence so they would be seated in their right places, and be sure they would all arrive and be on time.

While there was considerable experience and some standards of performance for a large group of vocalists, there was nothing similar for a large group of instrumentalists. For the Grand National Concert at New Orleans in 1864, Gilmore apparently had combined into a heterogeneous group the entire membership of twenty-five or thirty bands under his jurisdiction to form a giant band of five hundred pieces.

That is what every other bandmaster before him had done. Jullien in 1851 had assembled a big band in England by combining the players from three regiments of Household Cavalry, three regiments of Footguards, and one regiment of Royal Artillery to form a band of three hundred and fifty players. Before that, in 1838, the inventive Wieprecht, master of bands in the Prussian military forces, had assembled a band of one thousand by uniting the personnel from sixteen cavalry and sixteen infantry bands, to which he added two hundred drummers and fifers from field music units.

The instrumentation for Gilmore's thousand-piece orchestra was partly an artistic achievement and partly the result of fortuitous circumstances. He probably roughed out some general specifications, but he finally had to settle for what he could get. Although he advertised 1000 pieces, actually the orchestra totaled only 939. Even this total was no doubt reached by accepting more brass players than he wanted, for the brass section was out of proportion with the rest of the orchestra. The actual instrumentation for the National Peace Jubilee orchestra is given below.

Violins	215	Woodwinds	119
Violas	65	Brass	295
Cellos	65	Percussion	95
Basses	85		
Sub-Total	430	Sub-Total	509
		Total Players	939

The most specific recommendations regarding the instrumentation for large groups of instrumentalists were worked out by Hector Berlioz. Toward the close of his classic treatise entitled *Modern Instrumentation and Orchestration,* written in 1848, he dreamed up a large orchestra of 465 players and a chorus of 365 voices. He carefully analyzed the function of each kind of instrument and the number of each needed to give a pleasing ensemble and achieve the artistic ends Berlioz had in mind.

It is interesting to compare Gilmore's instrumentation with that recommended by Berlioz, as is done in the following tabulation. Both orchestras have been stepped up to a full thousand players, preserving the same proportions for each kind of instrument found in the smaller organizations. As a sort of side commentary, another thousand-piece orchestra has been added, made up by combining ten modern symphony orchestras, such as Philharmonic Society of New York, the Philadelphia Orchestra, and the Chicago Symphony.

	GILMORE	BERLIOZ	MODERN
Violins	225	260	450
Violas	70	90	75
Cellos	70	100	75
Basses	90	80	50
Harps		65	20
Total Strings	455	595	670
Woodwinds	125	135	150
Brasses	320	110	150
Percussion	100	110	30
Pianos		50	
Sub-Total	545	405	330
Total Players	1000	1000	1000

If we assume that Berlioz is correct—and he usually is in such matters—it is clear that Gilmore was striving for an artistic effect in selecting the instrumentation that he did. If he had merely been combining the personnel of a number of orchestras, he would have ended with an instrumentation more like that in the third column. If Gilmore and Carl Zerrahn had not found brass players more easily come by than string players, it is reasonable to believe that Gilmore's and Berlioz's instrumentations would have been even more nearly comparable.

Certainly both of them recognized the fact that a giant band or orchestra cannot achieve balanced instrumentation simply by combining a number of smaller units to make a greater whole. The instrumentation for a large group should have different proportions from that of a smaller group. Note the emphasis which both give to the percussion section, as contrasted with the additive percussion section in the third column. Their string-bass sections are also stronger in proportion than that in the standard symphony orchestra.

Where Gilmore sacrificed the artistic to the spectacular was in going to a thousand pieces. Berlioz stopped at less than half that number, believing four hundred and sixty-five instrumentalists were the maximum that could be expected to achieve an artistic performance. Gilmore's thousand-piece orchestra was undoubtedly anything but an artistic and musically balanced group, but if it had been selected and assembled along theoretically artistic lines, it probably couldn't have produced first-rate music because it was simply too large for musical purposes.

If anyone had attempted to talk about artistic performance to Carl Zerrahn while he was laboring to recruit one thousand instrumentalists of any kind he could obtain, he'd probably have answered by hurling a music stand. Unselfishly Harvey Dodworth in New York beat the bushes in his territory, trying to get the musicians needed for the Jubilee. George Lyon of Lyon & Healy, the great music house established in Chicago in 1864, did what he could to recruit musicians in the Middle West. Both men were close friends of Gilmore and wanted to see the Jubilee a big success. Other aggressive bandmasters over the country who could be counted on to send their bands to the Jubilee or help recruit players were D. W. Reeves of the American Band, Providence; Thomas Coates of the Easton Band (Pa.); William H. Minninger of the Allentown Band (Pa.); R. W. Carley of the Shelburne Falls Military Band (Mass.); Daniel H. Chandler of the Portland Band (Me.); Captain Price T. Barnetz of the Stonewall Brigade Band, Staunton, Va.; Professor C. E. Moscow of Moscow's Band, Newburgh, N.Y.; and Captain A. Goodman of the Goodman Band, Decatur, Ill.

To recruit ten thousand capable singers for a five-day festival required organized planning of a high order, but Tourjée was equal to the task. An informative circular was printed, giving the music numbers to be sung, outlining directions for rehearsals, and specifying that the balance in the great choir was to be in the following proportions: eight sopranos, seven altos, five tenors, and six basses; but, said the circular, "the volume of tone in each of the parts must be as nearly equal as possible."

Miscellaneous information was included, such as costs of living accommodations in Boston, provisions made to give singers half-fare rates on railroads, the spiritual rewards of participation in such a worthy undertaking, and a material reward of a bound copy of all festival music to each group attending the Jubilee. Entry blanks asked for the name of the music director and detailed information about him which would reveal his qualifications and fitness. The blanks also asked for the total number of singers in the group, broken down by voice.

A master mailing list of all the choirs, choral groups, singing societies, and music teachers in the country was compiled, and the circulars mailed.

In assuming that Tourjée was able to assemble a chorus of ten thousand singers in the proportion, as stated in the circular, of eight sopranos, seven altos, five tenors, and six basses it would be interesting to see what the composition of such a chorus of ten thousand would be and to compare it with a similar chorus of ten thousand made up in the proportions worked out by Berlioz for his chorus of three hundred and sixty-five voices. Berlioz specified forty child soprano voices and one hundred women soprano voices (first and second), one hundred tenors (first and second) and one hundred and twenty basses (first and second). Such a comparison is given below:

	GILMORE	BERLIOZ
Sopranos	3100	3875
Altos	2700	
Tenors	1900	2775
Basses	2300	3350
Total	10000	10000

Differences in nomenclature make it difficult to compare these two choruses, but even if second sopranos and first tenors in Berlioz's chorus take the place of Gilmore's altos, it is obvious that Berlioz is partial to basses.

When Gilmore began thinking about a pipe organ for the Jubilee, he of course thought in superlative terms: it had to be the largest ever built. It was only natural that he would go to E. & G. G. Hook in Boston. These two brothers were making pipe organs in Salem when Gilmore was director of the Salem Brass Band, and in 1868 had just moved their factory to Boston. Besides the attraction of friendship these two brothers had distinguished themselves by building "bigger and better" pipe organs.

In 1853 they had built "the largest pipe organ in America," for the First Tremont Temple in Boston. In 1863 they had built "the largest church organ in the United States," for the Church of the Immaculate Conception in Boston. The following year they hung up another record, this one being "the largest concert organ built in the United States," for the Mechanics Hall in Worcester. When Gilmore went to see them about the Jubilee organ, they had just delivered an organ to the church of the celebrated Henry Ward Beecher in Brooklyn, which was acclaimed as "the most noted organ of American manufacture."

Elias and George Hook listened to their good friend Pat Gilmore as he told them what he had in mind. This Jubilee organ had to have the greatest number of pipes, the greatest number of stops, the greatest number of manuals, the pipes had to be bigger than anything that had been made so far, it had to occupy more space and it had to weigh more . . . When Gilmore ran out of superlative specifications, the Hook brothers added one: it would have "the greatest wind pressure of any organ yet built—at least ten-inch wind."

"That's it," said Gilmore. "You have the right idea. And something else, boys: it'll have to be built in the shortest time, for the Jubilee must open in June of next year."

Everything was shaping up, but now Gilmore faced a most difficult problem. He wanted a soprano soloist—and what soprano had a voice powerful enough to make herself heard in the great and vast space of the coliseum? It just so happened that Euphrosyne Parepa-Rosa, the great English dramatic soprano, was appearing in America at the time with the Carl Rosa Opera Company. Although she had become noted for her opera roles, she was outstanding in oratorio and on the concert stage. She had a magnificent voice with a full two-and-one-half-octave range; besides she was a large and powerful woman.

Gilmore's appeal overwhelmed the great Euphrosyne. She would be more than glad to sing for the great Peace Jubilee; it would be a privilege and an honor. What would be her fee? The fee? Oh yes, the fee. Never mind the fee: she would not mention money in connection with such a wonderful and worthy cause, but would leave that entirely to Mr. Gilmore.

Gilmore no doubt talked fee with Carl Rosa, her husband and manager, but Gilmore evidently made a good bargain, for he ended up by hiring Euphrosyne as soloist and Carl Rosa as concertmaster of the thousand-piece orchestra! Rosa was eminently qualified for the job, for he was a fine violinist, having served as concertmaster in Hamburg, Germany, and later in London.

Following the Civil War, four songs vied with each other for the distinction of national anthem. These were *Hail, Columbia, The Star-Spangled Banner, America,* and *Battle Hymn of the Republic.* But Gilmore felt a new national anthem should be created especially for the Peace Jubilee. Henry Wadsworth Longfellow was the nation's most noted poet, and Gilmore began formulating a speech to convince the famous man he should write some special verses for the big event, only to discover that Mr. Longfellow was in Europe.

Apparently Gilmore had already selected the music for the new anthem, and all he needed was some new verses. The music was to be that composed by Matthias Keller for the *American Hymn*. Keller was a German violinist, bandmaster, and composer who had settled in Boston. He had written both words and music for the *American Hymn* and could probably have written new words appropriate to the Jubilee, for he was known to be an ardent patriot and a talented man. Keller, however, would not be "good box office." Oliver Wendell Holmes was finally selected to write the verses, and the new anthem was entitled *A Hymn of Peace*.

May 1, 1869, set Gilmore on the home stretch and on one of the busiest and most satisfying periods of his life. It was about two years since his "vision," and he was beginning to see this vision materialize in a dramatic way. "Two and one-half million feet of lumber" were going into the big coliseum and it was spreading out and growing higher every day. Rehearsals of choral and orchestral groups from nearby cities were going on in every available theater, church, and auditorium in Boston, and this busy hum was to mount steadily day by day until climaxed by the Jubilee itself.

Best of all, from Gilmore's standpoint, there were plently of news and feature stories for the press. Ole Bull, the famous Norwegian violinist, had consented to occupy a solo chair in the festival orchestra. Acceptances of invitations had been received from President Grant, members of his Cabinet, and other greats of Washington. The celebrated clergyman Edward Everett Hale had agreed to open the Jubilee with a prayer. Lowell Mason, the grand old man of music, would give his blessing by attending as a guest of honor. The Jubilee had become the greatest news subject in New England, and the newspaper and magazine writers exploited every angle they and Pat Gilmore could think up.

During the final days before the opening Gilmore invited members of the press to view the huge pipes of the world's largest pipe organ, being installed in the coliseum, and they were duly impressed. He also gave them a preview of the coliseum itself, from topmost balconies down through the spacious rest rooms. When the day came for the delivery of the giant bass drum, the men and women of the press were given ringside seats where they could see the monster, mounted

in all its majesty on a single flat car, switched to a side track for un-
loading. It was eight feet in diameter and was proclaimed to be the
biggest drum ever built in the history of the world.

Approaches to St. James Park began to take on the appearance of
a carnival. Concession stands were erected, lodgings in private homes
were advertised, and in vacant lots tents were put up and crowded
with cots and mattresses for the visitors. Some of the side shows
which usually followed the big circuses detached themselves and
came to Boston for what they considered would be a big and quick
cleanup. There were pink-lemonade stands, souvenir booths, and all
the other familiar sights of the carnival and circus.

The National Peace Jubilee opened in the afternoon of June 15.
The huge wood coliseum, bedecked with flags on the outside and
inside and smelling of freshly sawed lumber, was filled to overflowing.
At two dollars for single admission and another dollar to three dollars
for reserved seat, the box-office take was most gratifying. When the
place was packed and jammed to capacity, the doors were shut and
locked against hundreds of people who pressed to gain admittance.

After the invocation, a speech of welcome by the mayor of Boston,
and some other preliminaries, Patrick Sarsfield Gilmore gave the
huge audience a taste of things to come when he turned on the full
chorus, the full orchestra, and the big organ in *Eine Feste Burg*. Nothing like it had ever been heard before by mortal ears! This soul-
stirring hymn by Luther set the theme of the Jubilee. Against an instrumental background of one thousand instruments plus the
resources of several thousand pipes from the organ, the words rolled
out from the vast chorus: "A mighty fortress is our God, a bulwark
never failing." At the close of the hymn forty thousand pairs of hands
replied with applause that rocked the building. Gilmore knew then
that his Jubilee would be the success he had envisioned.

As Gilmore bowed himself off the podium, Julius Eichberg quickly
came forward, lifted his baton, and started an orchestra of six hundred players in the *Tannhäuser Overture*. Number followed number,
each one seeming to draw more applause than the one before, until
Madame Parepa-Rosa dwarfed all that had gone before with her
singing of *Inflammatus* from Rossini's *Stabat Mater*. She was one against
thousands—full chorus, orchestra, and organ—and yet so powerful
and penetrating was her magnificent voice that it soared clear and
free above the mass of tone from the vast ensemble. This deeply religious aria is said to have moved the audience to tears. In the words

of one reporter her voice rang like "a trumpet call above the noise of a thousand instruments, ten thousand voices, the roaring organ, the big drum and the artillery." Another wrote that "her voice was five hundred feet long and three hundred feet wide" (the dimensions of the coliseum).

Topping even the phenomenal vocal demonstration by Madame Parepa-Rosa was the *Anvil Chorus* from Verdi's *Il Trovatore*. As Gilmore, with six-foot baton, swung the unwieldly chorus, band, orchestra, and organ into this number, one hundred firemen, dressed in red, wearing regulation helmets and carrying blacksmith hammers at "right shoulder shift" like muskets, marched down the aisle in two files toward the stage. Reaching the orchestra, the two files separated and framed the orchestra on each side in red, each fireman stopping beside an anvil. At a signal from Gilmore the firemen lifted their long-handled hammers and started pounding the anvils in time with the music. From a desk beside the podium Gilmore began punching buttons, wired electrically to cannons outside the building, which created a tremendous boom at the beginning of each measure of the music. Simultaneous with the booming of cannons the bells of the churches and cathedrals in the city began ringing and clanging. Never, since the world began, had human ears been assaulted by such a cacophony of sound!

For five days the Jubilee rocked the rafters of the vast coliseum, the program changing each day but resulting in the same mass hysteria and frenzied applause. General Grant and other dignitaries came and went. Eichberg, Tourjée, Zerrahn, and other Gilmore lieutenants labored valorously to pass on the beat to the ponderous chorus and orchestra and enable all parts of the ensemble to end at the same time, even if they sometimes failed to start together and often strayed separately during a number.

When the Jubilee opened on June 15, John S. Dwight left town. Out of range of cannons and anvils, he still was able to obtain sufficient reports of the goings-on to write in his *Journal of Music:*

Whether the Festival, considered musically, was good or not, it musically did good. At any rate, to all those singers and performers it has given a new impulse, a new consciousness of strength, a new taste of the joy of unity of effort, a new love of co-operation, and a deeper sense of the divine significance and power of music than they ever had.

To the surprise of everyone, including Eben Jordan, the Jubilee showed a net profit of seven thousand dollars. This, added to the profits of a testimonial concert for Gilmore, brought him a total of forty thousand dollars. With his energies well exhausted but with his purse newly filled, he and his wife Ellen set out for an extended vacation in Europe.

One would think that the National Peace Jubilee would have enabled Gilmore to rid his system of the "bigger and better" ague, but a year or so later he suffered another and still more violent attack. This resulted in the World Peace Jubilee, staged in Boston in 1872. The professed occasion was the termination of the Franco-Prussian War. The symptoms and course of the disease were the same as those which resulted in the National Peace Jubilee three years before, but this time they were exactly twice as violent. He developed an orchestra and band of *two* thousand instrumentalists, a chorus of *twenty* thousand adult voices, and a coliseum seating *one hundred* thousand. The world, or international, flavor was obtained by importing musical talent from Europe. Among these were the Grenadier Guards Band from England, the Garde Républicaine Band from France, the Kaiser Franz Grenadier Regiment Band from Germany, and Johann Strauss from Austria.

This time over three hundred choral societies in the United States sent their singers, and Eben Tourjée, now a veteran in the matter of colossal choruses, took on the responsibility of controlling them. Besides the foreign bands there were the U. S. Marine Band, Gilmore's Band, and bands from twenty-six cities. These were placed in the capable hands of J. Thomas Baldwin, who later distinguished himself as leader of the Boston Cadet Band.

The volcanic musical monster started to erupt shortly after three o'clock on Monday afternoon, June 17, 1872. The first number on the opening program was the choral *Old Hundred*. The first verse was sung *pp* by a small group of voices, to the accompaniment of the orchestra only. If anyone in the audience thought for a while that this festival would be quieter and more musical than the previous one, the second verse swept all such thoughts away. At the second verse Gilmore turned everything on full blast—twenty thousand voices, one thousand-piece orchestra, one thousand-piece band, and full organ: all screaming and blasting away double forte!

For eighteen days the eruption continued. Mercifully there were

Two thousand musicians were placed in the capable hands of J. Thomas Baldwin, later conductor of the Boston Cadet Band.

some lapses during which quieter music was played and the audience could rest their eardrums. Such were the individual appearances by the visiting bands, and the Strauss waltzes, directed by Johann Strauss himself.

Strauss became an outstanding favorite. He brought along with him his Vienna orchestra of fifty-six players, and one of the most delightful experiences of the festival was to see and hear Johann conduct one of his celebrated waltzes. Johann would start to play his violin along with the orchestra. Soon he would become so swept away by his own music that he would stop playing but would retain his hold on violin and bow, waving them both in the air to mark the exuberant rhythm of the waltz.

One anticipated eruption did not happen. Every day the bands of different nations would march down the aisles of the great coliseum to their respective places. This pageantry was staged to give the audiences an opportunity to admire the resplendent appearance of these celebrated bands. They were small according to modern standards, the Garde Républicaine Band of France numbering fifty-five players, the Grenadier Guards Band of England numbering forty-five and the Kaiser Franz Grenadier Regiment Band of Germany numbering only thirty-five. What they lacked in numbers, however, they made up in rich uniforms and handsome mustaches.

Remembering that the Franco-Prussian War had just ended, many spectators feared that hostilities might break out anew when either the English or French bands came into contact with the German band. It is said that many scowls were exchanged during the marching and other contacts. Hatred and enmity reigned in the midst of this World Peace Jubilee until one day when the French Garde Républicaine Band played a number entitled the *Torch Light Dance*. This fine band played with such finesse and musicianship that the ranks of the Grenadier Regiment Band of Germany broke forth in enthusiastic applause. This generous and wholehearted act swept away hatred and prejudice and made them musician brothers.

Critics generally regarded the English band as good, the German band as too brassy, the French band as superb. The effect of the French band was partly owing to its unusual instrumentation. It carried eight saxophones, four bassoons, one contrabassoon, and some large, conically tapered tubas. The result, said one competent critic, "was so round, full and soft that all musicians were captivated with the deep diapason of sound."

Finally, on July 4, all was quiet in Back Bay Boston. The last rumble had rumbled and the World Peace Jubilee had ended. When the smoke and dust had cleared away, Gilmore was presented with two gold medals and fifty thousand dollars in cash.

So far as is known, John S. Dwight failed to give this festival a back-handed compliment as he had done previously, but others are on record that the festival justified itself by furnishing the world with the pun of the century. At one of the concerts the choir of twenty-thousand voices got completely out of hand. Tourjée and others gesticulated and shouted, trying to bring the various sections together. It was hopeless, however, and the discord increased with each bar of music. The audience finally broke out in hilarious, uproarious laughter when everyone realized the selection being performed was Handel's *All We, Like Sheep, Have Gone Astray*.

Gilmore had one more attack of the "bigger and better" ague, but it was so slight that it attracted relatively little attention. While Gilmore was in Europe in the fall of 1871, wheedling kings and premiers into sending their top bands to his World Peace Jubilee, the unprecedented two-hundred-million-dollar fire swept across Chicago. To commemorate the speedy rebuilding of the city, Chicago engaged Gilmore and his band for a three-day festival in June 1873.

This engagement was an eloquent testimonial to the position held by the Gilmore band. Chicago, "the city of GO," had to have the most outstanding attraction of the age to help celebrate its great triumph over the devastating fire. There could be no doubt in anyone's mind as to what was the most outstanding attraction of the age: it was Patrick Gilmore and His Band.

Little did the people of Chicago realize at the time he was engaged that Gilmore had taken the cure. The "bigger and better" ague, which had struck him three times and had driven him to ever greater

The volcanic monster started to erupt shortly after three o'clock on June 17, 1872.
BETTMANN ARCHIVE

and greater frenzied inspiration, had finally been brought under control.

In fact Gilmore began immediately reacting to the idea like a cured alcoholic reacts to a stiff drink. He professed being appalled when members of the Chicago committee requested that he put on the *Anvil Chorus*, with anvils, cannons, and bells, as he had staged it so many times. He tried to beg out of it, but it was useless. Like a character actor, Gilmore had become typed as the impresario of the *Anvil Chorus*. He finally compromised with the committee by staging the *Anvil Chorus* with anvils but without cannons and bells.

Gilmore arrived in Chicago on Tuesday evening, June 3. He was greeted with appropriate fanfare by leading citizens, almost as if he had been President of the United States. Rehearsals were at that

*Finally, on July 4, all was quiet
. . . the last rumble had rumbled and
the World Peace Jubilee had ended.*
CULVER SERVICE

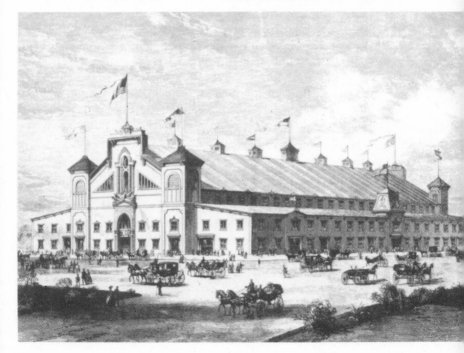

moment going on in the great new railway station. Gilmore presently left the festivities being conducted in his honor and went to observe and oversee the rehearsals.

In the dim reaches of the glass and steel and concrete edifice he discovered a chorus of one thousand singers, striving valorously with a number specially written for the festival by Campbell and entitled *New Chicago Hymn of Praise*. What he heard and saw worried him. The railway concourse was designed and built for railway trains and passengers and not for concerts. It was very long and relatively narrow, and the hard floor, walls, and ceiling reverberated violently. At the close of the number the sound continued to bounce around the great enclosure and echo and re-echo for several seconds. When Gilmore was introduced to the group, the cheers that went up fairly shattered the glass windowpanes.

The Gilmore "band" arrived from Boston the following afternoon and was hustled off to the Oriental Hotel. Gilmore had brought only thirty-odd players, about half his regular band. These players were to form the nucleus of the three hundred players who were to comprise the "giant" festival band, the rest of the band to be recruited from among Chicago musicians.

On June 4 the festival opened with the singing of the *New Chicago Hymn of Praise*. The musical results were appalling. The three-hundred-piece band and the thousand singers were placed at the far end of the concourse, and by the time the music had bounced around from side to side and from floor to ceiling of the vast structure, it was hardly distinguishable when it reached the audience. With dogged determination Gilmore struggled through this program, resolved never again to go through another like it.

During the night the position of the band and chorus was moved to the center of the building, with slight improvement. The narrow dimensions of the concourse compelled Gilmore to stretch out his band and chorus along one wall, the audience being seated at either end. This arrangement resulted in placement of some of the chorus so far to either side of the conductor's podium that Gilmore could hardly hear what was going on at the extreme ends. Nevertheless Gilmore did his best. He was all smiles and as full of bounce as the acoustics of the vast echo chamber. The listeners in the audience were not critical, and they reveled in the cracking, echoing discords.

The festival went on inexorably. The worst was yet to come, on the day that the regular chorus and band were augmented by a chorus of one thousand school children. More bunting and flags were strung along the steel supports and roof struts, in an effort to absorb some of the reverberation and deaden the lively echoes, but to little avail.

It was a relief to escape the railway depot torture chamber and give a band concert in Hyde Park on Saturday afternoon. That evening, however, a benefit performance for Gilmore was given in the railway station, by band, chorus, and soloists, and Gilmore concluded that he had earned every cent he collected for his efforts. With praise and encomiums ringing in their ears Gilmore and the remnants of his band entrained for New York, glad to escape further punishment.

Before Gilmore left Chicago he was interviewed by George P. Upton, leading music light of Chicago and music editor of the Chicago *Tribune*. This interview brought out an almost incomprehensible statement to Upton by Gilmore. About his use of anvils, cannons, and church bells, Upton noted that Gilmore "would be delighted if only he could have church bells, cannons and anvils with every piece he played, not merely for their effect upon audiences but because he enjoyed them himself. This passion for tumultuous noise and bizarre sensations," commented Upton, "was a curious feature in his musical make-up, for off stage he was very quiet, refined and unobtrusive."

Regardless of these professions by Gilmore, his wife Ellen and he privately concluded that he had effectively rid his system of the ague. In succeeding years, when he remembered the Chicago festival, the more sure he became that he was forever cured, and could thenceforth devote his talents and energy to revolutionizing the American concert band.

Four

GILMORE AND
THE 22ND REGIMENT
BAND

*For the next twenty years
Gilmore devoted his life to the
22nd Regiment Band.*
BETTMANN ARCHIVE

Shortly after Gilmore returned with his band from the jaunt to Chicago during the summer of 1873, he received word from the officers of the 22nd Regiment of New York that they wanted him to direct their band. For several years past he had been considering ways of breaking into New York. This offer seemed to be the opening he had been waiting for and he accepted. For the next twenty years he devoted his life to developing this band into what probably was the greatest in the world at that time.

The drive behind Gilmore's activities now was musical excellence in band performance. He had lost interest in bands of two thousand performers, one thousand, or even five hundred, and, as he said to a friend, "I'm through with tornado choruses." Having immunized his system against "bigger and better," he now saw, figuratively, that there was more skill and finesse displayed in a baseball game with nine good men on the team than there could possibly be with ninety or two hundred men. Ninety men on the diamond might create a spectacle, but they couldn't play winning baseball.

European band performance had made him see the need for improving American bands. When he went to Europe for a vacation, following the National Peace Jubilee in 1869, he received his first eye opener. At the International Exhibition in Paris in 1867 a band contest had been conducted to select the finest bands in Europe. Nine countries sent bands, and twenty of the leading musicians of Europe were the judges. First prizes were awarded to the Prussian eighty-five-piece Imperial Guards Band under Wieprecht, to the French sixty-five-piece Garde de Paris Band under Paulus, and to the Austrian seventy-six-piece 73rd Regiment Band under Zimmerman. England sent no band to the contest, even though the French Government had asked that the Royal Artillery Band under Smyth be entered as a contestant. Many English musicians thought that the Grenadier Guards Band under Dan Godfrey should represent England rather than the Royal Artillery Band, but the issue was resolved when no band at all was sent.

With such authoritative guidance as the band contest it was easy for Gilmore to "have a listen" to the best bands in Europe and England, and what he heard was not flattering to American bands, even to his own band in Boston.

On the second trip to Europe, in 1871, he was able to engage the Grenadier Guards Band under Dan Godfrey and the Garde Républicaine Band (the Garde de Paris Band with a new name) under Paulus. According to twenty distinguished judges four years before, the Prussian Imperial Guards Band was the finest across the seas, but for some reason Gilmore either didn't try for it or was unsuccessful in his efforts to bring this famous band to the United States. It may have been because the sixty-nine-year-old Wieprecht felt he was too old to make the trip. Wieprecht may have been at the time failing physically, for he died the following year. In any event, Gilmore settled for the Kaiser Franz Grenadier Regiment Band under Saro.

At the Jubilee, for ready comparison with these imported bands, were three of America's better-known bands: Gilmore's own band, the U. S. Marine Band under Henry Fries, and the 9th Regiment Band of

New York under D. L. Downing. Gilmore, as he listened to these bands from overseas, was too much of a musician not to be fully aware of their superiority. They had a more pleasing balance of reeds and brass, greater smoothness of performance, more flexibility and shades of tone. He believed he knew the secret of their superior playing, and he began making definite plans for a better band of his own.

Not only was he deeply impressed by their outstanding performance, but he also was struck by the kind of music these overseas bands played. Typical programs contained fewer quicksteps and marches and polkas and popular songs, and more of the classics. Gilmore had long been celebrated for using more of the music from the classic operas and symphonies than other bandmasters, but these overseas program makers went far beyond the overtures to *Tannhäuser* and *William Tell* and the *Anvil Chorus* from *Il Trovatore*. Since 1850, led by Wieprecht, bandmasters in Europe had been arranging for band most of the entire symphonies of Beethoven and many of the symphonies of Mozart, Mendelssohn, Berlioz, Schubert, and Schumann; overtures and other music from the operas of Von Weber, Meyerbeer, Wagner, Rossini, Verdi, Gounod, Auber, and Thomas.

In Boston, Gilmore had been a "big duck in a little puddle," but he had no qualms about bucking the big bands in New York. The most famous of these was the Dodworth Band under Harvey B. Dodworth.

For nearly forty years the Dodworth Band had led all other bands in musical excellence because of an aggressive and progressive attitude toward all things musical. As Gilmore himself said of the Dodworth Band a few years later, "To be a member of the organization, or to have graduated from it, must mark a man as a star in the profession." Many improvements in the instrumentation of American bands were the result of innovations championed by Harvey Dodworth and his elder brother Allen, who led the band from 1836 to 1860. Better instruments were always sought, and some of them were invented by the Dodworths, such as the "ebor cornos," a valve alto and a valve tenor to supply middle harmony before the saxhorns had been made available. Harvey was credited with introducing the saxophones, bass clarinet, and BB♭ bass tuba into American bands.

Besides directing the Dodworth Band, Harvey was conductor of the 13th Regiment Band, a duty he assumed in 1839, when he was only seventeen years old. Although but a youth, he was known for his exceptional native musical ability and sound musical training.

For fifty years he worked for the best interests of the band and brought it to a high state of musical performance. In 1860 his brother Allen wished to retire from band activity and devote himself entirely to teaching and coaching dancing. He urged his brother to take over the baton of the Dodworth Band. Harvey consented, but when he attempted to resign from the 13th, popular demand forced him to continue. He therefore found himself conductor of two of New York's best bands. Although the Dodworth Band was a superior organization musically, the 13th was very popular. In 1867 it became the "official" Central Park Band, and thousands of New Yorkers were regular patrons of these summer concerts. It was generally considered as the fourth ranking band in New York.

The second most celebrated New York band was the 7th Regiment Band under C. S. Grafulla. Like most other early bands, it was at one time a brass band, but in 1853 it was reorganized as a reed and brass band by Kroll and Reitzel, one of the first bands in America to adopt the modern idea of reed and brass instrumentation. In 1860 it was merged with the famous Shelton band, then under the directorship of Grafulla, and the combined band, now numbering forty select players, became the 7th. Under Grafulla it rose to become the chief rival of the Dodworth Band. Grafulla was a talented and prolific arranger of band music, and the library of the band became one of the best; the performance of the band was outstanding.

Rated as the third greatest band in New York was the 9th Regiment Band under D. L. Downing. Fierce rivalry existed among the various regiments of the New York National Guard, and Colonel James Fisk, Jr., could no longer endure the band prestige enjoyed by the rival 7th under Grafulla and the 13th under Harvey Dodworth. In 1870 he decided to have a band second to none, and he called in Downing, well-known bandmaster, composer, and arranger. During three busy years Downing had recruited some of the best musicians, had built an extensive library of music, and had achieved a standard of musical performance that was widely praised.

Rivalry among the regiments was also probably behind the offer from the 22nd to Gilmore. Ernest Neyer was at that time director of the band. He was a talented cornetist and an able director, but he was young and his efforts did not seem to satisfy. Years later he was to demonstrate his ability by becoming director of the Dodworth Band after Harvey Dodworth resigned in 1890 and by distinguishing himself as director of the 7th Regiment Band, which he took over in 1897. But Gilmore was a proved leader with a reputation for doing great and unusual things, and subsequent years confirmed the wisdom of this choice.

It must not be assumed that these four prominent bands of New York were typical of the bands to be found throughout America. They were not typiçal: they were outstanding exceptions. These four bands and the Gilmore band had no peers anywhere in the land, and only a scattered few even approached them.

Although rightfully respected and celebrated, because it was the oldest band in America and the President's own band, the U. S. Marine Band at this time was a second-rate musical organization. During the seventy-five years of its existence the band had had fifteen different directors. The authorized number of performing musicians was only thirty men. Enlistment in the band was regarded by the players as a sinecure from which they could not be discharged, and there was little incentive to rise above the mediocre. The music library was meager and obsolete. No creditable band could function under such conditions.

Two of the best civilian bands at this time were the American Band, of Providence, R.I., under D. W. Reeves, and the Easton Band (Pa.) under Thomas Coates. Both men were what Gilmore termed "stars in the profession," for Reeves once played cornet and Coates once played French horn in the Dodworth Band. Coates became director of the Easton band before 1850, the band then being nearly twenty years old. He was among the vanguard to discard the keyed-bugle family in favor of piston instruments and later to add a generous complement of reeds. His high standing as a progressive musician was evidenced in 1862 when he was appointed a member of the U. S. Army advisory board on bands, along with such distinguished authorities as Harvey Dodworth, C. S. Grafulla, and D. L. Downing.

D. W. Reeves was an American, but he went to England for his musical training, and toured the British Isles and Europe as leader of the Newcombe Minstrels Band. He became a noted cornet soloist and composer of marches. In 1866 he accepted the leadership of the American Band, following Joseph Green, who had been director since 1842. Reeves was richly endowed with musical ability, good taste and judgment, and thorough training in the fundamentals of his art. Coupled with these were the experience and contact with some of the best bands across the seas. With such a background he had the vision and the ability to recruit and train a band which was, as early as 1873, far above the usual town band.

It is hardly fair to state that these two bands were the only good civilian bands in the country at the time, but it is enlightening to take a look at some of the other contemporary "leading" bands. For instance, the Allentown Band (Pa.), which claims to be the oldest civilian band in America and which today is undoubtedly one of our finest, in 1872 had an instrumentation of five cornets, two trombones, four clarinets, and about a dozen of the old Civil War over-the-shoulder valve instruments in assorted sizes—a total of twenty-five players.

The Ringgold Band of Reading, Pa., another of today's top civilian bands, was organized in 1852, but as late as 1885, under the leadership of Joseph Winter, this band had only twenty-three players. Still another band which has become famous is the Stonewall Brigade Band of Staunton, Va., but in 1875, during its thirtieth year of

Allentown Band (Pa.), "leading" civilian band of 1872, had only twenty-five players.

endeavor, it had only fourteen players. The Shelburne Falls Military Band (Mass.), a band that today can point to one hundred and twenty years of continuous existence, had only sixteen men in 1874, and these were equipped with German-silver, rotary-valve cornets and saxhorns plus tenor, baritone, and bass over-the-shoulder instruments of ancient design, manufactured by the Boston Musical Instrument Company.

As for new bands that were organized during this period, what was their idea of a band and what did they have to look forward to? The Brass Band of Glenville, N.Y., furnishes an interesting example. It was organized in 1876 and was comprised of ten players, equipped as follows:

2 E♭ cornets
2 B♭ cornets
1 B♭ valve trombone
2 E♭ altos
1 B♭ tenor
1 B♭ baritone
1 E♭ bass tuba

These were all made of German silver with polished brass bells and rotary valves, except the two E♭ cornets, which were made entirely of German silver. They were manufactured in Germany by a brother of Charles Schreiber, music dealer in Schenectady, from whom the instruments were purchased. The entire set cost $220 and each member paid $22.

Weekly rehearsals were held in a small one-room structure which previously had been a harness shop. The instruction book used was *The Amateur Journal,* written by J. F. O. Smith and published by E. A. Samuels of Boston. It contained thirty-two pieces of band music which were supposed to be "arranged in a progressive manner."

After a few years drums and cymbals were added, as well as a B♭ helicon bass and a B♭ fluegelhorn. When the organization had grown to nineteen members, it is recorded that the band struck a bonanza when it played for a political rally and received pay of $60. The band's idea of musical superiority was to blow louder than an oncoming band on the countermarch, and thereby drown it out. The supreme test of a bass drummer was to be able "to maintain a regular beat." Their show-off pieces were the quickstep *Triumphant* by Bleger and *Garry Owen,* the music General Custer always used when he started the charge of his cavalry against the Indians.

Gilmore was well acquainted with the status of bands in America: the half-dozen really progressive bands, the few above-average bands scattered here and there, and the hundreds and hundreds of small town bands to be found in increasing numbers wherever he went. These last were poorly equipped, inadequately trained, and doomed to a low level of artistic performance because they knew of nothing better.

Gilmore was the most traveled, the most cosmopolitan, and the best-informed bandmaster of his age. His bands in Salem and in Boston had accepted engagements from outside their territories. He had twice journeyed to Chicago with his band and had played in whatever towns he could book, going and coming. He obtained a wide knowledge of service bands during the enlistment in the Civil War of his band with the Massachusetts 24th Regiment. Hundreds of players came under his observation later when he was reorganizing the state militia bands of Massachusetts and when he had charge of all bands under General Nathaniel Banks, commander of the Department of the Gulf in New Orleans. He had an unparalleled opportunity to know about bands in the hinterlands when he was recruiting musicians for the two Peace Jubilees in Boston. Twice he had crossed the Atlantic and had become acquainted with the best bands in England and in Europe.

The band Gilmore had in mind when he accepted the offer from the 22nd Regiment was one not only as good as the Dodworth Band or the 7th Regiment Band but much better. It would be even superior to anything in England or Europe. In America it would be so far above any band yet developed that it would be for years to come THE BAND after which all other good bands would be patterned. He would tour the country with this great band and he would play Wagner and Liszt, Mozart and Beethoven, Verdi and Rossini along with the quicksteps and polkas and popular songs. He would spread the gospel of good music throughout the United States and Canada. He would engage the finest musicians and soloists and give the people from coast to coast a new idea and a higher ideal of musical performance. He would even tour Europe and demonstrate that the New World could play as well as, if not better than, the Old World.

Gilmore's plans for the future were, as always, ambitious and bold,

*Famous Stonewall Brigade Band, Staunton, Va., organized in 1845.
In 1875 it had only fourteen players.*

but he had a way of making the most superlative plans become a reality.

In a little less than four months after accepting the offer to form a new band for the 22nd Regiment, he assembled sixty-five of the best musicians he could find and gave his first concert on November 18 in the Academy of Music in New York City. He was able to bring a number of good men from his old band in Boston, among them E. A. Lefebre, virtuoso of the saxophone, and Matthew Arbuckle, virtuoso of the cornet, both of whom Jullien had brought to America nearly twenty years before.

The personnel of the band was not everything Gilmore could ask for, and there was too little time for rehearsals, but it was a competent group which carried out the assignment satisfactorily. The program was not what Gilmore had dreamed of, but it had to be ar-

ranged to fit the talent he had so hastily gathered together. The band
performed to advantage when it played the stirring overture to *Der
Freischütz* by Von Weber and the brilliant and showy overture to
Semiramide by Rossini, with its dazzling opening followed by the
beautiful choral for brass instruments and the principal theme played
by the clarinets. There were also melodious selections from Von
Flotow's *Martha* and two new marches composed by Gilmore. Lefebre and Arbuckle, the two great soloists, displayed their unequaled
virtuosity, Arbuckle especially spellbinding the audience with the intricacies of De Bériot's *Seventh Air Varie*.

The program closed with a dramatic flourish, as seven cornetists
marched out to the front of the stage with their instruments, to be
joined a moment later by Gilmore himself with his cornet. Accompanied by the band, this octet of cornets played the *Concert Polka* and

brought the house down. Gilmore had made the most of everything he had; the officers of the 22nd and their friends were elated, and they talked of much greater achievements to come.

This opening concert by the new Gilmore band was followed by a series of his famous promenade concerts every Saturday evening in the 22nd Regiment Armory. These informal concerts became very popular in New York, as they had been in Boston, and every Saturday night large crowds of New Yorkers forgathered at Fourteenth Street near Sixth Avenue to hear the band and promenade around the armory.

Emma Thursby's name has been tied with Gilmore's Band ever since that night of November 27, 1874, when the band played at her recital in Plymouth Church in Brooklyn. Miss Thursby was a promising twenty-nine-year-old coloratura soprano who had been attracting considerable attention by her singing in the Plymouth Church, and by her appearance with the Brooklyn Philharmonic Society, conducted by Theodore Thomas. She was sponsored by the church and received from the church a salary of modest amount. Although always a devout young woman, she wanted to put on a paid recital which would be out of the ordinary. She contacted Gilmore and explained her idea to him. He was captivated by her charm and her glorious voice and agreed to furnish his band for the recital at a fee of only $350, with Lefebre and Arbuckle thrown in at her request. She specifically stated that she wanted Arbuckle and Lefebre to accompany her in certain of her solos.

The recital was a success, artistically and financially, and the proceeds were donated to the church, to which Miss Thursby felt a strong obligation.

Gilmore must have had some explaining to do before the Musical Protective Union, because the $350 charged was less than the union scale. The musicians' union was something new to Gilmore; in fact, this union was a novelty to the whole country, and it is believed to have been the only union of its kind at the time. It had been organized originally in 1863 because of the plight of the great number of musicians who had located in New York City. The playing fee had been from $2.00 to $4.00 for musicians and $5.00 for the leader, but price cutting was rampant and the fee paid was usually less. Out of this fee the musicians were taxed 5 per cent for music and other expenses, although they never at any time had any equity in the music library. This tax was the original gripe which led to the formation of the union. The rules adopted by the union required the leader to buy and furnish all music, and they set the playing fees somewhat higher.

When the demands of the union were presented, the leaders refused to accept them. The deadlock was broken, however, by the fortuitous arrival of the Russian fleet in New York Harbor. A grand ball was held in the Academy of Music, the orchestra seats being covered with a temporary flooring. Besides the ball many other functions were arranged, and the demand for musicians far exceeded the supply. Rather than pass up this influx of business the leaders agreed to accept the union terms.

The Musical Protective Union was strengthened in 1865 by the postwar gaiety, over six hundred balls being held in New York City alone. By 1874, the year in which Gilmore sold the services of his band to Emma Thursby for $350, the union had twelve hundred members. It is not known exactly what the fees were that year, but two years later they were as follows: first-class ball, $9.00; ordinary ball, $7.00; regimental parade, $7.00; company parade, $6.00; concert, $7.00. On holidays musicians received $2.00 extra. The leader always received double the musician fee.

If the fee in 1874 was $7.00 for a concert, sixty-five men would have cost $455 and the director would have cost $14, making $469. Since soloists were paid more than regular musicians, the total probably ran close to $500. Just how Gilmore explained himself out of this difficulty is not known, but he was always a good talker, free with his Irish wit and blarney, and there is little doubt that he came out on top.

The year 1873 was an unfavorable one in which to start a new band, for this was the year of a great financial panic. Many banks across the nation failed, and conditions became so bad that the New York Clearing House was suspended from September 20 to September 30. The effects of this panic depressed business for several years afterward. Gilmore felt the squeeze along with all types of business, but it was especially serious with Gilmore because his band was new and not well established. The money paid by the 22nd Regiment was not sufficient to keep sixty-five good men, and outside jobs in New York were hard to get. Gilmore began to look elsewhere for sources of revenue.

It didn't take Gilmore long to figure out that his only salvation was to tour the country with his band. With three or four older, better-entrenched bands in New York, competing for a limited number of engagements, he could see a big advantage in taking his band to other cities that did not have top-notch bands.

If he could not reason the matter out for his own situation, he could read the lesson clearly in the previous experience of Theodore Thomas. In 1866 Thomas had formed a permanent symphony orchestra of his own, and had obligated himself to keep his sixty men busy with concerts. He opened in the Terrace Garden with a series of Summer Concerts and played his regular engagements during the winter. After two seasons at the Terrace Garden, the Summer Concerts were moved to the Central Park Garden.

At this time there were, in the whole United States, only two other permanent symphony orchestras: the New York Philharmonic under Carl Bergmann, and the Brooklyn Philharmonic Society, which Thomas himself directed. Boston had had an orchestra under Carl Zerrahn from 1855 until 1863, but it had been abandoned, and was not to be revived until 1881, when the Boston Symphony Orchestra was established by Major Henry Lee Higginson and conducted by Georg Henschel. Chicago had had its Philharmonic Society on an intermittent basis since 1850, under Dyhrenfurth, Ahner, Unger, and finally Balatha, but now it had given up, and was not to be revived until Thomas took over in 1891. In Cincinnati, Frédéric L. Ritter had formed the Philharmonic Orchestra in 1857, but it languished and died when Ritter went to New York in 1861. Not until 1895 was Cincinnati to have a symphony orchestra, when Van der Stucken took up the task. In 1866, when Thomas formed his orchestra, there was little more than the beginnings of an orchestra in Philadelphia, St. Louis, Cleveland, San Francisco, and other of our leading cities, all of which now have large and capably directed symphony orchestras.

Yet, in spite of competition from only the New York and Brooklyn orchestras, Thomas's concerts were not well attended and financial problems were constantly plaguing him. It was not that the other two orchestras got the business away from him: he did better than either of them. The facts were that in New York at that time there wasn't a sufficient number of people to support adequately even one fine orchestra. Finally, in 1869, he made his first tour. He had no competition from symphony orchestras in any of the cities where he booked engagements, and year after year for twenty-two years he was to take his celebrated orchestra on tour.

Several times during these weary years his hopes rose with the prospect that his orchestra would be afforded a permanent concert hall and assured financial support, but in the end all plans and promises fell through and Thomas was forced to resume his travels. He was booked into churches, opera houses, armories, and even railroad stations, and he brought great music to thousands of people for the first time. It was a grueling experience, but in this way he held his talented musicians together as a highly developed, top-ranking orchestra.

Gilmore arrived at the same conclusions reached by Thomas, and in January 1875 he left New York City with his band, spending part of two months on tour and traveling as far west as St. Louis. He played such cities as Boston, Washington, Baltimore, Philadelphia, Pittsburgh, Cleveland, Detroit, Chicago, St. Louis, Cincinnati, and Louisville, with some smaller towns to break the jumps.

Knowing what box-office attractions Jenny Lind, Patti, and other concert sopranos had been, he engaged Emma Thursby as soloist with the band. This bit of showmanship undoubtedly added thousands of dollars to the ticket sales. Gilmore limited her repertoire mostly to simple songs, like *Silver Threads among the Gold* and Mason's *Nearer, My God, to Thee,* but he also programmed a few "war horse" pieces which allowed her to show off her vocal gymnastics. Chief among these was Proch's *Variations,* which she sang with the band and with flute obbligato.

Arbuckle on cornet and Lefebre on saxophone displayed their instrumental virtuosity on every program, and there were novelty groups of instruments which never failed to produce applause. Altogether, the tour was a definite success. This band of Gilmore's, although not up to the standard Gilmore had dreamed about, was the finest most people had ever heard. Reviews by the music critics were uniformly warm in their praise of the musicianship of the group.

It must have been on this visit to St. Louis by Gilmore's Band that Charles Seymour, a local budding cornetist, went to see Ben Bent, the celebrated cornet soloist of the band. Years afterward, when he had become a well-known performer on the cornet and director of bands in St. Louis, Seymour related the incident. He had heard about Bent and his prowess with the cornet; in fact, being a youth and of susceptible age, he had developed a strong case of hero worship for the man. He attended a concert, taking a front-row seat so he could observe the great soloist and learn, if possible, some pointers that would help him in his own struggle for mastery of the instrument. What a disappointment, then, to watch the great Bent sit through the whole concert with his cornet across his lap!

After the concert Seymour screwed up his courage to the utmost and introduced himself to Bent. "I was greatly relieved," related Seymour, "to find Bent friendly and affable. During the conversation I made bold to ask him why he had not played at all during the concert. Bent replied that he had been engaged by Gilmore to play only when Arbuckle, who sat in the first chair solo cornet position, chanced to rest. Arbuckle, however, did not rest, and there was nothing for Bent to do but sit it out.

"Much later I learned of the jealous disposition of Arbuckle and his resentment against Bent as an understudy for his position. The story goes that Bent did not play a single note during the entire season. The following season, however, Arbuckle was paid back in kind, for the great Jules Levy was added to the band, and Levy made life so miserable for Arbuckle that Arbuckle forgot all about Bent."

Three months after returning to New York, Gilmore took his band into its new home, called Gilmore Garden. Such concert gardens were more or less common in Europe, and in New York Theodore Thomas had been conducting his orchestra for several years in the Terrace Garden and in the Central Park Garden. Refreshments of various kinds were served at tables while the customers listened to the music, conversed with companions, and enjoyed the cool breeze of the summer evening. Everything was very informal and relaxed, and somewhat bohemian in character.

Gilmore had taken over the old Hippodrome which P. T. Barnum had built two years before to house his "Greatest Show on Earth." This was a huge wood structure occupying a square block bounded by Madison and Fourth, Twenty-Sixth and Twenty-Seventh streets, with entrances on Madison and on Fourth. Gilmore had transformed the vast area into a quiet, green, cool garden, with broad gravel walks, growing plants, blooming flowers, and spouting fountains. Except on Saturday there were no concerts in the afternoon, but the garden was such an inviting place that it attracted many people even then. On Saturday afternoon and every evening, when Gilmore and his band appeared, the place was packed.

From May 29 until October 28, Gilmore and his band played one hundred and fifty consecutive concerts to overflow audiences. Gilmore considered this some kind of record, and he celebrated the final concert with a special gala program. Never a man to pass up an op-

Theodore Thomas had presented a long series of concerts for several years at the Central Park Garden.

portunity to toot his own horn, he reveled in the questionable distinction of having presented such a long series of concerts. Theodore Thomas and his orchestra had been doing it for several years at the Central Park Garden. In fact, during his first season there Thomas performed one hundred and eighty concerts, and the second season one hundred and sixty.

In order to help Gilmore celebrate his achievement it is said that ten thousand persons pushed their way into the garden, each paying the regular fifty cents for admission. Gilmore saw to it that they received their money's worth. After an otherwise thrill-packed program

of special music Pat sent them away with a final number that was the talk of the town for days afterward. This was performed by four of the greatest cornet players of that time—Matthew Arbuckle, Jules Levy, Ben Bent, and Pat Gilmore. They played a quartet and band arrangement of *Echo de Mont* by Suck, which gave scope to their individual and combined virtuosity.

After a farewell concert on April 1, 1876, at the 22nd Regiment Armory, Gilmore and his band left New York for a five-week tour, which took them to San Francisco. Concerts were given on the way in Buffalo, Detroit, Chicago, Omaha, and Salt Lake City. Utah was still a territory and was not to be admitted to the Union for another twenty years. Only five years before Gilmore's Band visited Salt Lake City, Brigham Young, leader of the Mormons, had been arrested for polygamy. In 1869 the city listened to its first opera: Offenbach's *La Grande Duchesse de Gérolstein*. In the same year the nation's attention had been focused on Ogden, Utah, about forty miles to the north, when former Governor Leland Stanford of California drove the famous gold spike uniting the Union Pacific and Central Pacific systems and establishing the first transcontinental railway.

Regardless of its frontier status Salt Lake City gave the band a tumultuous welcome. When Gilmore's troupe reached the city late in the evening of April 12, they were met at the station by a local band and half the people of the city, all cheering wildly. A torchlight parade escorted them to the theater where the band was to play. At the head of the procession pranced four beautifully matched horses, pulling an elegant barouche, in which were seated in regal style Gilmore and Emma Thursby, Arbuckle and Levy, the last two scowling at each other because of having to share the spotlight equally. The next day merchants closed their stores during the matinee performance, which was given in the Mormon Tabernacle by special consent from Brigham Young.

A copy of the April 12 program shows the names of the soloists and principal musicians in the band, headed by Emma Thursby as featured soprano. Then follow:

> Jules Levy, *The greatest cornet player living*
> M. Arbuckle, *The great favorite American cornet player*
> E. A. Lefebre, *Saxophone*
> Carl Kegel, *Clarinet*
> De Carlo, *Piccolo*
> F. Bracht, *Flute*
> F. Letsch, *Trombone*
> B. C. Bent, *Cornet*
> Letsman, *Tuba*
> Bernstein, *Tympani*

It is extremely amusing and a pointed example of the tact and diplomacy of Gilmore to read the words of appraisal following the names of Levy and Arbuckle. Levy comes off better, it must be admitted, because of top billing if nothing else. Arbuckle, however, is called "the great favorite" and it is brought out that he is an "American." Coming from Gilmore, these honeyed words sounded both to Arbuckle and to Levy as if Gilmore had given each top billing.

There are many anecdotes relating to this suave trait in Gilmore. Russian Princess Dolgorovsky was once engaged to play a violin number with the band, but just before the concert she came fuming to Gilmore when she noted that her name was printed on the programs in the same-size type as that of other artists, and she resolutely refused to appear. Not batting an eye, Gilmore looked at the program and soothingly replied, with one of his disarming smiles, "But I have placed your name at the top, where it rightfully belongs because of your high rank among the nobility and your outstanding ability as a musical artist." That did it! She murmured her thanks and appeared as programed.

During the National Peace Jubilee, while Madame Parepa-Rosa was "climbing the golden stairs" in *Let the Bright Seraphim,* a Mrs. Dunlap of Chicago became so overwrought with emotion that she died of heart failure. In an interview with the press about the fatality Gilmore released the following statement: "No one more pure and gentle, more tender and affectionate could have been chosen to bear to the angelic choir above, tidings of the glorious scene on earth, of the thousands listening in rapt reverence to the sacred songs that inspired the souls of the great masters." And so did soft words turn away wrath—and a possible lawsuit.

There apparently was no special reason to put adjectives after Lefebre's name, for he was regarded then, and is still regarded today, as the greatest saxophone soloist of all time. The "B. C. Bent—Cornet" was Ben Bent, mentioned before. Principal trombonist was F. Letsch, for several years previously solo trombone with the Theodore Thomas Orchestra. His presence in the band shows clearly the high-caliber men Gilmore was engaging.

As Gilmore and his band entrained for San Francisco, some four hundred miles to the north General George Armstrong Custer and his 7th U. S. Cavalry were skirmishing with approximately three thousand enraged Sioux Indians under Sitting Bull. These were the preliminaries which a few weeks later at Little Big Horn, Montana, were to build up into the celebrated massacre of Custer and his entire force. This massacre is now known as "Custer's Last Stand," thanks to the thousands of full-color and bloody pictures which for years decorated the saloons of America from coast to coast.

In 1840 San Francisco was a quiet town of four hundred population. Then, in 1848 gold had been discovered, and the population had leaped to nearly thirty-five thousand by 1850, when California had been admitted to the union as the thirty-first state. In that year gold miners viewed their first real play, when *The Wife,* by J. S. Knowles, had been staged at the Eagle Theatre, later called the Washington Hall. Two years later Italian operas were given in San

Francisco. The first was Bellini's *La Sonnambula,* which was followed by his *Norma* and by Verdi's *Ernani.*

When the French pianist Henri Hertz—he of the florid style and 'the thousand candles used for lighting the concert—came to California in 1849, he was compelled to play on the only piano which could be found, a dilapidated relic that was hauled in from some saloon. It had a compass of only six octaves, and half the keys were not working properly. The boisterous gold miners paid the admission in gold dust, which was weighed on scales by the ticket seller.

By the time Gilmore arrived, San Francisco boasted several large but gaudy theaters with expensive Steinway grand pianos, and admission was paid in gold and silver coins struck off in the San Francisco Mint, established in 1854 and the second in the United States. The city had already endured several disastrous earthquakes and a dozen terrible fires, but it had been quickly rebuilt with bigger and better buildings, and was a fabulously wealthy and prosperous metropolis of the Pacific coast.

Gilmore gave thirteen concerts from April 17 to 25, packing in twenty-five hundred each program at Mechanics Pavilion and ten thousand at Woodward Garden. Attending the final concert as special guests were Dom Pedro II, Emperor of Brazil, and his retinue, who were stopping in San Francisco on their way to the Centennial Exposition in Philadelphia. San Francisco had never before heard a band like this, and Gilmore brought to his audiences the music of the great classic composers, such as Beethoven, Wagner, Liszt, Rossini, Berlioz, as well as popular marches, polkas, and songs. Arbuckle, Levy, Lefebre, and Thursby performed solos that fairly stunned their listeners with their virtuosity. As the Gilmore troupe journeyed eastward to Chicago, they all agreed that they never had played before more appreciative and enthusiastic audiences.

In Chicago, Gilmore gave two evening concerts and a matinee in the huge Interstate Industrial Exposition Building on the Michigan Lake Front. This vast hall was two blocks long and nearly a block wide and was constructed so that no supporting pillars obstructed the view from wall to wall. One end had been converted into a sort of concert hall, with a stand for the band and wood chairs set in rows on a rough wood flooring for the audience. The other end was given over to a kind of German garden, with growing plants and small trees and many tables with chairs suitable for serving refreshments. It was a larger edition of the Gilmore Garden in New York, and the band felt very much at home, except for the trains that periodically rumbled by on the Illinois Central tracks and drowned out the music every time they passed. Enthusiastic audiences crowded into the giant hall and welcomed Gilmore on this his fifth visit to the city. The Gilmore program was Chicago's kickoff for the Philadelphia Centennial Exposition in celebration of the one-hundredth anniversary of the signing of the Declaration of Independence, and enthusiasm ran high.

Gilmore arrived back in New York the second week in May, and seven weeks later departed for Philadelphia to participate in the Centennial Exposition, planned on a lavish scale in the Quaker City. Nearly fifteen million dollars had been raised to put on the exposition, and the buildings covered two hundred and thirty-six acres. The Centennial opened in May and continued into November, attracting nearly ten million visitors. The Gilmore band was engaged for a series of sixty concerts in the main exhibition building, which had cost four and one half million dollars to construct. Jacques Offenbach, the celebrated French composer of comic operas, was also engaged for a series of programs, which featured his own compositions. The highlight of the entire exposition occurred on July Fourth, and Gilmore was placed in charge of the gigantic Fourth-of-July massed concert in Independence Square.

The Centennial Exposition was an important milestone in the history of the United States, marking, as it did, the one-hundredth anniversary of the Declaration of Independence. Although hardly recognized at the time, it also was an important event in the history of the American concert band, for participating in the music performed to celebrate the centennial of American freedom were the greatest bandmaster of the day and three talented young musicians who were to become great as conductors of their own bands—Frederick N. Innes, Signor Alessandro Liberati, and John Philip Sousa.

Although Pat Gilmore's band was technically known as the 22nd Regiment Band, it was popularly known simply as Gilmore's Band. In essential character Gilmore's Band was revolutionary. The band wore the uniform of the 22nd Regiment and was the "official" band of the regiment, but Gilmore had made it different from other regimental bands. In most important respects it was Gilmore's own band, and he led and directed it with few restraints from the military. Outside of acting as an important bit of window dressing for the 22nd it had little connection with the regiment. The money the regiment contributed toward its support was a small part of the total expenditure necessary to maintain it in the fashion Gilmore dictated. To all intents and purposes the Gilmore band was an independent concert band, mainly supported by the revenue realized from its musical performances. Gilmore was a musical czar, who ruled over the band with few restrictions from the regimental officers.

When Gilmore took over the band in 1873, the military probably did not fully realize what was in Gilmore's mind, but after three years at the helm he was beginning to make his intentions clear. Fortunately the regimental officers assumed an attitude of hands off and let Gilmore work out his own ideas. Ever since he took over the Boston Brigade Band in 1859 and formed Gilmore's Band, Pat had been dreaming of the new kind of band he eventually was to make of the 22nd.

All other bands of the day were either military bands attached to military organizations and supported almost entirely by military funds, town bands subsidized by the municipality, or industrial bands underwritten by a business firm. More often than not these civilian and industrial bands were also attached to some militia unit and they supplemented their meager incomes by such means. Gilmore's new idea was a great concert band operated on a free-enterprise basis and supported by popular demand for its musical services. When Gilmore's Band played in Philadelphia, it was well along its way toward this goal.

One of the trombone players in Gilmore's Band was twenty-two-year old Frederick Neil Innes. He was an accomplished player but had not yet achieved his standing as one of America's great trombone soloists. Innes had come to New York from England only two years before. After a year in New York, he went to Boston and took a job as trombonist in the Howard Street Theatre. His reputation as an unusually fine performer spread throughout Boston, and Gilmore signed him up.

Although Innes played with Gilmore only a short time, this engagement was a determining influence upon his later career. Jules Levy was a member of the Gilmore band at this time, and as Innes listened day after day to the cornet soloist, who was billed as "the world's greatest," he began experimenting with Levy's solos on his trombone. It is safe to say that he never tried to play one of these solos in the presence of Levy, for this irritable and jealous potentate of the Gilmore band would not have tolerated such impudence on

the part of the young musician. Innes did practice these solos assiduously, however, and occasionally performed one for friends.

It was not until a year or so later, when he became trombone
soloist with the Boston Cadet Band, that he dared play one of Levy's
solos on a program. This excellent band was under the conductorship of J. Thomas Baldwin, the capable gentleman who drilled the
giant band for Gilmore's World Peace Jubilee in 1872. Musicians for
the Cadet Band were carefully selected, and Innes' admittance to the
band is high testimony to his ability. Mace Gay, who later distinguished himself as cornetist and bandmaster of the Brockton Band
(Mass.), was principal cornet soloist when Innes joined. Removed
from the jealous stare of Levy, Innes first risked playing one of Levy's
solos in the Cadet Band. Young Mace Gay, although an outstanding soloist, could scarcely accomplish this feat on the cornet, for which
this difficult music was specially arranged, and he stood in awe as
Innes performed the impossible on his trombone. From that day
Innes threw down the gauntlet to the great Levy and took delight
in matching his technique against that of the older and more celebrated virtuoso of the cornet.

Another determining factor in Innes's life was the day-to-day experience of playing in the Gilmore band. He shared in its triumphs
and formed his standards of what a fine concert band should be. He
was especially impressed with Gilmore's skill in building programs,
and years later, when he had a band of his own, he patterned his
programs after those of the master.

When Gilmore conducted the giant massed band in Independence
Square, one of the bands participating was the Detroit National
Guard Band, directed by Signor Liberati. Few facts are known about
Liberati up to this time. He came across the border from Canada
only the year before, to direct the band of the Michigan National
Guard. For three years previously he had been the bandmaster of
a Canadian artillery band and cornet soloist in the services of His
Excellency, the Earl of Dufferin, in Ottawa.

We know Liberati was born in Frascati, Italy, in 1847, but how he
managed the trip to Canada is a mystery. The best conjecture is that
he joined a United States ship's band as cornetist when it put in at
some Italian port, and then resigned or jumped ship when it arrived
on the American side. Certainly this was at that time a common way
for Italian musicians to obtain passage to America, for the logs of
many American ships contain references to such happenings.

While the Detroit National Guard Band lingered in Philadelphia, Liberati stole every minute he could away from his duties to listen to the Gilmore concerts in the main exhibition building. Being an accomplished cornet soloist in his own right, he knew great cornet playing when he heard it. He sat spellbound as he listened to Arbuckle play some of his celebrated Scottish songs, as only Arbuckle could play them, and to Levy play his *Whirlwind* polka or the *Seventh Air Varie* by De Bériot as transcribed by John Hartmann. He resolved then and there that one day he would become a cornet soloist with Gilmore, and three years later he was to realize this ambition, sharing the spotlight with the great Jules Levy and Matthew Arbuckle.

He also marveled at the performance of Gilmore's Band. For five or six years he had directed service bands and he had listened to many military bands in America and in Italy, but he had never heard anything before which approached the musical excellence of the Gilmore band. He was quick to realize that this was not a military band of the usual kind. No band he had ever heard could boast of such virtuosos as Arbuckle, Levy, Lefebre, Kegel and Letsman, nor play with such smoothness, flexibility, and precision. Liberati was destined to conduct stereotyped military bands for several more years, but eventually he solved the mystery of Gilmore's greatness and years later established himself at the head of a successful independent band of his own.

In the main exhibition building Gilmore's Band alternated with Offenbach's orchestra, and one of the first violinists in the orchestra was John Philip Sousa, only twenty-two years old. Young Sousa practically lived in the exhibition building, for when he wasn't playing with Offenbach he was listening to Gilmore. Sousa's mind was pretty well made up to follow a career in music, but just what kind of musical activity he would follow was still not clear to him. As he watched Gilmore in action and listened to the performance of the celebrated band, he began to feel that his place was in the band field. Little did he know at that time that the mantle of the great Gilmore would one day fall upon his shoulders.

As a boy of six, Sousa began the study of violin under Professor John Esputa, who conducted a small conservatory in Washington near Sousa's home. After laboring under the stern Esputa for several months and receiving numerous raps across his knuckles Sousa had a falling out with the professor and for a time failed to show up for lessons. His understanding father Antonio, a trombone player in the

U. S. Marine Band, seemed to agree with his son and helped him secure a job as a baker's apprentice. This cured Sousa's debility. After a few nights at this distasteful work Sousa changed his mind about music and returned to his studies with Professor Esputa.

After a few years Sousa began taking small jobs with local orchestras and bands as violinist or baritone player. One day the bandmaster of a visiting circus passed Sousa's house and heard him practicing. He entered the house, made Sousa's acquaintance, and secretly offered him a job with the circus band. The circus was to leave town the next day, and it was agreed that Sousa was to slip away without his parents' consent and join the traveling troupe. Antonio got wind of the arrangement, and the next morning, after breakfast, the father suggested to Sousa that he dress in his best suit and take a walk with him. This fateful walk ended at the office of the commandant of the U. S. Marine Corps. There Sousa signed up for a hitch with the Marines. This was in 1868 and Sousa was not yet fourteen years old. He served as an apprentice in music for over seven years. He played triangle in the band at the same time his father played trombone. In 1875 both young Sousa and his father received special discharges, and Sousa was launched on his music career.

He soon landed a job as conductor of an orchestra on tour with "Matt Morgan's Living Pictures," a tableau which exhibited seven beautiful undraped girls. In Pittsburgh the girls were arrested for indecent exposure. Morgan hired a good lawyer, and when the case came to trial the lawyer showed the arresting officer a picture of the statue of Minerva. "Did you ever arrest this woman?" the lawyer asked. "I may have," the policeman replied. "I have arrested so many people you can't expect me to remember all of them." The girls were acquitted; the production was judged to be true art and not a violation of public morals.

The publicity obtained in Pittsburgh followed the troupe to St. Louis and business was good; so good, in fact, that plans were made for a tour to San Francisco. Sousa, however, had set his heart on attending the great Centennial in Philadelphia, and so he resigned his post and joined Offenbach.

Following the Centennial, Sousa elected to remain in Philadelphia. He accepted engagements in the various theaters, playing violin in the Chestnut Street Theatre under Hassler and in the Arch Street Theatre under Zimmerman. He also edited music for a local music publisher, J. F. Shaw, and began devoting as much time as possible to composition. One of his early efforts was *Free Lunch Cadets*, published in 1877. When Gilbert and Sullivan's *H. M. S. Pinafore* began sweeping the country in 1878, he accepted an offer to conduct the orchestra of a company organized in the city. In the company was Miss Jennie Bellis, an understudy for the part of Hebe, and she became Sousa's wife just before her seventeenth birthday.

At the close of their respective engagements at the Centennial, Liberati returned with his band to Detroit, Sousa left Offenbach, as related, and began playing violin in Philadelphia theaters, and Innes resumed trouping with Gilmore. The paths of all four musicians were to cross many times in the future, and in later years the bands of Liberati, Innes, and Sousa were to vie with that of Gilmore. Together, they were to establish firmly the popularity of a new kind of independent, traveling concert band.

Five

GILMORE,
MADISON SQUARE GARDEN
FIGHT PROMOTER

Jules Levy, who admitted he was "the world's greatest cornet player ALL THE TIME."

When Gilmore's Band wasn't on the road, it was busy with concerts in New York City. Unless some important engagement in New England or in the West interfered, Gilmore was to be found at Gilmore Garden from May until late in the fall. These concerts were amazingly successful because they always contained something new. Typical of this Gilmore showmanship was the program presented on October 11, 1877. For this big event Gilmore had recruited extra instrumentalists and had arranged four separate bands in a kind of company square, with Gilmore in the center. The program, as usual, gradually was built up into a smashing climax that sent the audience away in a state of semi-hysteria. This evening's climax was reserved for Emma Thursby's singing of Proch's *Variations* with the band. Miss Thursby had sung this exhibition number many times, with Gilmore's Band, with the Thomas Orchestra, and with the Brooklyn Philharmonic Society, but it is certain she never sang it so well and she never created such a tremendous effect as she did that evening.

Practically every music critic and writer in New York was present, and Gilmore received columns of space in newspapers and magazines. Not all of it was in approval, but hardly any of it failed to tell of the electric effect the program had on the audience. Ten thousand persons crowded into Gilmore Garden that night, and at the close of Thursby's spectacular display of vocal gymnastics, supported by the superb playing of the augmented Gilmore band, everybody in the place applauded and shouted and whistled and strained neck and eyes to obtain a good view of the beautiful little prima donna as she smiled and bowed in the center of the company square of four bands, close to Gilmore and his podium. This event has often been called "her greatest triumph."

One particularly graphic writer related in his newspaper article the next day how he found himself standing on a chair, trying to see over the heads of the people in front of him. All eyes and attention were trained on the lighted arena, where stood Gilmore and Thursby. He felt a tug on his coattail, and finally he became aware of some woman standing on the floor beside his chair. She was saying something to him, but he couldn't hear a word because of the din. He leaned down. With her mouth against his ear she asked: "Is her dress cut on the bias or is it gored?" The flabbergasted reporter craned his neck until he obtained a good look at Miss Thursby, and gallantly replied: "It's on the bias."

A moment later it occurred to him that he wasn't being very courteous to others standing on the floor level behind him, and so he descended from his chair so others might enjoy the sights. As he stepped down, the unknown woman hopped up into the chair. As the reporter started to move away, the woman turned, stooped down, and shouted into his ear: "No, it's gored."

Since Gilmore organized his band in Boston in 1859, the prodigious hoop skirt had been replaced by the provocative bustle. The "hourglass figure," achieved through the use of elaborately laced corsets, had become fashionable, along with voluminous "leg-of-mutton" sleeves. And after Miss Thursby's appearance a new "must" for a woman's dress probably was that it be gored.

Shortly after Miss Thursby's "greatest triumph," the twenty-year-old Lillian Norton came to Gilmore for an audition. Emma Thursby had become famous during the three years since she had hired Gilmore's Band for her recital, and she had more offers of engagements than she could fill. This left Gilmore without a soprano he could depend on, and he was looking for someone to fill the vacancy. Miss Norton proved to be the one, and Gilmore arranged a performance with his band that winter at which his new soprano made her concert debut.

The following spring Lillian Norton accompanied the band on its western tour. The European tour by Gilmore's Band followed soon after, and Miss Norton was engaged as soloist. The association of Norton with Gilmore's Band was cut short in London at the Crystal Palace, when Lillian and her mother had a clash with Gilmore. Lillian broke her contract and went to Milan for a year of vocal training. Miss Norton changed her name the following year to Lillian Nordica, and it is under this name that she later became famous as a dramatic soprano in opera.

Gilmore's European tour was an important milestone in Gilmore's life and in the development of American bands. For four years, since he took over the 22nd Regiment Band assignment, Gilmore had been working assiduously to improve his organization. He had started with sixty-five players and he stuck close to this number for twenty years, except for special events of a temporary nature. He constantly experimented with the make-up of the band, however, changing the instrumentation from time to time and replacing players with better ones whenever he could find them. Players who met Gilmore's high standards he kept for years, for he paid top wages and always dealt fairly and honorably with his men. E. A. Lefebre, saxophone soloist, and Charles W. Freudenvoll, clarinetist and later assistant conductor, joined the band in 1873 and were still with the band when Gilmore laid down his baton for the last time in 1892.

Playing with Gilmore was not a soft job, for he drove his men as he drove himself. He was a perfectionist when it came to musical performance, and every man in the band knew he had to be on his toes if he was to keep his position. Gilmore attempted the most difficult music and he made his players sweat to play it as he wanted it played. Arrangements of the classics for use by the band were kept as near like the originals as possible, and he refused to sacrifice the composer's intent by dishing up an easy version. He paid his men for their full time, and he never spared them when rehearsals were necessary to smooth out difficulties.

The instrumentation of the Gilmore band which toured Europe is given in the table on Pages 106–7, together with the instrumentation of six other bands—the three finest European bands as selected in the international contest in 1867, the English Grenadier Guards Band of 1888, the U. S. Marine Band under Sousa in 1891, and Sousa's band of 1900. It will be noted, with respect to the proportion of reeds to brass instruments, that Gilmore's Band had a stronger reed section than any of the three champion European bands but that it most closely resembled the Prussian Guards Band, considered the top band in Europe at that time. The English Grenadier Guards Band, ten years after Gilmore played in England, had increased the proportion of reeds to brass to 52 per cent, showing the trend overseas to stronger reed balance. Sousa's U. S. Marine Band, thirteen years after Gilmore's European tour, shows Gilmore's influence on Sousa, who had almost the same balance adopted by Gilmore in 1878. Sousa's band in 1900, however, goes still farther and reaches a balance of almost two reeds to one brass. In 1924 Sousa carried this emphasis to exactly two for one, having forty-eight reeds to twenty-four brass.

Thus it becomes clear that Gilmore was a trail blazer, and that he was pointing the way with his band toward improved musical performance by concert bands.

The Gilmore band sailed for Europe aboard the steamship *City of Berlin* on May 4 and returned to New York aboard the steamship *Mosel* on September 29. A total of one hundred and fifty concerts was given, an average of one a day. The tour took the band to the principal cities in England, then on to Dublin, Edinburgh, Glasgow, and Aberdeen. The band was at the Trocadéro in Paris during the World's Exposition, and visited Le Havre, Rouen, Lille, and other French cities. After an engagement in the famous Brussels Opera House, the troupe went to Rotterdam, The Hague, Antwerp, and Amsterdam. The longest stay was made in Germany, the tour of nearly two months beginning in Cologne and including Hamburg, Bremen, Berlin, Leipsig, and other of the principal cities.

At a dinner in Berlin, given for Gilmore and his band, a clipping

	Austria 73rd Reg. 1867	France Garde de Paris 1867	Prussian Guards 1867	Gilmore Band 1878	England Grenadier Gds. 1888	U. S. Marines Sousa 1891	Sousa Band 1900
Piccolo	1	1	2	2	1	2	1
Flute	2	2	2	2	2		3
Oboe (Eng. Horn)		2	4	2	2	2	2
A♭ Clarinet	2		1	1			
E♭ Clarinet	4	4	4	3	4		2
1st B♭ Clarinet	12	8	16	8	14	6	9
2nd B♭ Clarinet				4		4	4
3rd B♭ Clarinet				4		4	3
Alto Clarinet				1	1	2	2
Bass Clarinet	2			1	1		2
Bassoon	2		6	2	2	2	3
Contrabassoon			4	1	1		
Sop. Saxophone		2		1		1	
Alto Saxophone		2		1		1	2
Tenor Saxophone		2		1		1	2
Barit. Saxophone		2		1		1	1
Bass Saxophone							
Total Reeds	25	25	39	35	28	26	36
Per Cent Reeds	35	45	50	56	52	56	62
E♭ Cornet				1			
1st B♭ Cornet	2	4	4	2	6	2	2
2nd B♭ Cornet				2		1	2
3rd B♭ Cornet						1	
B♭ Trumpet	12	3	8	2	2	2	2
Fluegelhorn	6	3		2		2	2
French Horn	6	2	4	4	4	4	4
Trombone	6	5	8	3	3	3	4
Alto Horn	3	3	4	2			
Tenor Horn				2			
Baritone Horn	3	2	4		1		1
Euphonium	2	5	2	2	4	2	1
E♭ Bass Tuba		2			4		
BB♭ Bass Tuba	6	2	6	5	2	3	4

	Austria 73rd Reg. 1867	France Garde de Paris 1867	Prussian Guards 1867	Gilmore Band 1878	England Grenadier Gds. 1888	U. S. Marines Sousa 1891	Sousa Band 1900
Total Brass	46	31	40	27	26	20	22
Per Cent Brass	65	55	50	44	48	44	38
Percussion	5	4	6	4	3	3	3
Total Players	76	60	85	66	57	49	61

from a New York newspaper was handed to him. In it he read a report that his European tour was a complete failure. Since this was toward the close of the tour, Gilmore waited until he returned to New York to refute this false report. To reporters who came aboard as soon as the *Mosel* docked at Hoboken, he defended both the financial and artistic success of the tour.

He admitted that "we have not come home with a ship-load of money," but he intimated that they were satisfied with the financial results. "After paying all expenses," he said, "every man received nearly four times as much money as the best musicians in Europe would have received." As further evidence of the affluence of the band, he continued, "We came home by the German steamer, which cost us $15 each more than by other lines we could have taken, and that does not look as if we had no money."

If his defense of financial success was a little lame, he was outspoken and positive about the artistic triumph of his band. "We did not cross the ocean to make our fortunes," he said, "but to compare our skill with that of foreign organizations, and to show if possible, that America has the best musicians in the world. While we were abroad we played with fifteen or sixteen of the best bands in Europe, and public opinion, as expressed through the newspapers, was that not one of them could compare with us.

"In London, at a reception at the Crystal Palace, we were met by five fine bands belonging to the 'Guards.' The five united in one grand orchestra of two hundred and fifty pieces. We felt a little uncertain about playing after this tremendous band, for fear our sixty pieces might sound weak; but the boys did splendidly, and the audience began cheering us in the midst of the performance. . . .

"Franz Abt, composer of *When the Swallows Homeward Fly,* said to me one day: 'You have the best band in the world; you may feel satisfied of it.' Saro [director of the Prussian Guards Band] and Ferdinand Hiller both complimented us highly. Gumbert, the author of *Ye Merry Birds,* came into one of our concerts while we were playing his composition and he became so overcome he burst into tears."

Gilmore had invaded the territories where the greatest bands of England and Europe played, and the performance of his band was praised everywhere as equal to any, if not superior. In Germany, Gilmore made a vast number of friends by his superb playing of the music of Wagner and Liszt. In England the playing of such difficult and "modern" music created widespread awe, for English bands generally steered clear of such music.

Henry George Farmer, in his *The Rise of Military Music,* states that various visiting bands had brought "splendid opportunities for improvement to military bands in England and Europe, the "most important" of them being "the French Garde Republicaine, the Belgian Guides and the New York Twenty-Second Regiment (Gilmore's), all most artistic combinations, the latter especially."

As related above, Gilmore lost the services of Lillian Norton in London, toward the beginning of his tour. He was also completely deprived of the services of Arbuckle, for Arbuckle was a deserter from the English army and feared he would be detained in England if he risked putting in an appearance there. Jules Levy did not make the trip either, but the reason is not known. The solo-cornet duties therefore fell on Ben Bent, a young cornetist named Bagley, and a new star whom Gilmore engaged just before the tour began: Walter Emerson of Boston, only twenty-four years old but a finished artist.

While Gilmore was in Europe, Theodore Thomas and his orchestra took over Gilmore Garden, giving one hundred and thirty-one concerts from May 25 to September 28, one day before Gilmore arrived at the Hoboken pier. The September 23 concert was a benefit performance for yellow-fever sufferers. Another epidemic was raging through the South and many died despite the widely used remedies of long black cigars and liberal doses of whiskey. The Thomas Orchestra shared the spotlight with the 7th Regiment Band under Grafulla and the Dodworth Band under Harvey Dodworth. Jules Levy appeared as soloist and was billed modestly as "the great Levy, the most wonderful cornet soloist in the world."

A few weeks later Gilbert and Sullivan's comic opera *H. M. S. Pin-*

afore began breaking out like the measles all over the United States. It was first heard on November 25 at the Boston Museum Theatre, and on December 23 it made its double debut in San Francisco, two separate companies opening the same night at the Bush Street Theatre and at the Tivoli Opera House. Another company opened in Philadelphia at the Broad Street Theatre on January 6 and still another in New York at the Standard Theatre on January 15. On February 10 two other companies opened simultaneously in New York at Niblo's Garden and at the Fifth Avenue Theatre. Such a strange condition of affairs was possible because of the complete lack of protection by international copyright, a condition that was not corrected for nearly forty years.

Notwithstanding this hubbub in the theaters, Gilmore carried out a series of winter concerts at the Grand Opera House, featuring a saxophone quartet comprised of the inimitable Lefebre plus Walrabe, Steckelberg, and Schultz. Following this, he opened on January 20 at Madison Square Garden with afternoon and evening concerts. The old Hippodrome, which Barnum built in 1873 and which had been known as Gilmore Garden for the past four years, was now back under the management of Barnum and was renamed Madison Square Garden, a name it was to retain until 1925, when the new Madison Square Garden was built farther uptown in its present location. The New York Life Insurance Building now occupies the site of the old Garden. When Gilmore left New York on his regular spring tour, Madison Square Garden was taken over by the Dodworth Band for a series of summer night concerts.

To most people Madison Square Garden means prize fights, and Patrick Sarsfield Gilmore was probably the first fight promoter in this famous arena, a promoter, however, not of a boxing match but of a cornet-playing match. Both Matthew Arbuckle and Jules Levy were back on the Gilmore band roster in the fall of 1879, when Gilmore's Band opened a series of promenade concerts in Madison Square Garden. As noted three years before, when the band made a tour to San Francisco, these two great cornet soloists were bitter rivals and extremely jealous of each other. This feud had grown in intensity year after year, until it was at white heat by the time the first program was printed for the promenade concerts. Gilmore had them both under contract, and he could see great box-office possibilities with these two cornet gladiators on the same bill.

Like a good fight promoter, he called in the press and by slyly dropping a hint here and there he divulged the animosity that existed between his two soloists. The newspaper writers ate this up and immediately devoted columns of space to needling the two players. This rivalry spread to the audience, and some took sides with Arbuckle and some with Levy. When Arbuckle played his solo, his fans applauded and whistled, while the Levy crowd sat on their hands and booed. When Levy played, his cohorts made the garden resound with their bravos, while the Arbuckle clique hissed. Meanwhile Gilmore remained neutral: Arbuckle money and Levy money counted the same at the ticket window, and the attendance grew night after night until there was standing room only and many were turned away.

Arbuckle was a star pupil of Herr Koenig, the great German cornet virtuoso whom Jullien had brought over from Europe in 1853. As conjectured in the chapter on Jullien, it is probable that Arbuckle accompanied Koenig, but Koenig returned to Europe while Arbuckle stayed in America the rest of his life. It was Koenig who had worked with the French instrument maker Antoine Courtois in developing a medium-bore cornet of superb solo qualities, which came to be known as the Koenig cornet. Arbuckle, being a pupil of Koenig, naturally adopted this instrument too.

Joseph Jean B. L. Arban was a French cornet soloist of the same era, best remembered today for his *Arban Methods for Cornet* and for some cornet solos he composed. He collaborated with the French instrument maker Besson, and helped develop the large-bore Arban Model Besson. This cornet became popular in the military bands but proved to be too large for most soloists and never reached the wide acceptance of the Koenig cornet.

Jules Levy liked neither model, and prevailed upon Courtois to build for him a small-bore instrument using the Koenig cornet bell. While this small-bore instrument proved to be ideal for Levy and his style of playing, few besides Levy could produce a good quality of tone from it, although it lent itself to technical execution, for it was easy to blow.

Not only did the type of cornet influence the characteristic styles of playing of Arbuckle and Levy, but the training each received also was a factor. Koenig was a romanticist, and he excelled in the production of beautiful tone quality and in the lyrical phrasing of ballads and in expression and interpretation. Arbuckle modeled his playing after his great teacher, and he became celebrated for his pure tone and the emotional impact of his playing. He was especially noted for his rendition of Scottish songs, for he was a Scot by birth and loved the old Scottish ballads. He had great technical resources, also, but he seldom resorted to pyrotechnics, preferring to achieve fame by playing simple songs more musically than anyone else.

Jules Levy received his training in the English Guards bands. We do not know who his teachers were, and it is believed he was largely self-taught. Nevertheless he was a superb musician. His repertoire was more extensive than Arbuckle's, and he delved into the classics for many of his solos. During the season of Summer Concerts in Central Park Garden in 1869 with the Theodore Thomas Orchestra, his solos included a cavatina from Rossini's *Una Voce, Cujus Animam* from Rossini's *Stabat Mater, Adelaide* by Beethoven, a canzonetta from Meyerbeer's *Dinorah,* a romanza by Hugo-Pierson entitled *Elle m'aimait tant,* and Schubert's *Serenade* and *Adieu.*

However, this classical binge was not characteristic of Levy and may have been owing to the influence of Thomas. Even Thomas could not entirely suppress Levy, for the programs contained also a few of Levy's showpieces, such as *Carnival of Venice* by Paganini as transcribed by Levy, the *Seventh Air Varie* by De Bériot as transcribed by Hartmann, and three Levy compositions: the waltz *Maud,* the *Levy Athens* polka, and the *Whirlwind* polka. These showpieces probably account for Thomas's entry in his notebook during the following season at Central Park Garden (when Levy was not on the program): "At last the Summer programs show a respectable character and we are rid of the cornet! Occasionally a whole symphony is given."

Levy's forte was fireworks. He loved to play a simple air of a few bars and then repeat it endlessly with all sorts of intricate and showy variations, finally closing with a flourish of runs and trills and ending on an altissimo note of prodigious volume and length. His execution was phenomenal. He played the impossible with the greatest of ease and artistry, like a Paganini. He cultivated mannerisms calculated to impress and fill his hearers with awe and wonder. He refused to wear the uniform of the 22nd Regiment and always appeared in a dress suit, with medals adorning his breast and a monocle stuck in his eye. He was a colossal egoist and was not content with ordinary praise: it had to be spread on a foot thick or Levy felt slighted and became offended. This egotism made him obnoxious to everyone, and he was continuously quarreling. He liked money, demanded and obtained prohibitive fees for playing, but died a poor man.

James F. Boyer, for many years connected with a band instrument company, was the originator of an often repeated story about Levy. The two were drinking cocktails in Levy's home in Elkhart, Indiana. Boyer asked him if he'd ever thought about becoming President of the United States. Levy's surprising reply gives a quick insight into the Levy personality. "Why would I want to be President?" he asked. "After four years I'd be kicked out of office. As it is, I am Jules Levy, the world's greatest cornet player, ALL THE TIME."

Hi Henry, an outstanding cornetist in his day and leader for many years of Hi Henry's Minstrels, was in the audience night after night during the Levy-Arbuckle duel. Years later he set down his impressions of these two great performers. Since this account is the opinion of a well-qualified listener, it is quoted here at length.

"It was an exceptional privilege," he says, "to hear these two great masters, Levy and Arbuckle, night after night in the same program, each great and so different, the former exciting wonder and admiration by his wonderful cadenzas, his spirited staccato and rapid chromatic runs, his wonderful intervals and extreme high and low notes; the latter with his beautiful, passionate tone, his heart winning sympathy, his artistic breadth, his deliberate lights and shades; the former stirring his listeners to highest enthusiasm, the latter hushing them to the stillness of the sleeping chamber; the former retiring amid clapping of hands, the latter drawing tears and retiring only for his hearers to find themselves spell-bound by his skill.

"A just comparison of these two great artists is no disparagement to either. They were not at all comparable. Levy may be said to play that which no other living man can as brilliantly repeat. Arbuckle, while playing nothing others could not render, delivered it in such finished style that none could simulate it."

Hi Henry was a pupil of Arbuckle and one would expect him to side with the Arbuckle faction, but he is fair and objective in his appraisal. Not so the majority of the listeners. They egged and needled until the two men lost control of themselves. Arbuckle was a big man while Levy was short and stocky, but Arbuckle was fifty-one years old against Levy's thirty-nine. Nevertheless one night they finally came to blows. Gilmore intervened, and in the shuffle he tore Levy's coat and disarranged some of the medals adorning his ample chest. Levy's wrath then turned on Gilmore, but players in the band stopped the fracas before violence was done.

Levy boiled with rage and immediately challenged Gilmore to a duel to the death with pistols. Friends entered the parley and finally persuaded Levy to settle the argument with pistols, but at a nearby shooting gallery. Thus the protagonists, with their seconds and a couple of newspaper writers, repaired to the shooting gallery. Six shots were allotted to each; the one making the fewer bull's-eyes was to pick up the check for dinner at Delmonico's for the whole crowd.

Levy won the toss and elected to lead off with the first shot. He raised the pistol and watched it quiver with his nervousness. He lowered it, took a deep breath, slowly raised the pistol until it bore on the target, and fired. The bell clanged, showing a bull's eye. Surprised at his good marksmanship, he jumped up and down like a kid in his excitement. It was now Gilmore's turn. He fired and missed. Levy was jubilant. He turned to Gilmore with triumph in his big red face and said, "You see, if this was a real duel you'd now be dead after my first shot, and I'd still be alive, for your first shot missed."

The duel proceeded in deadly fashion. Each man took aim as if his life depended upon it. But the final results plunged Levy into the depths, for Gilmore came out high scorer. The group made their way to Delmonico's, and after much eating of rich food and much drinking of vintage champagne, Levy paid the big check and they staggered to their several homes.

The next day Levy, bleary-eyed and with a head the size of a pumpkin, read in the pages of the New York *Sun* the complete story about the duel of the previous evening. The writer, who was present, spared no details. He related how the proprietor of the shooting gallery had connived with the seconds of the duel to load the pistols with blanks and to have a boy behind the scenes strike a bell with a hammer as prearranged, so as to give Gilmore the high score.

Levy was seized with a paroxysm of anger and shame, and rolled over in his bed and bawled.

Levy led a checkered career following his break with Gilmore. His foul disposition and obnoxious personality kept him from holding any position very long. A typically flagrant example of his egoism is related by R. E. Trognitz, who was saxophone soloist of the City Guard Band of San Diego along about 1890. The band was giving a concert at Redondo Beach, and Levy was to play some solos. The band started playing before Levy appeared, and Trognitz was taking a bow for a solo he had just finished, when Levy arrived at the bandstand. Hearing the applause, Levy cried, "That's for me," and he shoved Trognitz aside and took the bows himself.

He followed a career of featured soloist and appeared with many different bands from coast to coast. At times he taught, but he limited his instruction to advanced or very talented players, Edwin Franko Goldman, the great bandmaster, being one of his relatively few students. He also established the Jules Levy American Military Band around 1892, but in 1895 he advertised: "Jules Levy, the greatest cornet player in the world, offers for sale 40 uniforms, coats red and gold, 40 coats, blue trimmed with braid. Library of Military Band music and string band music."

A year later he moved to Elkhart, Indiana, where he became an instructor of cornet in the Conn Conservatory of Music and acted as tester of cornets in the Conn instrument factory. After a couple years of almost incessant wrangling with Colonel Conn, Levy left in high dudgeon and went to Chicago. There he died in 1903.

Shortly after Levy left the Gilmore band, Arbuckle followed. As far as we know, Arbuckle had no trouble with Gilmore, but the four years of battling Levy had probably soured him on the Gilmore band. In 1880 he accepted the directorship of the 9th Regiment Band, following D. L. Downing. Directing was not to Arbuckle's liking, and the following year he accepted a position as soloist with the 7th under Signor Cappa, who had succeeded Grafulla. Two years later Arbuckle died.

With both Levy and Arbuckle gone solo cornet duties devolved upon the dependable Ben Bent and young Walter Emerson, whom Gilmore had recruited for his European tour. Gilmore also had another ace in the hole in the person of Signor Liberati. After Liberati returned to Detroit with his Detroit National Guard Band, following the engagement at the Philadelphia Centennial, he became dissatisfied with the humdrum life of directing his mediocre band, and he began to yearn for the glamorous life of soloist with Gilmore. His countryman and good friend, Signor Cappa, was trombone soloist with the 7th. Through Cappa he opened negotiations with Gilmore for a job as cornet soloist. In the fall of 1878 Gilmore signed him to a contract.

At that time Gilmore was well supplied with cornet soloists, carrying on the roster not only Levy and Arbuckle but also Ben Bent and Walter Emerson. But Gilmore, no doubt, sensed that the animosity between Levy and Arbuckle was coming to a head, and he realized that he might lose one or both of his great soloists. Bent and Emerson were both capable soloists, but Liberati was known as the "neatest

Walter Emerson of Boston,
only twenty-four years old but
a finished artist.

and most dashing" cornet soloist of the day. That was the kind of talent Gilmore liked, and he hired him as a hedge against the expected blowup of Levy and Arbuckle. That Gilmore had the right hunch was borne out a few months later when both of his great soloists left him.

At first Liberati was only one of four talented soloists with Gilmore, and he had little opportunity to play. Late in the following year, however, Gilmore began to build him up by programing solos by Liberati. On a program given by the Gilmore band on November 23, 1879, at the Grand Opera House in New York, Liberati shared honors with Levy as cornet soloist. This must have been a bitter pill for the jealous Levy and may have had something to do with his quitting soon afterward. The fiasco of the Levy-Arbuckle duel clinched matters, and within a few weeks Levy broke his contract with Gilmore and left.

We do not know exactly how long Liberati played with Gilmore, but it is believed that he left the band in 1880. We are fairly certain

he was not with Gilmore in 1881, for in that year Liberati was engaged as soloist at the Yorktown Centennial celebration. Liberati has said he was employed as cornet soloist to entertain European celebrities who visited the celebration, but we do not know what band he was with. It most probably was the 13th Regiment Band under Harvey Dodworth. This great band, augmented to one hundred and thirty players especially for the event, was a big attraction and was regarded as the "official" band of the celebration.

As for Emerson and Bent, neither was destined to be with Gilmore to the end. Emerson left the band in 1881 and became cornet soloist with the Boston Cadet Band, playing alongside of trombone soloist Frederick N. Innes. Ben Bent stayed with Gilmore until 1890. At that time he had been Gilmore's right-hand man for nearly twenty years and had worked himself up to three hundred dollars per week. He struck for three hundred and twenty-five, Gilmore refused, and Bent quit. Soon after, he teamed up with his brothers, Fred, Tom, and Sam to form the Bent Bros. Military Band, for several years a star attraction with circuses.

Not long after Gilmore hired Liberati, he signed up a young trombone player by the name of Thomas Preston Brooke. This young recruit was destined to have a band of his own before Gilmore died and in later years was to have one of the most meteoric careers in the whole history of the traveling concert band.

Gilmore first met Brooke when he brought his 22nd Regiment Band to Boston for a series of concerts. Brooke was at that time a young music student in Boston. He had composed several marches, and he made an appointment with Gilmore to have the band play some of them, following an afternoon matinee. With his compositions, arranged for a sixty-five-piece band, he arrived backstage after the curtain had been lowered and just in time to hear Gilmore tell the band, "Take ten minutes."

Brooke was greatly relieved to find Gilmore "as common as an old shoe." With natural friendliness Gilmore greeted the young composer and asked to see the music he had brought. With practiced eye Gilmore rapidly ran through the conductor's scores while Brooke sat by his side and fidgeted. After several minutes Gilmore called his librarian over and said to him, "We'll try this one first and this one will be next." The librarian had just finished putting the parts on the music stands when the last musician returned to his place on the stage.

Then Gilmore, ever courteous and considerate of others, asked Brooke if he would like to direct the numbers himself. Would he! Here was the greatest band in America—probably in the world— and he was invited to conduct this band in two numbers, two of his own compositions. With mingled feelings of both elation and apprehension, Brooke mounted the podium, picked up Gilmore's baton, and started the first number. At the close Gilmore applauded and called out so the whole band could hear, "Bravo! Very good!" After the second number Gilmore shook his hand warmly and told him he considered the marches as showing unusual talent, and he said he felt sure that great things lay ahead for the young composer and conductor.

Although Brooke lived to compose two comic operas, numerous concert pieces, and over two hundred military marches and two-steps, it is safe to say that no other of his compositions gave him such satisfaction and made him feel so important as these two early marches played for the first time by the celebrated Gilmore band.

Brooke was not only a composer and conductor but an unusually good trombone player, and after he had finished his music studies in

Boston he applied to Gilmore for a job as trombonist. Gilmore arranged an audition and Brooke was accepted. Brooke found himself in fast company, but he was a musician to his finger tips and he held down the job with credit for about two years. After that he resigned, returned to his home in Dubuque, Iowa, and married Miss Minnie Fox of La Crosse, Wisconsin. This was in 1880 and Brooke was twenty-four years old.

Six

GILMORE'S
MOST PRODUCTIVE
YEARS

*Signor Carlo Alberto Cappa
was eminently well fitted
to conduct such a band
as Gilmore had.*

Although less spectacular than previous periods in his life the years
from about 1880 until his death in 1892 were probably Gilmore's
most productive and influential. He was fifty-one years old in 1880.
His band was without peer in America, if not in the entire world. He
had established a successful and profitable routine of engagements
which varied little from year to year. All summer he usually played
at Manhattan Beach and in the winter at Madison Square Garden.
In spring and fall he toured America under the management of
David Blakely.

The Gilmore band was the only touring band in the country, almost up until the time Gilmore died. Year after year, for nearly
twenty years, Gilmore and his superb band brought to hundreds of
communities the only first-class music they were privileged to hear.
Gilmore did not look upon himself as an educator or missionary of
good music, but he nevertheless functioned as one. For years he
alone brought Wagner, Liszt, Mendelssohn, Berlioz, Rossini, Verdi,
and other of the great classical composers to many cities from coast

to coast. The visit to any of these cities along Gilmore's tour was a community music festival, in which many listeners heard great music for the first time.

Herbert L. Clarke, who was to become cornet soloist with Gilmore and with Sousa, has related in a very poignant way his feelings upon the occasion when the Gilmore band visited his home town of Indianapolis in 1884. Clarke was then seventeen years old and had begun to play the cornet. "I remember a date when the famous Gilmore's Band was booked for a concert," he said, "and on the morning it arrived in town I was at the depot to have a look at these wonderful musicians, who were supposed to be the greatest instrumental performers in the world. When the train pulled in and the men left their cars, I stood back in awe as they passed me, although I gladly would have helped 'tote' grip or instrument to the hotel if I had had the nerve to approach any of them. I wanted to speak with the celebrated Ben Bent, solo cornet, and question him as to the correct way of practicing so that I might become a good player myself. But I could not muster up enough courage to brazen it out and approach him, and so he too walked off with the rest of the bandsmen. I realized that with his going I had let an opportunity slip by, and for so doing never really quite forgave myself, as perhaps I might have learned more in a few minutes' conversation with this solo cornet player, than so far, I had from all my studying.

"Anyway, I attended the concert and was enthralled beyond words by the playing of this magnificent aggregation. . . . Oh, how tame our own town band sounded at our next rehearsal! For the first time I began to notice the mistakes we all made that were allowed to pass by the leader, and to observe how little he made of dynamic and expression marks, carrying everything through without trying to produce contrasts, and without paying any attention whatever to proper interpretation. Right then and there I made up my mind that if I became a good cornet player I would make every endeavor to become a member of Gilmore's great band, which was the best in the world; and well it might be as it was made up of picked men from all countries, and was comprised of the best players that could be procured."

Two years later Herbert Clarke's idols were playing in St. Louis, where the Triennial Conclave of the Knights Templar was being held. He was a cornetist in the When Band of Indianapolis, a commercial band sponsored by the When Clothing Company. This band was engaged to escort a Knights Templar commandery to St. Louis, and Clarke spent all his spare time during the week listening to the Gilmore concerts. "I heard Ben Bent play several solos. He was an excellent cornetist, with the most natural and musical tone I ever heard," Clarke related.

"One morning Mr. Gilmore invited every band in town to report at the fair grounds for a massed band concert, and there must have been a thousand or more musicians playing under the direction of the great bandmaster. It was a wonderful experience, and my enthusiasm for band music mounted higher and higher. My! but was I proud to play under him."

Clarke has said that there "were at least a hundred bands in the city that week. . . . It was here that I first met Fred Weldon, who came down from Chicago with the Second Regiment Band, at the head of a Chicago commàndery."

Gilmore was engaged for the entire conclave, which lasted about four weeks. The band played four times daily at the Music Hall of the Exposition Building. Although Gilmore played much solid music during this engagement, the piece which probably caused the most comment was the *Passing Regiment.* This is a descriptive piece, in which the band begins softly, as if heard from a distance. As the music gradually increases in loudness, it simulates the regiment drawing nearer and nearer. Then the music blasts forth as if the regiment were passing directly in front of the listener. The piece ends in reverse dynamics, simulating the regiment as it marches on and finally passes out of sight.

The way Gilmore and his men handled the very gradual crescendo and diminuendo was a revelation to most bands in attendance, for seldom had any of them heard sixty-five men play so softly and build up to fortissimo so smoothly. Many bands, returned home to their own practice hall, tried to imitate the artistry of the Gilmore band. If they did not succeed too well, they at least raised their sights and strove to become better bands.

With Gilmore piling success on top of success with his new kind of band the question constantly arises: Why weren't there other bands like his? Why didn't other bandmasters cash in on this lush business? For more than ten years Gilmore had been showing them how it was done. Surely there were other bandmasters capable of doing the same thing as Gilmore. A run-down on the well-established bandmasters of about 1886 reveals that all of them were contented to follow the conventional pattern; at least they were unwilling to take a try at something new.

Signor Carlo Alberto Cappa, who in 1881 had succeeded Grafulla as bandmaster of the 7th, was eminently well fitted to conduct such a band as Gilmore had. At this time he was regarded as Gilmore's only rival. Born in the Piedmont, Italy, in 1834, he studied music for five years in the Royal Academy at Asti and for four years played first trombone in a band of the 6th Lancers. When twenty-two he enlisted in the U. S. Navy and served two years aboard the frigate *Congress,* after which he landed in New York and soon became trombonist with the Boston Brass Band.

When Grafulla took charge of the 7th in 1860, Cappa went with him as solo trombone and remained for seven years. He then joined the Theodore Thomas Orchestra as solo trombone for seven years. In 1876 Cappa went back to the 7th for a five-year stretch as solo trombone and then became director of this crack band. For the past five to six years he had been enjoying outstanding success and popularity in this position.

In addition to being one of the most capable musicians in the country Cappa was a showman. He featured virtuosos on various instruments, the same as Gilmore, one of his current prizes being Walter Rogers, cornet soloist. Cappa also composed special music for his band, one number being strangely suggestive of Mons. Jullien. It was called *Reminiscences of Veteran Firemen* and it was descriptive music such as Jullien liked so well. It started out with conversation in the enginehouse, then came the fire alarm, the commotion to get started, the thrilling run to the fire, the battling of the flames, the collapse of a wall, the eventual triumph over the conflagration, and the grand finale.

Surely a man like this ought to be traveling with a sensational band such as Gilmore's Band, but for some reason Cappa preferred to stay in New York and play drills, guard mount, parades, and summer concerts for the commanding officers of the 7th Regiment. He played every Saturday and Sunday afternoons from May until October on the Mall in Central Park, and occasionally he made a trip as official band of some group going to a convention. This routine seemed to be all that Cappa desired out of life.

Although not on the same high plane as the 7th, the 9th and 13th followed the same pattern. William Baynes, bandmaster of the 69th Regiment Band of New York, began forging to the front about this

*In Chicago,
Fred Weldon was becoming
prominent as bandmaster of
the 2nd Regiment
of Illinois.*

time. He tried for several years to do some touring with his band, but the tours were short and intermittent. In Chicago, Fred Weldon was becoming prominent as bandmaster of the 2nd Regiment of Illinois. He made some trips through the Middle West and was highly regarded as cornetist, teacher, and bandmaster, but he could not bring himself to launch an independent band.

The civilian bands of about 1886 were not much different from the military bands. Most if not all were "official" bands for some military unit in addition to being a municipal band. The renowned American Band of Providence, directed by David Reeves, was also official band for the 1st Massachusetts Volunteer Militia. Jean Missud had established the Salem Cadet Band (Mass.) in 1878 and had built it into one of America's finest civilian bands. This band did more traveling than most bands of the time, but its bread and butter were the money it drew for acting as the official band of the Second Corps of Cadets of the Massachusetts Volunteer Militia, a source of income it clung to for forty years. Mace Gay formed his Brockton Band (Mass.) in 1880 and soon built it into one of New England's most famous bands, but until the turn of the century his band relied on the 5th Regiment of Massachusetts for much of its support.

Three of Pennsylvania's leading bands of this era were on the pay roll of the Pennsylvania National Guards, the Ringgold Band of Reading being attached to the 1st Brigade from 1881 to 1898, the Alexander Band of Wilkes-Barre being attached to the 9th Regiment from 1887 to 1907, and the Allentown Band being official band of the 4th Regiment from 1885 until 1900. The historic Stonewall Bri-

The Alexander Band of Wilkes-Barre was attached to the 9th Regiment of Pennsylvania.

gade Band of Staunton, Virginia, was incorporated in 1875 as the official band of the First Division, Second Corps, Army of Northern Virginia, and this is still its official name.

All of these bands, both military and civilian, took outside engagements when they could get them and when they could work them into their schedule of military and civilian duties, but these engagements were few and irregular. They usually consisted of leading some Knights Templar commandery to a conclave or some Shrine or Elk's lodge to an annual convention, of a parade at the annual G.A.R. convention, a trip to Washington for a presidential inaugural, a short series of concerts at some fair or exposition, or a college commencement concert. Not one of these established and leading bands was an independent, traveling concert band, depending upon popular demand at the ticket window for its support.

And what of Liberati, Sousa, and Innes? Ten years had passed since these young and aspiring musicians had listened to Gilmore at the Philadelphia Centennial. And what of the great promise of Brooke as predicted by Gilmore when Brooke directed the Gilmore band in his two new marches?

Liberati was the first to try Gilmore's formula for success as a bandmaster. In 1883 he formed a band of his own. We do not know much about this band except that F. A. Maginel, who was to become one of America's star performers on the saxophone, was a member. Apparently it didn't cut much of a figure and expired soon. This kind of band was more than Liberati could master. A few years later Liberati was back in the routine service-band fold, becoming conductor of the 71st Regiment Band of New York. He held this job for the following three years.

Sousa also got cold feet and accepted an appointment as director of the U. S. Marine Band in 1880. After Sousa had married Miss Jennie Bellis he had started earning a livelihood for himself and bride by going on the road as orchestra conductor for the musical comedy *Our Flirtation*, for which he composed the music. When the show reached St. Louis, Sousa received a letter from his father Antonio saying that the U. S. Marine Band was looking for a new conductor, that he had talked with the commandant, and that the position would be granted to young Sousa if he would return to Washington and accept it.

From some viewpoints the offer was not attractive. Sousa was already a successful composer and conductor, and he was making three times as much annually as the Marine job would pay. He would receive the pay and wear the uniform of a Marine captain, but his actual rank would be that of a noncommissioned officer, a rank of no distinction.

However, the U. S. Marines were strong in the Sousa blood. He had served over seven years in the Marines as an apprentice in music, and he had played triangle in the band while his father played trombone. His brother George had also played cymbals in the band and acted as librarian at one time. Furthermore Sousa considered directing this noted military band an unusual opportunity. He was strongly drawn toward band work, and if he couldn't see his way clear to forming an independent band, such as Gilmore directed, he would at least gain experience in conducting a band, and he would have the security of regular pay checks, even though small. Eventually he returned to Washington and took up his duties as conductor of the U. S. Marine Band on October 1, 1880. Here he was to remain for twelve years.

We do not know much about Brooke after he returned home in 1880 and married Miss Minnie Fox, but we know he didn't have a band of any kind for nearly a decade. Only Frederick N. Innes had the courage and the stamina and the ability to launch a successful band, patterned after the one Gilmore was making so successful.

After several years with the Boston Cadet Band, Innes had joined the Mapleson Opera Company orchestra and had spent three years touring the United States with this successful organization, under the direction of Luigi Arditi. In the cast at one time was Lillian Nordica, the Lillian Norton who began her career with Gilmore's Band while Innes was still occupying solo trombone chair.

After Innes had been in the New World for more than ten years, he began hankering after a visit to his homeland. Arriving in New York a fledgling but talented trombonist, he returned to England a finished and seasoned virtuoso. For a year or more he appeared as trombone soloist in London, Paris, Vienna, and Berlin. During these months he established himself as one of England's all-time greats on trombone.

But opportunity beckoned and he returned to America, where, in 1887, he established his own band. His travels with the Mapleson Opera Company and with Gilmore's Band had impressed him with the money and fame that could be his as conductor of a top-notch, traveling concert band. Gilmore was alone in this alluring field, and he had more engagements than he could fill. Innes decided the time was ripe for him to cut himself in on this lucrative business.

Innes called his organization Innes' Great Band. It was in essentials a copy of Gilmore's Band. Like Gilmore, Innes assembled an imposing array of competent soloists who could enliven the programs with solos and novel ensembles. In addition to a saxophone quintet, comprised of Fagotti, Conway, Williams, Klose, and Trout, he featured F. Austin on cornet, Tobin and himself on trombone, Delany on euphonium, Herr Stross and Herr Broatmann on clarinet, and Monsieur Meert on piccolo. His programs were carefully built along the lines he had observed Gilmore used when he traveled with Gilmore's Band. He included plenty of solid music from the classics, but he interspersed popular music numbers.

He secured a manager, who arranged bookings for a tour. He was now in business, and he was entirely on his own. He had no military officers to report to and he was untrammeled by obligations to subsidizing city fathers. He was determined to succeed as the Mapleson Opera Company had succeeded, relying wholly upon popular demand for patronage. In this he was even more advanced than Gilmore, who had certain obligations to the 22nd, however tenuous.

The tour took Innes' Great Band across the country as far as San Francisco, and the reception he received in most places augured well for his bold venture. In San Francisco he was engaged for two weeks. There he played afternoon and evening concerts at the Mechanics' Institute Fair, from September 9 to September 24. As ill luck would have it, Innes had as competition in San Francisco on September 16 and 17 the greatest band in America next to Gilmore's—the famous 7th Regiment Band of sixty men under Signor Cappa. This celebrated band had been engaged by a New York drill team of firemen to accompany them to San Francisco for a firemen's convention. The concerts given in the Grand Opera House by Cappa detracted from Innes's concerts, but Innes is said to have had a successful engagement nevertheless.

In San Francisco, Innes could not help wondering about the wisdom of his plunge into the new field. While he was worrying about ticket sales and expenses, he was sure Cappa led a serene existence, untouched by such business matters and completely free to give his whole attention to things musical. He couldn't keep from envying Cappa his security and regular pay check. While Innes had a chance of making two or three times what Cappa made in a year, he also ran the risk of losing a fortune and fastening upon himself a debt that would take years to repay. With these unhappy thoughts passing through his mind he left San Francisco and headed back East on the tour.

Not much is known about Innes' Great Band after this auspicious beginning. It is likely that the bright hopes of Innes were not realized as soon as he had expected. It is even probable that he was not able to maintain his band regularly and that he was compelled to abandon it for months at a time. In any event, when in 1890 Harvey Dodworth decided to retire from directing the 13th Regiment Band, Innes accepted the job with alacrity and held onto it until 1896. Although what Gilmore was doing looked easy, Innes learned that it was not as easy as it looked. The idea of an independent, traveling concert band was alluring, but apparently Gilmore was the only bandmaster who could make it work.

Perhaps for the present, thought Innes, he had better stick with the conventional band pattern. The 13th at least furnished steady employment and he could always be sure he could pay his room rent when it came due. Better times were ahead, Innes told himself. As he had traveled about the country he could see that the band idea at the grass-roots level was growing by leaps and bounds. Maybe the time wasn't ripe for his entry into the new field. If he would wait a few years, there would be more interest in bands and band music. When that day came, he would launch another band. He still believed the idea could be made to work for him as well as it was working for Gilmore.

In line with Innes's observation that the band idea was on the upsurge, there appeared an article in *Harper's Weekly* in 1889, entitled *Military Bands in the United States,* written by Leon Mead. In this article the author states: "At present there are over ten thousand military bands in the United States. In the smaller cities they average twenty-five men each. In small country towns they number twelve to eighteen members. The average band, composed of twenty-five men, is usually made up in this wise:

1 piccolo
1 E♭ clarinet
4 B♭ clarinets
2 E♭ cornets
4 B♭ cornets
2 alto horns

3 trombones (or tenor horns)
2 baritones
2 tubas
1 small drum
1 bass drum
1 cymbal
1 bandmaster

It is worth noting that the proportion of reeds to brass is only 35 per cent reeds to 65 per cent brass. This is the reverse of the proportion in the Gilmore and a few other of the finest bands. The fact that the average band contained even 35 per cent reeds was a big advancement over conditions fifteen years before, when Gilmore made his first tour; and Patrick Gilmore, more than any other person in America, was responsible for this gain.

"To several influences is attributed the vast improvement in military bands in this country within the past twenty-five years," Mead continues. "Notable among them may be mentioned the larger musical field which military bands have entered, and which was formerly monopolized by the stringed orchestras. Bandmasters have learned that marches are not the only type of music which a band can render effectively. The gavot, the waltz, the polka, and compositions reaching into the classics are now the common property of military bands.

"Within the limits allowed for this article it would not be possible to name the many bands from Maine to California which are more or less celebrated."

Mr. Mead then names and comments at some length on the U. S. Marine Band under Sousa, the American Band of Providence, R.I., under D. W. Reeves, the 7th Regiment Band under Signor Carlo Alberto Cappa, and Gilmore's Band. He also says that in the South good military bands are unknown, but that in the Eastern and Middle Western states "hundreds of excellent brass bands exist, and then there are others which, to put it mildly, should not be taken seriously." Among the best he names the Fitchburg Band in Massachusetts [Gustav Patz was bandmaster], the Salem Cadet Band (Mass.) under Jean Missud and the Boston Cadet Band under J. Thomas Baldwin.

In the West he names the First Brigade Band of Greeley, Colorado, with twenty-six men; the Elgin Watch Factory Band of Elgin, Illinois, "with an ensemble of seventy-six musicians, under the leadership of Professor J. Hecker"; the Cleveland Gray's Band, the Toledo City

Band, the Metropolitan Band of Dayton, and the Kansas City Band. Mead says there are several bands along or near the Pacific seaboard which "are among the foremost in the country," but he doesn't name them. He also refrains from naming the best bands in the larger cities.

Such is the quick roundup of bands in the United States by a contemporary authority in 1889.

Liberati may have failed to establish his band and Innes' Great Band may have found the going tough, but Gilmore's Band went on to one great triumph after another. In 1888, Gilmore made his first tour of the South, and the following year he made his first tour of Canada but combined it with another tour of the United States, traveling to San Francisco and back. This last tour was something special, being the twentieth anniversary of his famous National Peace Jubilee of 1869.

This was probably the greatest tour ever made, on the basis of the poundage of the baggage, for Gilmore carried along a set of anvils and six bronze cannons! The latter were specially made for the occasion. They were loaded at the breech and each was fitted with two sets of wires, one set to fire the cannon and one set to show on the podium that the cannon was loaded and ready for Gilmore to touch the button which would set it off. Each cannon was capable of twenty shots per minute, according to Gilmore's advertising, and the six must have required a gunners' crew of several men, thoroughly drilled in ordnance.

Listed as soloists with the band at this time were the following twenty-two stars:

Herman Bellstedt, famous German cornetist
B. C. (Ben) Bent, cornet
Albert Bode, cornet
Michael Raffayolo, euphonium
August Stengler, clarinet
Stockigt, clarinet
Matus Uri, E♭ clarinet
Bruggman, alto clarinet
E. A. Lefebre, alto saxophone
John Cox, flute
Mons. De Carlo, piccolo
Signor de Chiari, oboe
Rupp, bassoon
Cavanagh, bassoon

Ernest Weber, bass clarinet
Wilson, trombone
Ernest Clarke, trombone
Harry Weston, French horn
Herman Conrad, bass
Elden Baker, bass (antoniophones)
Herr Ritze, fluegelhorn
Harry Whittier, euphonium

It was this great wealth of solo talent which enabled Gilmore to enliven his programs with such variety and novelty. In any one week Gilmore's programs were studded with the appearance of fifteen or twenty different soloists. At the church services, held every Sunday morning in the ampitheater at Manhattan Beach, Gilmore simulated the church organ by employing a quartet of French horns. The rendition of four-part songs was for several years a feature of Gilmore's programs there. An unusual effect was produced by employing a solo instrument or a solo voice, which was accompanied by a quartet of French horns, headed by Harry Weston.

In a typical program given in St. Louis on October 18, 1891, the following unusual numbers were presented. Lefebre played a saxophone solo, accompanied by a French-horn quartet comprised of Weston, Vohkins, Miel, and Zilm, with background music by the whole band. Bode on cornet and Raffayolo on euphonium played a duet called *The Sweetest Name,* with band accompaniment. On the same program appeared a novel arrangement of the *Miserere* from *Il Trovatore,* presented as a trio by Bode, Raffayolo, and Baull, with band accompaniment.

The Gilmore band was now at its peak. Every member was an artist carefully selected and trained to follow the conductor in all the niceties of tempo, phrasing, dynamics, tone, and other subtleties which marked Gilmore's superb interpretation of great music.

The band library aggregated ten thousand pieces, and Gilmore employed two to three full-time experts who were kept busy making arrangements of new music for the band. It is said that the players were such finished musicians that Gilmore often set on their stands new music of the most difficult kind, and that the band could read it off at sight without rehearsals.

The instrumentation of the band at this time was just about what Gilmore had dreamed of years before. Of course he used a quintet of antoniophones, but these were treated as novelty instruments and were not considered as a standard part of his instrumentation. During the decade following his European tour he had made some needed changes, such as adding more clarinets and a bass trombone, and cutting down on the percussion section and the brass section. Roughly he now had one-third clarinets, one-third other woodwinds, and one-third brass. The brass section he had trained to play as softly as the woodwinds when the occasion demanded, and the band as a whole had the softness and smoothness and disciplined flexibility of the finest stringed orchestra.

It is obvious today, when viewed from the vantage point of later developments, that the trend was toward more clarinets, with divided parts; the use of saxophones as a blending agent for woodwinds and brass; fewer trumpets and trombones; elimination of the solid front of saxhorns, and a more refined percussion section. But Gilmore had no guide and had to feel his way along as he ventured into the unknown, relying entirely upon his artistic judgment. Back of everything he did was this over-all desire to develop a band which would be able to play the great classical music as effectively as the symphony orchestra. He had no illusions that he could make a wind band sound like a stringed symphony orchestra, but he believed it could perform as musically.

Discussing this subject once with a friend, Gilmore put it this way: "Figuratively speaking, the stringed orchestra is feminine, the military band masculine. The stringed orchestra may be as coarse as a very coarse woman, or made as refined as the most accomplished lady. So, too, the military band may remain like a rough street tramp, or he may undergo a polishing that will make him a perfect gentleman, equally fit, from a critical standpoint, to occupy the concert-room with his more sensitive sister. That is what I have tried to make of my band. Somebody may bring the stringed orchestra to such a degree of perfection as to make it the very queen among its kind, but my military band shall be king."

In the late fall of 1891, at the age of sixty-two, Gilmore was planning still greater exploits for his band. He envisioned what he termed the Columbian Tour with a band of one hundred players. He was to open at the St. Louis Annual Exposition in September of 1892 for six weeks and then continue the tour through the fall, returning to New York for Christmas. The following spring the tour would be resumed, culminating at the Columbian Exposition in Chicago. For 1894 he planned his second European tour.

Such grandiose plans sound a bit frenzied, as if Gilmore had fierce competitors at his heels and was trying desperately to outdistance them. Nothing could be farther from the actual situation. As far back as Gilmore could see, he had no competitors of any kind. He found himself running superbly but alone. Gilmore, however, was a man who, if he couldn't find competitors to run against, liked to run against time, against his own record.

In other musical fields great activity was found. New faces had appeared before the public, such as Marcella Sembrick, Ignace Jan Paderewski, Master Joseph Hofmann, and Master Fritz Kreisler. The Metropolitan Opera House had been opened and had presented the complete Wagnerian *Der Ring des Nibelungen*. Theodore Thomas had finally come to the end of his travels and had established the Chicago Symphony Orchestra.

In the professional band field, nothing much was going on. Innes was securely pocketed in the 13th and showed no disposition to change. Concerning Brooke, we have little to go on. There is some evidence that he formed a band of his own in 1889, but if he did it was not successful enough to establish a mark in the records. It is believed that Brooke was devoting most of his time during these years to composition.

Signor Liberati was making his second try for a band of his own. After three years as conductor of the 71st band, he again got the fever to have a band like that of Gilmore. He forsook the shelter of the militia and established a new band in 1889. Among the players he hired was a boy wonder trombonist from St. Joseph, Missouri, by the name of Arthur Pryor, who a few years later was to develop into the greatest of all virtuosos on the trombone.

We do not know by what name this new band was at first known, but in 1890 Liberati was bravely advertising it as "The World Renowned Liberati Band." This title was especially incongruous with the engagement which occupied him most of the year, for he traveled with the C. D. Hess Grand Opera Company and played short selections between the acts of *Il Trovatore* and other operas. Such small chores were not liable to add to his "world renown."

Liberati hung on as long as he could, but finally he was compelled to throw in the towel again. This idea of an independent band might be all right for Gilmore, but Liberati could not figure out how to make a go of it. This was the second time he had gone through all the labor and worry of auditioning and hiring musicians, of selecting and rehearsing the music, of haggling with booker and manager —only to play a few months and then have to disband. Liberati was thoroughly discouraged, thoroughly disgusted, and thoroughly broke.

He could have gone back to some military organization, but the few months he had conducted his own band had spoiled him for the drab routine of the service band. Instead he decided he would take a whirl at personal appearances as cornet soloist. Accordingly he put his cornet under his arm, packed his solos, with band arrangements, and started out. He was successful as soloist, for he was a real virtuoso; besides he had a stage personality that was worth as much as his musical ability. Everywhere he went he was enthusiastically received. Eventually he went to England for a series of engagements, among them being a stay at the Alhambra Theatre, London. But Liberati wasn't happy. He kept looking back at his ventures as bandmaster and he still felt he could be a success with a band of his own. He was soon to demonstrate to all the world that he could.

As for Sousa, he was still conducting the U. S. Marine Band. But he had broken with age-old tradition and had taken the band on a tour of five weeks. In order to do so, he had to get the consent of the President of the United States of America, no less! This epochal break with tradition occurred in 1891, and the following year Sousa was able to take the band on a tour of seven weeks. This second tour was momentous. When the band reached Chicago, Blakely, the manager, met Sousa, induced him to resign from the Marine post and form "Sousa's New Marine Band."

Meanwhile Gilmore was very busy with preparations for the Columbian Tour and the European tour which was to follow. For his one-hundred-piece band he needed a new and extremely talented solo cornetist. He had heard of a phenomenal, twenty-four-year-old star named Herbert Clarke, at that time playing in Toronto, Canada. Ernest Clarke, featured trombone soloist with Gilmore and elder brother of Herbert, finally persuaded Herbert to try for the job. The graphic, intimate account of his meeting the great Gilmore is so typical of the experiences of scores of young musicians whom Gilmore took under his wing and portrays Gilmore in such a warm and human light that it is worth repeating in this connection.

"So in February, 1891," Herbert relates, "I mustered enough confidence to go to New York City, arriving there on a Sunday morning and going direct to Mr. Gilmore's home, without any notice to him. On my reaching his house, his maid informed me that he could not be disturbed this morning, as he was resting after a hard week's work, preparing for his regular spring tour, but she made an appointment for me for three o'clock in the afternoon.

"I did not go home with my brother Ern, but walked around in Central Park for several hours all alone; for Mr. Gilmore's home was close to the Park, on the West side. During this time I nearly lost courage and was going to back out and return to Toronto. . . . However, the trip to New York was expensive, and I was not going back a coward, even if I failed in the examination. Anyway, I would have the honor of playing before Mr. Gilmore, and perhaps learn something from any suggestions he might offer; and when I grew older, I would be in a better position and condition to make another trial at that time. I made up my mind that I would do my very best, even if I failed to satisfy him.

"With this thought uppermost in my mind, I walked bravely to Mr. Gilmore's home and rang the bell. I was ushered into his beautiful library and told to wait a few moments. While looking around the room I discovered a photo of myself and wondered how it came there. It was beside a picture of my brother Ernest, who had probably given it to the great bandmaster. Mr. Gilmore was a man who kept in touch with every soloist in the world, and I felt proud that my picture was exhibited in his home.

"After I had waited in his library for about half an hour, he appeared and greeted me so affably, a characteristic that made him such a lovable man to all, that I really forgot my excitement for the moment. He talked quite a while about conditions in Canada, asking after his old friend Dr. Torrington, and then requested me to take out my cornet and play something for him. Before starting, he advised me to 'warm up a bit,' but I could not think of a single piece to play. He noticed my hesitation and began to encourage me, saying that he realized just how I felt. His manner was so delightful that I forgot my self-consciousness and commenced playing one of my most difficult solos; I think it was Levy's *Whirlwind Polka*.

"When I had finished this number in a creditable manner, Mr. Gilmore simply nodded his head and said, 'Go on.' I then played a difficult 'air varie,' finishing on a very high note, top F, that was not in the music. His exclaiming 'Bravo!' encouraged me to play another solo with more execution, or technique. I was then told to rest, during which time he asked me some questions regarding what experience I had had in the band field, also what music I had been used to playing. I told him that my education in playing had been under the direction of Dr. Torrington and Mr. John Bayley, who were efficient musicians, as he well knew, and that I had been drilled in all the standard oratorios, symphonies and operatic selections. He next asked me if I could play some simple ballad, suggesting *The Last Rose of Summer,* which I well knew and interpreted to his astonishment and satisfaction.

"Then suddenly he asked me if I knew the popular soprano aria from *Robert the Devil,* by Meyerbeer. I answered 'Yes.' 'All right, play it,' he said. So I carefully blew all the water out of my cornet, and at the same time braced myself for this number, for I knew it required more endurance than any polka to interpret properly. Taking a little time in starting, I felt my confidence return, as I had been coached many times in this aria by my old bandmaster, who had explained its words and sentiment as well as its dramatic meaning in the opera.

"After I had finished, Mr. Gilmore came over to me, patted me on the back, and told me that he had been looking for a great cornet player who could play musically, with the endurance I had displayed this afternoon, and that he had found one! I nearly fell over on hearing this expression of enthusiasm regarding my playing, and had to sit down. All the playing I had just done had completely exhausted me, and his encouragement, coming on top of it all, actually knocked my legs from under me.

"The position I had long sought was now offered me. I was told to report in New York early in April for rehearsals, these taking place before the regular Spring Tour through the New England States, which was succeeded by a month at Madison Square Garden, the entire summer at Manhattan Beach, with six weeks at St. Louis Exposition, and later a Fall Tour, returning to New York for Christmas.

"Mr. Gilmore dismissed me cordially, thanking me for the treat I had given him, and impressed upon me the importance of being at rehearsals promptly in April. He also told me that in order to play in his band I must join the New York Musical Union, an act compulsory for every member, that I was to provide myself with a Gilmore uniform and the necessities of traveling, as well as all my solos with full band arrangements."

Gilmore selected his soloists, but the recruiting of the extra thirty-five musicians necessary to bring his band to its full complement of

*Gilmore
became a heavy drinker
a few years before
his death, in 1892.*

one hundred men he left entirely to his trusted assistant conductor, Charles W. Freudenvoll. This work occupied Freudenvoll several months, but the great band was ready in time to fulfill the opening engagement of the Columbian Tour at the St. Louis Annual Exposition early in September. The concerts were given in the Music Hall, and they were enthusiastically received. Gilmore's name was well known in St. Louis, for he had stopped there repeatedly on his tours. His big band of one hundred men topped anything he had ever brought to St. Louis before, and each concert augured unbounded success for the long tour that lay ahead.

But Gilmore conducted his final concert on September 23. Stricken that night, he died in great pain the following evening in his room at the Lindell Hotel. Gilmore became a heavy drinker during the last years of his life, but whether this was directly or indirectly the cause of his death is not known. Freudenvoll had visited his great mentor briefly that afternoon, and had then gone to the Music Hall to conduct the evening concert. The band was playing *Old Folks at Home* when Frank Gaiennie, general manager of the exposition, approached the bandstand. At the conclusion of the number Mr. Gaiennie walked to the podium and stood beside Freudenvoll, facing the audience. In a choked voice he announced that Patrick Gilmore was no more, and that under the circumstances the remainder of the concert would not be given.

The evening following Gilmore's death the Gilmore band marched at the head of the cortege bearing the body of their revered and beloved leader to the train which would take it to New York for burial. As they marched in slow cadence, they played Gilmore's own composition *Death at the Door* and Handel's *Death March* from *Saul*. Only strong men could play under such emotional tension. When the body was placed aboard the train and the band broke ranks, many of the musicians wandered into the night to cover their unrestrained grief.

The next day, only a few hours after the body of Gilmore had been taken from the train in New York, a newly formed band gave its very first concert, at the Stillman Music Hall in Plainfield, N.J. The very first number of this initial concert was Gilmore's own composition *The Voice of a Departed Soul,* played as a memorial tribute to the great bandmaster. The conductor of this new band was John Philip Sousa.

Exactly two weeks later the new Sousa band played a concert at the exercises held to dedicate the new but empty buildings of the Columbian Exposition in Chicago, where Gilmore had planned to end his grand Columbian Tour the following year. Many of Gilmore's finest musicians were to keep this rendezvous, but the baton which was to swing over them was not that of the immortal Gilmore but that of Sousa.

The Gilmore band, under Freudenvoll, finished the engagement in the Music Hall, and speculation was rife concerning the rest of the Columbian Tour. Freudenvoll was urged to continue, but he advised against it. He had been taken into Gilmore's confidence concerning the management of the tour and its financial risk, for Gilmore had suspected it would be difficult to make a profitable tour with an expensive one-hundred-piece band. With the magic name of Gilmore removed the tour was more certainly headed for financial trouble. Freudenvoll refused to be saddled with the responsibility and eventual blame.

At the insistence of a faction in the band D. W. Reeves, for twenty-six years leader of the highly respected American Band of Providence, was asked to assume the conductorship of the band. He confessed grave misgivings, but the opportunity to lead such a magnificent band was more than he could resist. He resigned from his old band and started out on the tour. After the band had played in a few towns, financial conditions became so bad that in Cincinnati the tour was abandoned, and Reeves returned to Providence. Without the guiding genius of Gilmore the grandiose Columbian Tour was doomed to dismal failure.

By the following spring many of the Gilmore players were ready to acknowledge defeat, and quite a number of the best men secured jobs with Sousa. Others, however, still believed that Gilmore's Band could be continued. They lashed out against those who they felt had deserted the cause, especially those who had joined the Sousa band, now looming as a strong rival. In the March 15, 1893, issue of the *Musical Courier* magazine the die-hard Gilmore men published a scurrilous attack upon the deserters who had joined Sousa, calling them "fossilized" musicians.

This brought a quick reply from the men who were with Sousa. In this statement they questioned the right of the die-hard Gilmore men to call themselves Gilmore's Band, saying that perhaps a total of two thousand men had, at one time or another, played under the baton of Gilmore. The statement was signed by:

> Raffayolo, euphonium soloist
> Lefebre, saxophone soloist
> A. Bode, first cornet
> H. L. Clarke, solo cornet
> F. W. Wadsworth, first flute
> F. Urbani, first clarinet
> J. Lacalle, first clarinet
> Thos. Shannon, bass saxophone
> Herman Conrad, Bass tuba
> Ernst Mueller, drum and typmpani

D. W. Reeves, now back with the American Band of Providence and no longer involved in the dispute, joined in the battle of words. He sent in a statement to the *Courier* upholding the right of the men to use the Gilmore name for the band they planned to form. He said that four of the signers had already deserted the band when he took over but that the other six had promised him they would stick with the band because of their undying respect for Gilmore. Now, he said, they had shown their small regard for Gilmore and had deserted the cause. It was evident that he was bitter and that his sympathies were with the men who were trying to carry on.

*David W. Reeves,
of American Band,
Providence,
became conductor of
the 22nd after
Gilmore died.*

Herbert Clarke states that when he joined the Sousa band, in April 1893, there were thirteen ex-Gilmore men enrolled. In addition to the ten who signed the *Courier* statement, there were also August Stengler, clarinet, Frank Seltzer, cornet, and Elden Baker, bass tuba. Eventually there were nineteen Gilmore men who joined Sousa.

In the fall of 1893 fifty Gilmore men decided to revive Gilmore's Band under Victor Herbert, then cellist with the Metropolitan Opera Orchestra and the New York Philharmonic. However, by November 26, when the first concert was given, there were only twenty-eight Gilmore men in the band. Herbert Clarke, who played the Columbian Exposition during the summer with Sousa, returned to the Gilmore band as cornet soloist, and continued for six weeks. At various times during Victor Herbert's regime, which continued until some time in 1897, Clarke was solo cornet with the Gilmore band.

Victor Herbert did a creditable job under great difficulties. The band was outfitted in new blue and red uniforms and the men were kept busy with engagements. They spent much time on the road, making one tour after another. The tour in 1895 covered fifty-one towns, in which the band played sixty-two concerts in fifty-three days, and extended through the South to New Orleans, back through St. Louis and Chicago as far north as Toronto, ending finally in Salem, made hallowed ground to the Gilmore band by the early efforts of Gilmore.

During these years Herbert often accepted solo cello engagements with various orchestras. He was also in demand as a composer. While director of Gilmore's Band he had produced his first light opera *Prince Ananias* and had collaborated with Harry Bache Smith in producing the successful comic opera *The Wizard of the Nile.* Under such pressure Herbert finally decided he had had enough, and in the early summer of 1897 he resigned.

E. A. Lefebre,
greatest saxophone soloist of
all time,
played with Jullien,
Gilmore, and Sousa.

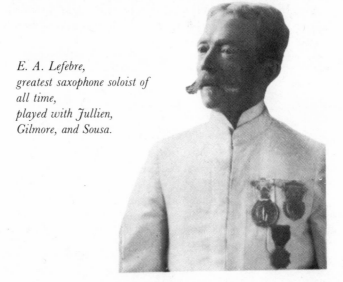

In June, E. A. Couturier, well-known cornet soloist from Easton, Pa., announced that he had acquired the entire Gilmore band library of "eighteen thousand pieces," through arrangements with Gilmore's widow, and that a tour was being arranged under the management of Thomas Ebert, which would extend through the United States and Canada. Whether or not this tour materialized is unknown, but the following spring a tour was started under the management of H. C. Fast. Failure dogged the enterprise, however, and the band folded on July 3, the musicians departing for their homes without being paid.

In 1905 it was learned that Mrs. Gilmore and her daughter Minnie were in destitute circumstances, living in one room in Boston. Victor Herbert and three other prominent conductors organized a benefit concert in New York for them, but the musicians' union stepped in at the last moment and required that the musicians who had donated their services be paid union scale, the excuse being that "the concert had been well advertised." This left a mere pittance to be turned over to the widow and daughter of the famous Gilmore.

The last we hear of the Gilmore dynasty was in this same year. The P. S. Gilmore Band Library Publishing Company was established in St. Louis. An announcement issued by the firm stated that all the best music in the Gilmore library would be "rescored and condensed" and republished for sale.

But by this time such an announcement could scarcely be heard above the resounding harmonies of the great new bands of Sousa, Innes, Liberati, and Brooke.

Seven

*Sousa's boyish face
was camouflaged by
a black beard, which added
dignity to his appearance.*

When Gilmore died and his band broke up, Sousa's New Marine Band became the principals in the story of the independent concert band. The name for Sousa's new band was chosen in order to capitalize on the fame and prestige Sousa had gained during the previous twelve years as conductor of the U. S. Marine Band, from 1880 to 1892.

Sousa was only twenty-six years old when he became conductor of the Marine Band, and most of its members were old enough to be his father. Accordingly the first thing Sousa did upon arriving in Washington was grow a heavy, black beard. By the time he faced the Marine veterans, his boyish face was camouflaged by the severe black beard, which added years and dignity to his appearance.

Sousa had found the U. S. Marine Band in a demoralized condition. As he says, the music library contained "not a sheet of Wagner, Berlioz, Grieg or Tschaikowsky or any other of the modern composers who were attracting attention throughout the musical world." He immediately bought pieces from various European publishers and proceeded with "most rigid rehearsals." This new regime brought protests and typical Marine gripes from the players. They began making threats that they would obtain discharges if Sousa didn't ease up, knowing full well that their threats were groundless, for there was no machinery at the time whereby they could obtain discharges. Sousa, however, called the turn by securing new regulations under which it was possible to grant speedy discharges. At the end of the first year the membership of the band had shrunk to thirty-three men, but he began recruiting young replacements and gradually the band was built up to its original strength.

Modern music and improved performance began to attract more favorable attention for the band. The White House concerts grew in popularity until regular attendance ran into the thousands. Every Thursday concerts were given in the Marine Barracks, and every Wednesday in the Capitol grounds. Discipline in parades was tightened so that the band regularly played from assembly point to the end of the march, and instead of the tempo being regulated to suit the decrepit oldsters it was stepped up to the regulation one-hundred-and-twenty cadence per minute. This brisk pace, as much as anything else Sousa did, helped weed out the superannuated and fill the ranks with young men. The Marine Band became a spectacular marching unit, with the front rank filled with trombones and basses, stretching from curb to curb. This was the marching formation which was being used by Gilmore and by the 7th Regiment Band under Cappa. Sousa had witnessed how effective it was, and he had adopted it.

The hard-working Sousa brought about other reforms. For the receptions at the White House he discontinued the opera numbers, overtures, and marches customarily played while the guests were entering, and played instead quiet, subdued music. As the guests filed past the President, Sousa changed to lively, spirited music. President Hayes commended Sousa for this change, saying that the lively music enabled him to shake more hands in less time and left him less tired when it was over.

At a reception in the East Room during President Arthur's term Sousa led the band in *Hail to the Chief* as the President appeared and led the way to dinner. Later President Arthur slipped away from his guests and sought out Sousa, asking him, "What piece did you play when we went in to dinner?" Sousa told him he played *Hail to the Chief,* the customary piece. President Arthur then asked, "Do you consider this piece appropriate?" Sousa said only the title was appropriate, that the music was originally an old Scottish boating song, and that he considered it non-military, empty, and pompous. President Arthur's reply was short and to the point: "Then change it." Sousa did, composing the *Presidential Polonaise,* and this number became standard for all indoor affairs.

A few years later Sousa composed *Semper Fidelis* for review purposes outdoors. This composition was adopted as the official march of the U. S. Marine Corps, the only composition, even today, which can claim official recognition by the government.

Although the authorized number of playing musicians was only thirty men, in some manner Sousa managed to maintain a band of about fifty. During these years Gilmore and his band often included Washington on their tours, and these appearances made Sousa restless and eager to take his own fine band on the road. The routine official functions had palled on Sousa, and in 1891 he obtained the consent of President Harrison to take the Marine Band on a tour of five weeks. David Blakely, who had managed the tours of Gilmore for several years, was engaged to make bookings. Dressed in dark blue trousers and scarlet coats, lavishly trimmed with yards of silk cord, fancy epaulets, and gilt buckles, the band of forty-nine men made a striking appearance.

On this tour Sousa learned some lessons about public taste in music which he never forgot, and which guided him in making his popular programs for the Sousa band years later. A Washington newspaper correspondent warned him about the high-brow music demanded in Pittsburgh. He told Sousa that if he played light or popular numbers there, he would be hissed off the stage. Sousa therefore prepared a heavy program of Wagner, Bach, and Brahms. After the first heavy number he expected to receive heart-warming approval but found the audience strangely silent and unmoved. He concluded that the highly cultured audience found even this number too trivial. The next was sure to please, however, for it was the *Procession of the Grail* from Wagner's *Parsifal*. But when he turned to the audience after this number, he found them half asleep. He sensed that his newspaper friend had given him a bum steer, and he decided to find out. He switched to *Annie Rooney*, a popular music-hall song from London which had been published in the United States only the year before, and under his breath he warned the men close to the podium to be prepared to be hissed off the stage. The playing of this sprightly little piece aroused the audience from their high-brow lethargy, and they applauded with enthusiasm. Sousa then fed them some more of the same, and the balance of the program was a big hit.

Later, in Fayetteville, N.C., he risked playing *Dixie* as an encore, and was rewarded with clapping, whistling, and shouting. Nothing he played was so enthusiastically applauded, and he figured that he could be a big success throughout the South if he could play *Dixie* after every number on the program.

Blakely had laid out a strenuous schedule for this first tour. Two regular concerts were booked each day, and in addition Sousa found himself attending luncheons, civic demonstrations, and other functions in practically every town. When he had nothing else to do, he boarded his train and traveled through the night to the next town. As a result he suffered a nervous breakdown by the time he returned to Washington, and the post surgeon sent him to Europe to recuperate.

The following March, however, Sousa set out on his second tour. This jaunt lasted for seven weeks, and extended as far as San Francisco, where he arrived April 9, having played the larger cities along the route. When he reached Chicago on the return lap, Blakely was there to meet him. He asked Sousa how much he was being paid as conductor of the Marine Band, and Sousa told him about fifteen hundred dollars a year. Blakely asked him if he would be interested in heading a private concert band at a salary of six thousand dollars a year plus 20 per cent of the profits. Seeing the incredulous look on Sousa's face, Blakely assured him he was not talking through his hat. He said he had already lined up a syndicate of business men who would put up the money for such a venture. He revealed that he had recently broken with Gilmore and was looking for a comparable band to manage. Sousa said he would accept the offer if he could be released from his duties with the Marine Corps, and he showed his faith in such a project by buying one thousand dollars' worth of stock in the syndicate.

Blakely did not reveal the reasons for his break with Gilmore, but it most likely was over Gilmore's Columbian Tour with a band of one hundred players. Gilmore had his heart set on touring with this augmented band, even though experience told him such a tour could hardly be made profitable. Blakely had been through tour after tour with Gilmore, and he knew how difficult it had been to make a profit even with sixty-five men. Some of the tours, when weather, railroad strikes, or other unforeseen events interfered, had been conducted at a loss, a few with heavy losses. He advised strongly against the hundred-man tour, but Gilmore persisted, and the long business association was broken off. Even as Blakely talked with Sousa in Chicago, Gilmore and his assistant conductor Freudenvoll were making contracts with players for the tour, which was to be launched in September, only four months away.

Sousa's resignation from the Marine Corps was accepted late in July. When it was announced that Sousa had left the band, the Washington newspapers expressed regrets that the Marine Band was to be deprived of the services of the man who had made it great. They eulogized him in the strongest terms and wished him success with his new band.

The *Evening Star* editorialized: "There has probably never been a military organization in the country which has given more pleasure than the U. S. Marine Band." In a news story details of the new band were divulged. "Professor Sousa leaves here to take personal charge and leadership of a magnificent military band which is to have its headquarters in Chicago," the story stated.

In an interview with the press Sousa told how and why the band came about. "The new band is not being planned," he said, "with any special reference to the Chicago World's Fair, as many people imagine, and as yet no engagement has been made with the Fair people. The stock of the organization is held very largely in New York, and the company holds a New York charter. Chicago was chosen as headquarters on account of the facilities offered; and as a matter of fact, the band will spend comparatively little time in that city.

"The organization grew out of the general knowledge that all over the country there is a demand for high-class military music. Outside of the Marine and Gilmore bands there are no organizations in the country which meet this want in any sort of satisfactory manner."

Those two sentences are an eloquent preamble to Sousa's declaration of inde_i ndence from the conventional band pattern of the time.

T. P. Brooke had made a feeble stab at forming a business band. Liberati had tried twice but had failed both times. Innes had put everything he had into Innes' Great Band, but eventually he had to take conventional employment with the 13th Regiment Band. And now Sousa had taken the big step.

He immediately set about recruiting a band of the finest players he could find, and he personally auditioned every man. One of the first men he signed up was a young trombone soloist by the name of Arthur Pryor. When he was eighteen, Pryor had played solo trombone with Liberati and two years later had almost accepted a similar position with Gilmore but instead had taken the job of conductor with the Stanley Opera Company, a traveling opera company based in Denver. Pryor turned out to be one of the greatest stars in the Sousa band for eleven years, until he organized his own famous band in 1903.

Walter Smith had been solo cornet with the U. S. Marine Band under Sousa, and he cast his lot with Sousa's new band. Smith formerly had been cornet soloist with the Coldstream Guards of London, and was one of the finest of his time. Other greats in Sousa's first band were Staats, clarinet, a graduate of the Paris Conservatory; Henry Koch, one of the finest French horns in America; F. Jabon, bassoonist, graduate of the Paris Conservatory; J. S. Cox, celebrated Scottish flutist; Robert Messinger on oboe; Frank Holton on trombone; and Signor Joseph Norrito, clarinetist, who played with the Sousa band for thirty-two seasons.

Rudolph Becker, the last surviving member of this first band, related sixty years later how he happened to sign up with Sousa. He was playing baritone saxophone with the Wanamaker Band in Philadelphia when he heard that Sousa and Harry Coleman, his music publisher from Philadelphia, were scouting players in and around this city for the purpose of selecting men for his new band. Sousa seemed to know just who the better players were and he invited those he wanted, to try out for the band. Sousa in person held these auditions, and he was very critical and particular about whom he selected. Becker was given Sousa's okay, and he signed the contract.

Becker preserved this contract, and it is an interesting document. The printed contract is headed: "Sousa's New Marine Band, under the direction of the Blakely Syndicate, Incorporated; D. Blakely, President and General Manager, John Philip Sousa, Musical Director." Signing for the Blakely Syndicate was Howard Pew, secretary. Pew was also the booking agent, with offices in Chicago, and Frank Christianer was associated with him.

Rudolph Becker signed up on the twelfth of September, and he agreed "to render services in said band, and to perform therein at all Parades, Concerts, Rehearsals, etc., during the season of about nine weeks, commencing on or about Sept. 26, 1892, and ending on or about Dec. 18, 1892, at a salary of Thirty-five dollars per week."

Another paragraph specifies that Becker "agrees to rehearse for twelve (12) days prior to the commencement of the season without compensation." There is also a no-strike clause and a clause outlining grievance procedure. No salary is to be paid during a transcontinental tour "for days necessarily consumed for travel when no concert can be given, nor for time unavoidably lost by any railroad or other accident or Providential interference or epidemic which shall prevent the fulfillment of engagements."

Personal friends of Becker who signed up with him included Marv Lyons, trombone, who also became baggage manager; William Foster, bass drummer, who also functioned as librarian; Gus Grosshurt, trumpet, who became a one-man clipping service of local newspapers in the towns where the band played; and Otto Blauert. In all Sousa recruited seventeen men from the Philadelphia area, most of them Germans. These included two men from the Allentown Band (Pa.): S. Schaich, clarinet, and Ed Fritz, cornet.

Rehearsals were held in New York. The men soon learned that they were playing for a man who knew what he wanted, and he wanted plenty! Never before had they been made to watch the conductor more closely and to play so precisely. Sousa deliberately increased tempo unexpectedly or slowed it down, just to determine if the men were following him. By the end of the series of rehearsals the fifty men were "hanging from the end" of Sousa's baton, quick to follow the beat of that imperious stick of wood. The band had a new sound, too. The usual loud brass was held in check, and the reeds played as one man. In tutti passages the blend of brass and reeds was smooth and oily.

After the rehearsals in New York the band set out for nine weeks of hectic traveling. The "spit and polish" tradition of the Marine Corps was carried by Sousa into his new band. Each man was required to keep his uniform immaculate, his cap and his shoes shined to a high luster. The men often grumbled, and they delighted in citing to each other that Sousa had a valet to do this, and besides Sousa's uniforms were made to fit! There was only one consolation: there were no more rehearsals on the trip—there wasn't any time for rehearsals.

At the beginning of the tour each man was given a "tour sheet," which listed all the places and dates for concerts to be given so that the men could inform their families where mail could reach them. On Saturday night every man received a yellow envelope with his name on it, and inside was cash payment for the week. With it was a hectograph sheet with transportation schedules, showing the exact time the trains left each town to be played during the following week. Out of the thirty-five dollars each man had to pay his own living expenses, including hotel accommodations, which usually could be had for fifty cents a night. Transportation was furnished without cost, and the band usually traveled in private cars attached to through trains.

The tour proceeded through Pennsylvania, New York, Connecticut, Rhode Island, and New Hampshire to Boston.

David Blakely met Sousa in Boston with a long face. Receipts from the tour had been lean, and Blakely insisted that the balance of the tour be canceled. This was Sunday, November 20. Gilmore's Columbian Tour had already folded, and Reeves, who had been hastily called in to take Gilmore's place, had returned to his old band in Providence. The Gilmore men were bewildered and like sheep without a shepherd. Gloom was everywhere. Sousa's men sensed the bad state of affairs, and were privately speculating about what they would do when the band was broken up and they were sent home.

One thing was clear to the players in both bands: this idea of an independent, traveling concert band was no good. To this idea could be traced all their present troubles. Gilmore had made a success of it because he was a genius of some kind, but everybody else who had tried it had failed. There was Gilmore's Band, sailing along as prosperous as you please, but the very minute Gilmore died the band started losing money. Neither Freudenvoll nor Reeves nor anybody else could be successful with a band like that.

The others who had tried to manage a band like Gilmore's had failed. And now Sousa, with even the advantage of having the guidance of Gilmore's former manager, had failed. The U. S. Marine Band had been going for nearly one hundred years, but Sousa couldn't keep his New Marine Band going for two months. There was something fundamentally wrong with an independent band. For any band to succeed it had to be backed up by the military, the town, or some industry. No band could make enough money to support itself.

Such were the obvious conclusions to be drawn from all previous experience with the independent-band idea. But Sousa looked at it differently. To him the idea was sound; only the management of the band had failed. And Sousa was angry. He and his men had been on the road six weeks, playing two concerts a day, traveling interminably, living on sandwiches, and sometimes sleeping on top of their trunks. They had done their level best. They had played in small towns and large, in opera houses, lodge halls, armories, and theaters, with their cramped stages, rickety stairs, and dusty scenery and curtains. If the tour had not so far been the success that Blakely had hoped, whose fault was it? Who booked the band into those Godforsaken little crossroads? Sousa had expected better things from the clever and experienced and successful Blakely and from Howard Pew, the booker Blakely had delegated to lay out the tour. Hot words passed between them, and Sousa refused to call the tour off. He felt his whole future was at stake, and he meant to go on. Finally Blakely reluctantly consented. He had never before reckoned with a man of Sousa's determination, and he hoped Sousa knew what he was doing.

Providentially business picked up in Maine and continued to improve during the remaining three weeks. The *William Tell* overture, selections from Massenet, popular selections from De Koven's *Robin Hood*, and Strauss waltzes had proved to be favorites on the tour, and these were programed at each concert. Occasionally a Sousa march would be played, and it always brought enthusiastic applause. By the time the tired band arrived at the Broadway Theatre in New York City for the final concert on Sunday, December 11, everybody felt better. After the final concert had been played, the troupe was disbanded, to be reorganized the following spring.

Eleven days before the tour ended, the Sousa band played a matinee in Northampton, Mass., and an evening concert in Springfield. The jump was only fifteen miles or so, and the band arrived in

INITIAL APPEARANCE

OF

SOUSA'S NEW MARINE BAND

MR. JOHN PHILIP SOUSA, Director.

D. BLAKELY, General Manager.

WESTERN OFFICE: EASTERN OFFICE:

186 MONROE STREET, CHICAGO.   1441 BROADWAY, NEW YORK.

SEPTEMBER, 1892.

Mon.	26	Eve.	Stillman Music Hall	Plainfield, N. J.
Tue.	27	Eve.	Taylor's Opera House	Trenton, N. J.
Wed.	28	Mat.	York Opera House	York, Pa.
		Eve.	Grand Opera House	Harrisburg, Pa.
Thu.	29	Mat.	Opera House	Danville, Pa
		Eve.	Lycoming Opera House	Williamsport, Pa.
Fri.	30	Mat.	Opera House	Corning, N. Y.
		Eve.	Opera House	Elmira, N. Y.

OCTOBER.

Sat.	1	Mat.	Hale's Opera House	Towanda, Pa.
		Eve.	Wilgus Opera House	Ithaca, N. Y.
Sun.	2	Eve.	Music Hall	Buffalo, N. Y.
Mon.	3	Eve.	Lyceum Theatre	Detroit. Mich.
Tue.	4	Mat.	Grand Opera House	Ann Arbor, Mich.
		Eve.	Hibbard Opera House	Jackson. Mich.
Wed.	5	Mat.	Salisbury's Opera House	Owosso, Mich.
		Eve.	Academy of Music	Saginaw, Mich.
Thu.	6	Mat.	Music Hall	Flint, Mich.
		Eve.	Baird's Opera House	Lansing. Mich.
Fri.	7	Mat.	Hamblin's Opera House	Battle Creek, Mich.
		Eve.	Academy of Music	Kalamazoo, Mich.
Sat.	8	Mat. / Eve.	Opera House	Muskegon, Mich.
Sun.	9	Eve.	Hartman's Hall	Grand Rapids, Mich.

Mon. 10	
Tue. 11	
Wed. 12	Grand Formal Opening
Thu. 13	at
Fri. 14	The Auditorium,
Sat. 15	Chicago.

Sun. 16	Sunday

Mon. 17	Grand Concerts at Dedication
Tue. 18	of the
Wed. 19	World's Fair Buildings, Chicago,
Thu. 20	by engagement with
Fri. 21	The Columbian Exposition,
Sat. 22	Theodore Thomas, Musical Director General.

Direct Mail these Two weeks in care of D. BLAKELY, 188 Monroe Street, Chicago, Ill.

Sun.	23	Eve.	Faurot Opera House	Lima, Ohio.
Mon.	24	Mat.	Ada Opera House	Ada, Ohio.
		Eve.	Masonic Temple	Fort Wayne, Ind.
Tue.	25	Mat.	Opera House	Bucyrus, Ohio.
		Eve.	Memorial Opera House	Mansfield, Ohio.
Wed.	26	Mat.	Adair's Opera House,	Johnstown, Pa.
		Eve.	11th Ave. Opera House,	Altoona, Pa.
Thu.	27	Eve.	Grand Opening of	Washington, D. C.
Fri.	28	Mat. Eve.	Metzerott Music Hall,	

Sat.	29	Mat. Eve.	Academy of Music,	Philadelphia, Pa.

Sun.	30	Eve.		New York

"Who booked the band into those god-forsaken little crossroads?" Sousa asked Blakely.

SOUSA'S BAND.

ROUTE SHEET NO. 2.

NOVEMBER, 1892.

Sun.	13	Eve.	Broadway Theatre,	New York.
Mon.	14	Mat.	Bunnell's Theatre	Bridgeport, Conn.
		Eve.	Delavan Opera House,	Meriden, Conn.
Tue.	15	Mat.	Opera House,	New Britain, Conn.
		Eve.	Hyperion Theatre	New Haven, Conn.
Wed.	16	Mat.	The Middlesex	Middletown, Conn.
		Eve.	Foot Guard Armory	Hartford, Conn.
Thu.	17	Mat.	New Opera House	Woonsocket, R. I.
		Eve.	Music Hall	Providence, R. I.
Fri.	18	Mat.	Opera House	Amesbury. Mass.
		Eve.	Academy of Music	Haverhill, Mass.
Sat.	19	Mat.	Opera House	Exeter, N. H.
		Eve.	City Opera House	Dover, N. H.
Sun.	20	Eve.	Music Hall	Boston, Mass.
Mon.	21	Eve.	Lowell Opera House	Lowell, Mass.
Tue.	22	Mat.	Town Hall	Brunswick, Me.
		Eve.	City Hall	Lewistown, Me.
Wed.	23	Mat. } Eve. }	Bangor Opera House	Bangor. Me.
Thu.	24	Mat.	Coburn Hall,	Skowhegan, Me.
		Eve.	Augusta Opera House	Augusta, Me.
Fri.	25	Mat.	Alameda Opera House	Bath, Me.
		Eve.	Farwell Opera House	Rockland, Me.
Sat.	26	Mat. } Eve. }	City Hall	Portland, Me.
Sun.	27	Eve.	Music Hall	Boston, Mass.
Mon.	28	Eve.	Cadet Armory	Salem, Mass.
Tue.	29	Mat.	Marlboro Theatre	Marlboro, Mass.
		Eve.	Mechanics Hall	Worcester, Mass.
Wed.	30	Mat.	Academy of Music,	Northampton, Mass.
		Eve.	City Hall,	Springfield, Mass.

DECEMBER.

Thu.	1	Mat.	Centre Street Opera House	Schenectady, N. Y.
		Eve.	Kasson Op. House. With Cho.	Gloversville, N. Y.
Fri.	2	Mat.	Skinner Opera House	Little Falls, N. Y.
		Eve.	Opera House	Utica, N. Y.
Sat.	3	Mat.	Monroe Opera House	Oneida, N. Y.
		Eve.	Washington St. Opera House	Rome, N. Y.
Sun.	4	Mat. } Eve. }	Lyceum Theatre	Rochester, N. Y.
Mon.	5	Mat.	Linden Opera House	Geneva, N. Y.
		Eve.	Burtis Opera House	Auburn, N. Y.
Tue.	6	Mat. } Eve. }	The Alhambra. With Chorus.	Syracuse, N. Y.
Wed.	7	Mat. } Eve. }	Academy of Music	Scranton, Pa.
Thu.	8	Eve.	Ninth Regiment Armory	Wilkes Barre, Pa.
Fri.	9	Mat. } Eve. }	Music Hall	Allentown, Pa.
Sat.	10	Mat.	New Grand Opera House	Pottstown, Pa.
		Eve.	Academy of Music	Philadelphia, Pa.
Sun.	11	Eve.	Broadway Theatre,	New York.

Springfield in the late afternoon. It is not recorded, but when the players walked from the train to their hotel, and wandered around town before going to the city hall for the concert, they probably saw a rare sight, more intriguing than a high-stilt walker or a man with a trained bear. They saw a sort of buggy come wheeling along the street without a horse either pulling or pushing. This buggy sounded like an old Gatling gun, and smoke puffed out with each bang! bang! and trailed along behind for a block or more. In the seat sat two grimy young men, one steering the strange vehicle with a piece of bent pipe, the other sitting with a wrench in each hand, ready to hop down and administer suitable treatment in case the little monster coughed and died. These two young men were bicycle makers in Springfield, and they had put this contraption together and had ridden about the streets for the first time only a few weeks before Sousa and his band arrived. Their names were Charles and Frank Duryea, the first to make a gasoline car in America.

The Sousa band and the horseless carriage grew up together. While Sousa was playing at the Chicago World's Fair in 1893, Henry Ford was driving his gasoline buggy around the streets of Detroit. The following year in Kokomo, Indiana, Elwood Haynes broke up a parade by driving his buggy down the streets at six miles per hour, accompanied by a frightening noise and a cloud of black smoke. Before Sousa started his world tour in 1910, nearly a dozen automobile companies had been organized, including Olds, Winton, Buick, Pierce-Arrow, Packard, Cadillac, Ford, Reo, General Motors, Hudson, and Hupp. Two years after he returned, there were a million automobiles running loose on our streets and highways. By the time Sousa laid down his baton for the last time in 1932, there were more than thirty million automobiles in operation.

In the spring of 1893, Sousa began looking not only for new players for his band but for a new publisher. Between 1886 and 1891 he had written five marches: *The Gladiator, Semper Fidelis, The Washington Post, The Thunderer,* and *High School Cadets.* These he had sold outright to Harry Coleman of Philadelphia for thirty-five dollars each. When he sold *Semper Fidelis* he included arrangements for piano, for orchestra, and for brass band, hoping to obtain more money for the composition if it could be published in these three forms. Harry Coleman made a long dissertation about all the expenses of publishing and the risk he was taking when he published numbers by an unknown composer such as Sousa. Although disappointed Sousa accepted the thirty-five dollars, because this stipend seemed to be standard, at least with Coleman.

After three years of touring with a band, however, Sousa had a better idea of the acceptance of his music and the potential sales. In 1893 he took the *Manhattan Beach* and *Liberty Bell* marches to the John Church Company in Philadelphia, and these were published on a royalty basis. The *Liberty Bell* march alone earned royalties for Sousa which eventually amounted to over thirty-five thousand dollars. All other marches from then on Sousa took to the John Church Company, and left Harry Coleman to kick himself the rest of his days for not being more astute.

William Fletcher, who joined Sousa's Band in 1904 as a clarinetist, was a printer's devil and office boy with Harry Coleman at this time, and he recalled years afterward the days when Sousa and his band played in Philadelphia. Sousa and some of his players came to visit the store, and Arthur Pryor was usually among them. Fletcher often listened to him "prelude" in the store and marveled at his extraordinary ability, little dreaming that twelve years later he would be among this select group of fabulous musicians.

These were the days, Fletcher recalled, when the piano arrangement of Sousa's *High School Cadets* was selling in large quantities. Some of the bigger dealers ordered in lots of twenty thousand, to be delivered five thousand at a time. One day the store received an order for ten copies of "Ice Cold Cadets." Later, when Fletcher was playing in the band, Sousa received a request to play "Ice Cold Cadets" on one of his programs.

About this time Sousa acquired the title of "The March King." His publisher had read an article in an obscure brass-band journal published in England in which the author commented on the outstanding marches being composed in America. Among the prominent composers of American marches were listed Grafulla, Downing, Reeves, Missud, Brooke, and Sousa. "The last name," the article read, "is entitled to the name of 'March King' quite as much as Strauss is to that of 'Waltz King.'" The publisher showed Sousa the article, and also an ad he had prepared which ended with the sentences: "You can hear this music from the Atlantic to the Pacific, from the St. Lawrence to the Gulf Stream. The March King reigns supreme."

With the breakup of the Gilmore band Sousa selected many top-notch players, calling for rehearsals in New York beginning in April.

This first rehearsal has gone down in history as an example of the thoroughness of Sousa and the lengths to which he was willing to go in order to obtain just the right sound in the band. Sousa was engaged to play a long series of concerts at the Columbian Exposition in Chicago, popularly referred to as the Chicago World's Fair. This was the plum Gilmore had expected to pluck, but fate had dropped it into the lap of Sousa. It was the big opportunity to establish his name far and wide, and Sousa was determined not to muff it. He set about developing a band which would insure success.

For two and one-half hours in this first rehearsal he drilled the different sections of the band on how to play sixteen bars of an overture! He started with the clarinet section. If this section had been a bunch of dubs, the long time he spent with them would not have been so remarkable, but these men were the cream of clarinet players, the best in the land, each chair occupied by a finished artist, personally selected by Sousa for the job.

First Sousa asked the solo clarinet to play a few bars of the music alone. This he did, and to other members of the band his playing was above criticism. Then Sousa asked him to play it again, this time using a little different breath control and somewhat different phrasing and tone quality. The solo clarinet began to sweat, and he became a bit irritated when Sousa asked him to play it again and again, like a beginner. Finally he grasped what Sousa was striving for, and when he had played it to Sousa's satisfaction, he was a little surprised at how much more musical it sounded.

Then Sousa turned to the assistant solo clarinet and asked him to play it exactly the same way. After a few trials the assistant solo clarinet protested that it was asking too much to expect his playing to sound the same as that of his partner. He had his own style of playing, he said, and he had his own individual quality of tone. Patiently Sousa persisted and asked him to try it. Eventually the second man played the passage so it was indistinguishable from that of the first. Then Sousa proceeded to the next stand, of first clarinets, and in time this man was playing the passage so it had the same sound produced by the first two men. Eventually Sousa had all six first clarinetists playing the passage with the same breath control, same phrasing, and same quality of tone, and when they played together, they played as one man.

The same procedure was followed with each section in each family of instruments. Each part in those sixteen bars was played again and again, until every man in the band was breathing and phrasing and interpreting the music so that the whole ensemble blended perfectly and performed smoothly as a unit. At no time did Sousa show impatience, but neither did he compromise with a single man or a single note. The skepticism and even rebellion of the men were turned to admiration and wholehearted co-operation. As Sousa opened their minds to the amazing musical potentialities in this short passage, they marveled at the artistic grasp of their leader.

Sousa dismissed the band with this parting shot: "Now, gentlemen, you know what I want in the future. You reed players will discard your coarse military reeds and adopt the narrow, light symphonic reeds. And you cup mouthpiece players will look to your mouthpieces and play with a delicate embouchure. Forget how you may have played in other bands. I want this band to play great music with the precision and polish of the finest symphony orchestra."

The Sousa band was a big hit at the Chicago World's Fair, attracting many thousands at each concert. Theodore Thomas, who had established the Chicago Symphony Orchestra two years before, was musical director of the exposition and had planned an elaborate cycle of musical programs of the highest order. The enthusiasm created by the Sousa band was a sad reminder of his experiences at the Philadelphia Centennial, where Gilmore and his band stole the show. The exposition had progressed only a few weeks when Thomas saw history repeating itself. The expensive and elaborate symphonic and choral events were poorly attended, while the crowds that came to hear Sousa's Band continued to swell. Reluctantly Thomas advised the fair authorities that the remainder of the events he had planned be canceled. As he said, people at such a fair do not come to be educated but to be entertained, and Sousa's Band filled this want much better than the educational programs he had arranged to present.

The year before the Fair, Charles K. Harris had published a sentimental song called *After the Ball* ("After the ball is over, after the dance is through . . . many the hearts that are broken, after the ball"). With an uncanny ability to pick what the people like Sousa made an arrangement of this song for the band. He brought the piece to his desk and in less time than it would take a half-dozen arrangers to copy the parts he had dashed off a little masterpiece. Not a superfluous note was scored, and not a note had to be changed after he had finished. This catchy song, dressed in the new garments

Sousa had created, became a tremendous hit. Sousa played it daily throughout the rest of the fair, and thousands and thousands of people returned home humming this melody. Sousa is credited with putting this song over, and eventually it sold more than a million copies.

Another tune which scored a hit almost as great was *"Ta-ra-ra-bom-der-e.* This piece was originally a bawdyhouse song, its origin shrouded in the dull glow of the red-light district. Students of ragtime say it was first sung by a colored mamma in a St. Louis dive. Sigmund Spaeth says it was a public-domain number when it gained fame, but this didn't prevent Henry S. Sayer from copyrighting the words and music in 1891, under the slightly altered title of *Ta-ra-ra-boom-deay.* Sousa liked its swing and roistering drive, and he dashed off an arrangement for full band which set the fair-goers on their ears.

One evening at the fair, Sousa and Mr. Tomlins, Chicago choral leader and vocal director of the exposition, were chatting about things musical, when Mr. Tomlins suggested to Sousa that he invite the big audience at his concerts to sing some familiar number with the band. The next evening Sousa played *Old Folks at Home,* and he invited his listeners to join in and sing the next chorus with the band. Sousa then remained with his back to the band, and with baton in hand, he directed the audience and the band, encouraging the people with emphatic gestures to sing louder and louder. The singing began timidly, but so friendly and sympathetic did Sousa appear that the volume mounted and grew into a mighty chorus. The applause with which the audience greeted their own efforts was deafening, and an encore was necessary. So successful was this venture into a different kind of entertainment that it became a featured part of Sousa's concert at the fair every evening afterward.

It must not be concluded that Sousa limited his repertoire to such popular music; quite the contrary. His programs were studded with Wagner, Liszt, Beethoven, Bach, and other great composers, but he felt that the mission of his band primarily was to entertain the people. In a conversation with Theodore Thomas, Sousa was comparing notes with the great symphony conductor on the subject of proper programs. Thomas was celebrated for the continuous battle he had been waging for nearly forty years to create acceptance of the great classic compositions. He adamantly refused to program anything popular or trivial. Sousa did not fully agree with this lofty purpose.

Finally Sousa summed up their respective attitudes by saying, "You are an educator but I am an entertainer."

On a later occasion Sousa clearly stated his convictions on the subject by saying: "If they will listen to a Liszt *Rhapsody,* I will play *Has Anybody Here Seen Kelly?* Or I will play a Brahms *Hungarian Dance* and follow it with *Put Me Off at Buffalo."*

This policy of program building was firmly established by the time he played the Chicago World's Fair, and Sousa saw no reason to change it during the following thirty years of his career. Like Gilmore, he did not consider himself a missionary for good music, but he unwittingly became such by constantly playing some of the great classics in a superb manner at every concert.

Following his great triumph at Chicago, Sousa took his band to Manhattan Beach for an engagement of a month. Sitting night after night in the great band shell where Gilmore had been the star attraction for over a decade must have filled the nineteen ex-Gilmore players in Sousa's Band with poignant memories. Comparisons between Gilmore and Sousa were inevitable. Gilmore had been more warmly human, more dramatic and colorful. While Sousa was quiet and businesslike in front of the band, every player felt his sincerity and respected his artistic honesty.

From Manhattan Beach the Sousa band journeyed to St. Louis for the Annual Exposition. The Music Hall was filled with sad memories for the men who had played here the year before under Gilmore. For the first few concerts it seemed to many of these men that they were playing in a dream and that the much-admired and beloved Gilmore must suddenly take up the baton and lead them in a fiery number, as he had many times before.

If Gilmore and Theodore Thomas had resorted to tours in order to enable them to hold their organizations together for the better engagements in New York, Sousa looked upon touring as the first and real purpose of the band. It was primarily a road band from the beginning, and it became more so in later years. The men who were selected to play in Sousa's Band had to be not only good musicians but real troupers. Russ Henegar, who played cornet with Sousa in 1923 and 1924, recalls:

"Although I played with the band only two seasons, I played in every state in the Union and in Canada. With the exception of thirteen weeks at Willow Grove, Pa., the longest booking in any one city was two or three days. Often the band played a matinee in one city and a concert that same evening in another. To complete its heavy year-round schedule, the band traveled by special pullman train. It was when on these train trips that the members talked informally with Sousa, while the latter smoked specially-made cigars that had his picture on the seal."

In 1894 the band started out early in the year for a long tour to San Francisco, where it played an engagement at the Mid-Winter Exposition, and arrived back in New York in time for the Manhattan Beach season. It was here that Sousa started breaking attendance records. After hanging up a record at Manhattan Beach the band journeyed to St. Louis for its second engagement at the Annual Exposition, and again broke all attendance records for this popular attraction.

The following year the travel pattern was similar: the spring tour, Manhattan Beach, St. Louis Exposition. Then Sousa took his band to the Cotton States Exposition at Atlanta, Georgia, which opened September 15. This engagement again showed David Blakely the temper of the man he was managing. One week before the band was to appear Blakely received a wire from the manager of the exposition saying: "Impossible to carry out contract. Consider canceled." Blakely was in a dither, and asked Sousa what should be done. Sousa replied without hesitation, "Wire the manager that the Sousa band will open as per contract." With many misgivings Blakely did as directed.

When Sousa and his band arrived in Atlanta, a series of long conferences began with the directors of the exposition. Sousa pointed out that it was impossible for him to change his plans. To take his band back to New York, without bookings ahead, would result in a loss to him of ten thousand dollars. The directors would not alter their position, however, and Sousa finally made a proposal that the management be released from the contract and that Sousa would give daily concerts in the Festival Hall at fifty cents admission, all profits to go to Sousa. The directors accepted this proposal. They privately thought Sousa was crazy, but they had nothing to risk by the deal. Blakely shared their view, but he knew that once Sousa had made up his mind there was nothing he could do. Only Sousa had confidence in the drawing power of his band.

The concerts were started, and Blakely left to round up some future bookings. Attendance was good, and for three weeks Sousa made a substantial profit. The directors liked the arrangement, for the exposition was making money at the general-admission gate without having to pay Sousa anything. At the end of three weeks, however, Blakely had lined up some good bookings for the band, and he notified the directors that after one more week the band would leave. The directors could hardly believe their ears, and they protested vehemently. But there was nothing they could do about it, for the bookings had been made and had to be filled. At the end of the fourth week Sousa and his band packed up and left for a swing through the Eastern states.

For the spring tour the next year the band again played its way to the West Coast and back to New York in time for the Manhattan Beach season. This incessant traveling had taken its toll, and after the final concert at Manhattan Beach, Sousa went to Europe for a rest. He had journeyed leisurely through Europe as far as Naples, when he read a newspaper dispatch that David Blakely had died. He immediately secured passage aboard the S. S. *Teutonic* for return to New York.

This trip has become historic. As Sousa walked the deck, saddened by the loss of Blakely and trying to look into the future to see what was in store for Sousa's Band, he began hearing in his mind a musical theme. Day after day this theme forced itself upon his consciousness. It grew insistently and it repeated itself incessantly. It seemed to Sousa as if it came from a source outside himself and independent of his will.

When the ship steamed into New York Harbor, he looked up and saw the American flag whipping in the breeze. The music in his mind quickened, and by the time he set foot on American soil it was complete. He went immediately to his desk and started to set it to paper. Without effort the music flowed from his pen, and feverishly he tried to keep up with the surge of notes that insisted on being written down. Finally he had completed it, note for note as it had pounded in his brain. Without changing a note Sousa sent the manuscript to his publisher, and soon all America and within a few years all the world began listening to his greatest march, *The Stars and Stripes Forever.*

Sousa has gone on record several times regarding the supernatural quality of his musical inspirations. Near the end of his life, in a conversation with Dr. James Francis Cooke, then editor of *The Etude* magazine, Sousa said: "Composers think that they do it themselves.

Fools! They can acquire technic. They can learn the machinery of composition. They can build great musical structures, but they can't make living things. . . . All of my music, all of my melodies are not of my making; no matter how light, they came from a higher source. I have listened to a Higher Power."

Granted that *The Stars and Stripes Forever* was pure inspiration, it followed the formula Sousa had used before and was to use many times afterward. As Sigmund Spaeth has pointed out, this march is a "perfect example of Sousa's favorite march form." First is an arresting introduction; second, a light, skipping melody; third, a broader tune; and finally, the "immortal strain itself, the trio."

The popularity of this march mounted quickly and found a spot on practically every program the band played. Although often programed it was mostly used as an encore, and all the bandsmen who played with Sousa remember it as the most played number in the entire repertoire.

Frank Sullivan, saxophonist with the band during the last six years of its existence (1926–31), recalls: "During the six years I toured with Sousa, I played in every state in the union and in every province in Canada except Prince Edward Island. I estimate I played Sousa's most famous march *Stars and Stripes* twelve hundred times, twice a day at each city where the band played." Another player has said, "I played it so many times I could play it backward, and so I always watched the audience to observe their reaction. They invariably became terrifically excited, probably because it reminded many of them of war experiences."

Sousa dramatized the number on his programs by building it up to the most intense patriotic climax. After the band had played it in the normal manner, up popped flutes, piccolos, cornets, and trombones from various spots in the band. These quickly marched to the front of the stage and lined up in military fashion, while the rest of the band continued to play. The stir and the motion in the band brought the audience to the edge of their seats in expectation of something about to happen. When the band cut loose on this closing strain, with the brass blaring forth in power and the piccolo screaming above the whole band, the audience often involuntarily stood up, as they were trained to do when *The Star-Spangled Banner* was played; and when the number was finished, they broke into waves of cheering. No wonder a volatile Frenchwoman once told

Sousa that this march "sounded like the American eagle shooting arrows into the aurora borealis."

While this great march was always the high point in most of Sousa's concerts, and is still one of the most popular marches played, for some curious reason it has evolved into a warning signal in the circus. The circus band never plays *Stars and Stripes Forever* as a part of its regular program. It is reserved only for emergency use. If an animal gets loose, a high wind threatens the tent, or a fire breaks out, the band plays this march as a warning signal to every worker on the circus lot that something is wrong. This peculiar circus quirk has probably evolved over the years, as have various superstitions and various expressions. Some circus band may have been playing *Stars and Stripes* at a time when disaster hit the lot in one form or another, and the association established. In any event, to circus people it means "panic," and it has come to be known among circus personnel as the "Panic March."

For his new manager Sousa engaged Everett R. Reynolds, who had been manager of Manhattan Beach for several years. While the manager was different, the tour pattern remained the same: constant traveling. Wherever Sousa went, he usually fraternized with the local bandmaster. In Providence, R.I., it was his good friend D. W. Reeves, of the American Band. In Boston it was T. M. Carter, of Carter's Band; and J. Thomas Baldwin, of the Boston Cadets. In Brockton it was Mace Gay, and in Salem it was Jean Missud. These men were respected by Sousa because they all had exemplary bands and were pioneers in better band music.

On tour westward he could quaff a stein of good German beer with Martin Klinger, Allentown, Pa.; Joseph Winter, director of the Ringgold Band at Reading, Pa.; and Herman Bellstedt, of the Bellstedt & Ballenberg Band, Cincinnati. In Chicago were the well known Fred Weldon and Frederick Phinney, and in St. Louis the top bandmasters were Charles Seymour and William Weil. And so across the nation, east and west, north and south. Most bandmasters were glad to have Sousa's Band play in their cities, for it always stirred up local support and interest in their own bands.

In Providence, R.I., one night in 1897, the March King played to a packed house, and there was standing room only. Another king, Bob Fitzsimmons, world heavyweight titleholder, who had taken the crown from "Gentleman Jim Corbett" a few months before, stood

throughout the concert. Fitzsimmons was barnstorming the vaudeville circuits, and while in Providence he suddenly had a desire to
hear a concert by the noted Sousa band. When he appeared at the
box office, he was told there were no seats available, but he could
pay an admission and stand.

After the concert Fitzsimmons elbowed his way backstage to the
dressing room and announced he wanted to "see the little guy who
led the band" and who "could draw more people to a concert than
would come to see the world heavyweight champion." Sousa was a
boxing enthusiast, and he and Fitzsimmons immediately became
friends. The two of them repaired to the Narragansett Hotel, where
David Reeves joined them. There then ensued a hilarious gab fest, for
Bob was an uninhibited conversationalist and Sousa had a sense of
humor to match. Reeves more or less sat on the side lines, but
he thoroughly enjoyed the gibes and banter between the two "kings."

After that first meeting Sousa and Fitzsimmons met whenever they
could arrange it. Bob had become a sort of advocate of "the little
guy who led the band." During one of these meetings, shortly before
Sousa was to leave for a tour, Sousa stated that he hoped the audiences would like the Sousa band. Bob resented the doubt expressed
by Sousa, and he said in a blustering voice: "Like you? Why, you'll
knock hell out of 'em."

When Victor Herbert left Gilmore's Band, in 1897, it was evident
to all that the end of this great band had come. Herbert Clarke, who
for six years had vacillated between Gilmore's Band and Sousa's
Band, playing first with one and then the other, now cast his lot
with Sousa, and for the next twenty years he was the principal cornet soloist with Sousa and His Band. Shortly after, Bohumir Kryl
joined Sousa as assistant cornet soloist.

It is probable that Clarke's recommendation of Kryl was responsible for Kryl's securing this contract, for Clarke was well acquainted
with Kryl's schooling and rise to fame. His career started in Chicago.
When he was in his early twenties, he studied cornet under Fred
Weldon, a personal friend of Clarke's. Weldon was a celebrity in
the band field throughout the Middle West. He was not only an excellent cornet soloist and teacher but was director of the 2nd Regiment Band of Chicago. It was through his travels with this band
that his fame spread far and wide around Chicago.

The first paid job of any importance held by Kryl was as cornet
soloist with the When Band of Indianapolis. This band, sponsored

by the When Clothing Company as an advertising medium, had been in existence for fifteen or twenty years. Clarke was also an alumnus of the When Band, having served an apprenticeship with the band in 1886. After playing with the When Band for several years Kryl began to establish quite a reputation and in 1898 Sousa signed him up. For a young man less than twenty-five years old this was doing all right. It was like Kryl to begin his illustrious soloist career near the top.

Simone Mantia and Arthur Pryor were in the Sousa band when Kryl joined, and they often recalled the fun the older bandsmen had with the young bohemian when he arrived fresh from Indianapolis. Upon the occasion when the Sousa band played in Buffalo, N.Y., Kryl expressed the desire to behold the wonders of Niagara Falls, which he had never visited. It so happened that the engagement was on Sunday, and the men in the band convinced Kryl that the falls were turned off on the Sabbath. They said, however, that they knew the mayor of the city well, and they would intercede on Kryl's behalf to induce him to have the falls running on Sunday. When Kryl visited the falls and found them pouring forth in their spectacular glory, he was profoundly grateful to his associates for this favor.

During Sousa's spring tour in 1898, from January to April, the Spanish-American War was begun. The battleship *Maine* was blown up in Havana harbor in February, Congress appropriated fifty million dollars in March, for possible war, and Spain declared war on the United States in April. In May Admiral Dewey destroyed the Spanish fleet in Manila, becoming one of America's greatest heroes. During this year of war Sousa crowded more than the usual number of patriotic numbers into his programs.

As a sort of victory celebration the following year Sousa outdid himself, making one of his longest and most arduous tours, a total of forty-eight thousand miles through twenty-eight states and Canada. As he says, he toured from coast to coast and from the St. Lawrence to the Gulf. He also did another most unusual thing: he marched his band in a parade! On the last day of September Admiral Dewey was given a tremendous reception in New York, and Sousa's Band, with many others, marched in the long procession.

Although Sousa was known as the March King, Sousa's Band seldom marched. During the first seven years of its existence the Sousa band had marched a total of exactly four times: in 1893 at Chicago's World Fair, in 1898 at a send-off of Spanish-American War troops from Cleveland, a welcome back of troops in Pittsburgh, and in the Dewey parade. Sousa gave no explanation of this anomaly, but it is probable that he had had enough marching to last him a lifetime during the twelve years as director of the U. S. Marine Band (at the fast cadence of one hundred and twenty to the minute!).

Even if Sousa didn't march, he "talked a good march"—to borrow a phrase from sports. "A march," said Sousa, "should make a man with a wooden leg step out." The five most effective street marches, according to a list made out by Sousa some years later, were the following: *The Thunderer, The National Emblem, Semper Fidelis, Washington Post,* and *High School Cadets.* The second of these was written by E. E. Bagley, the other four by Sousa. During his lifetime Sousa wrote over one hundred marches, approximately half of his entire composition output.

During World War I, when Sousa was in charge of bands at the Great Lakes Naval Training Station near Chicago, Sousa again did considerable marching, but after that he almost never marched. Many players attest to this fact. As Frank Sullivan, saxophonist with the band, recalls: "It's a funny thing, while Sousa is known as the March King and the band may have done some marching in the early days, during the six years I was with the band, from 1926 until 1931, none of us ever marched a step."

Many protests were voiced by old Sousa men when the Twentieth Century-Fox Technicolor movie *Stars and Stripes Forever* was released in 1953. This movie was based on the life of John Philip Sousa, but it left the impression that Sousa's Band was a marching outfit, whereas it was really a concert band. This protest was a slight variation of the perennial complaint that "the movie did not follow the book."

In the fall of 1899 the program passed out to concert audiences contained a summary of some formidable statistics about the achievements of Sousa and His Band during its seven years of existence. This summary reveals in a forceful way the intense activity of the band during these years and the popularity it was building up.

6 weeks at Chicago World's Fair
5 weeks at Mid-Winter Fair, San Francisco
4 weeks at Cotton States Exposition, Atlanta
6 weeks at Madison Square Garden, N.Y.
54 weeks (5 seasons) at Manhattan Beach, N.Y.
24 weeks (4 seasons) at St. Louis Annual Exposition

One week at Food Fair, Boston, playing to 200,000 people
Two weeks at Pittsburgh Exposition, playing to 300,000 people
Festival Tour of 6 weeks
14 regular tours of United States and Canada, including 4 transcontinental tours, ocean to ocean
More than 3500 concerts in more than 400 different cities

From an uncertain beginning in 1892, Sousa had built up a sound and thriving business. Music was Sousa's business, and his band was strictly a business band. Although Gilmore had conducted a similar business in music for twenty years with the 22nd Regiment Band, Sousa's Band was the first simon-pure business band ever to succeed, for he was completely divorced from military, town, or industry subsidy. After that first critical tour in the fall of 1892, Sousa went on year after year and proved to other and less courageous bandmasters that the business band was the band of opportunity.

Eight

*In those days, hardly any event
could be properly
observed without a band.*

Without detracting in any way from Sousa's success and achievement it should be pointed out that he was riding the crest of an upsurge in band interest. If he had launched his business band ten years earlier than he did, he probably would have been successful, for he was a man of determination and good business instincts, but the fact remains that his road was made easier by his good fortune in starting his band after this upsurge had begun. Liberati, Innes, and Brooke—all of whom had previously tried and failed—finally rode this same crest to successful formation of their own business bands.

Leon Mead stated there were, in 1889, over ten thousand military bands in the United States. These were all adult amateur bands, and although the term "military band" was applied to them, the majority were local town or industrial bands.

Rupert Hughes, eminent musicologist and writer on music, is the authority for the statement that "by 1897 Sousa marches had been sold to eighteen thousand bands." We have no way of knowing how reliable are these figures of Leon Mead and Rupert Hughes, but if we accept them, we are led to the conclusion that the number of bands must have doubled from 1889 to about 1899, roughly from ten thousand to twenty thousand.

In Sousa's summary of achievement, published in his 1899 programs, it is stated that from 1894 to 1899 "more than three million copies of Sousa's marches have been sold." These, of course, were not all band arrangements; in fact, the great majority of the sales were of sheet music for piano and organ. However, the total sales show a wide demand for march music. Marches are the substantial fare of bands, and such popularity tends to show that the populace was not only march-minded but band-minded.

We know from other sources that these were years of great band activity. In 1893 seventy-one bands marched in the parade held in connection with the inaugural exercises of Grover Cleveland. In August 1895 one hundred and thirty-six bands marched in the parade of the Knights Templar conclave held in Boston. The majority of these bands were from New England, but some of them came from considerable distance, from Maine to Kansas. Among those from the "west" were:

Metropolitan Band of Detroit, 26 men
Metropolitan Band of Chicago, 25 men
Allentown Band of Allentown, Pa., 32 men

Veterans Corps Band of Baltimore, 23 men
3rd U. S. Cavalry Band, St. Louis, 25 men
Carthage Light Guard Band, Carthage, Mo., 23 men
Marshall's Band of Topeka, Kans., 36 men

An indication of the intensive band activity of the period is given in 1896, when the 3rd Regiment Band of Arapohoe, Nebraska, was awarded the contract to furnish music for the state fair at Omaha, from August 27 to September 5. Two hundred bands filed bids for the ten-day engagement! Mr. Elia Barnes, president of the fair, must have had a ticklish time of it in making his selection.

Today it is difficult to imagine the great number of adult amateur bands and the intense interest everybody took in them during this band-craze era. It must be remembered that these were the days before the automobile. In 1896, according to one authority, there were, in the whole United States, "only sixteen horseless carriages capable of being operated." The famous Model T Ford did not go into mass production until 1909. Villages, towns, and cities were isolated to a degree we can hardly comprehend today. People "belonged" to a community and took pride in their community in a way we do not generally feel today. Each of these communities had to have a band. It was a rallying point for civic interest. Hardly any event could be properly observed without a band. In those days a village or small town without its own band was considered "a back number."

These were also the days before the phonograph and the motion picture, to say nothing of radio and television. The hours of entertainment supplied by these modern devices today were to some extent supplied in the old days by the town band. The phonograph from 1889 to 1900 was a coin-operated machine with listening tubes, found in the penny-arcade type of amusement place. Its impact was not felt until after 1905 or thereabouts.

People also began going to see the movies about 1905 or shortly thereafter. In 1896 Edison first showed his Vitascope, which could project a moving picture on a screen, but for nearly ten years it remained merely an adjunct to the vaudeville program. It was not until 1904 that *The Great Train Robbery* was produced and shown, and not until 1905 that the first "nickelodeon" was established, in Pittsburgh.

In such an era, without the automobile, the phonograph, the movies, or radio, adult amateur bands answered a need and soon became a kind of craze. If one town formed a band, all the surrounding towns felt they should have one, and from about 1890 to 1905, new bands sprang up by the hundreds and thousands.

A set of fifteen or twenty instruments cost from eight or nine hundred to fourteen or fifteen hundred dollars, depending upon the grade of instrument bought and the number of "big horns" included, such as baritones and basses. Usually 20 per cent down was required by the manufacturer, the balance being guaranteed by responsible citizens and paid in installments over a period of ten months to a year.

The merchants in the town usually bore the brunt of the cost of forming and supporting a band, since they were believed to benefit most from a band's activities. Usually solicitors signed up the merchants and other businessmen for a dollar or two per month for a year or more. Additional money came in from fund-raising activities, such as the ice-cream social and amateur theatricals, or from paid band engagements of certain kinds, such as political rallies, fairs, picnics, and excursions. During the summer months the band was expected to play an evening concert once a week, which was a free treat for the community.

Sometimes a bolder approach was taken, as is shown by the following clipping from the Lacon, Illinois, *Journal* of May 7, 1896: "Arno E. Anske comes before the council and asks for an appropriation to help buy a set of instruments for a brass band to be organized in our city, the said instruments to be the property of the city."

A cynical writer in 1897 describes a typical experience of a beginning band. "A desire is manifest in the community for a band," he says. "Men who aspire to things of this kind voluntarily organize into a body. Instruments are purchased and a 'professor' is secured to teach them. A room is engaged and the men are ready for their first lesson.

"Here a wonderful surprise awaits them—they cannot read a note of music. They don't know 'A' from a bale of hay. This is a condition to be deplored, but I can safely say that not one amateur bandsman in five is in the possession of the merest rudiments of music. They take the first lesson; they learn the natural key of C—all are anxious to learn and to play music.

"They try an exercise. They take another lesson and learn the scale of one flat, and get another exercise. Then two and three flats are looked at. They can play a piece (so everyone says). The 'professor' is dismissed and they go it alone. Music is ordered and it ar-

rives—it is written in four flats. Somehow—no one can tell why—
nothing harmonizes. The music is condemned, the author ridiculed,
and both are set aside as useless.

"Thus, the amateur band has had its first experience. What a
wonderful condition of things in this enlightened America."

Eventually, however, the new band learned to play. A bandstand
was erected in the park or on the square. It usually was circular or oc-
tagonal, a shape ill suited for concert purposes. With the stand barely
large enough for eight or ten players fifteen or eighteen were crowded
on. From the center of the high-peaked roof a single electric light cord
dangled, at the end of which was a feeble yellow light. This high-
peaked roof also served to trap a high percentage of the volume from
the band, making it sound more puny than it actually was. The
platform floor was low, and allowed small boys to climb aboard and
crawl among the music stands or sit around the edges, with their feet
dangling over the sides so they could pound the upright slats with
their heels. There they sat during the concert and cracked peanut
shells and munched popcorn.

Where the merchants heavily subscribed money, often a portable
bandstand was provided. This was set up in different locations for
each concert, so the various stores could be near the focus of activity
during a proportionate share of the concerts. Naked electric light
bulbs were strung around the band from upright two-by-fours. Bugs
swarmed around the lights by the millions, often getting into the
mouths of the players or becoming entangled in the key mechanisms
of the woodwinds.

The smell of hot dogs and hamburgers and mustard pervaded the
air, along with the smell of popping corn and roasting peanuts; and
the soft whistle from the roasting machine sounded a thin obbligato
to the band music. Families sat in farm wagons lined up along the
hitching racks. Carriages "with the fringe on top" were driven not so
quietly around the square or along the streets which were not roped
off. Boys met girls under the trees or around the lemonade stands.
The small fry, with a couple of liberty-head nickels burning in their
pockets, shopped around and finally settled for a big mass of fluffy
white spun candy, or a bottle of orangeade, pulled from a wood
chest filled with big chunks of ice, cut from the millpond the previous winter.

Meanwhile the band played on. The professor led the bandsmen
through the program prepared for this concert. Only the better

bands dared tackle *Stars and Stripes,* for it was difficult music. Neither did most bands include marches by David Reeves, for they had a habit of soaring into the ledger lines above the staff, and the ordinary musician could not read notes in this high altitude. They settled for Fred Weldon's *The First Brigade* or *The Gate City.* Favorites were the circus marches by Russell Alexander, such as *Columns of Columbus* and *The Crimson Flush.* Everybody gave attention to the music when the band played *For He's a Jolly Good Fellow* and *There'll Be a Hot Time in the Old Town Tonight.*

Along about nine-thirty the smartly uniformed band began to look less smart. The heat of the electric light bulbs and the warm summer air began to loosen the uniform coats at the neck or completely down the front. Wet locks of hair began to slide down over the brows of the steaming bandsmen and their caps were set back on their heads to give better ventilation. Their pants stuck to the hot chairs, and during intermission between numbers they arose and fanned the hot seats with their caps. The pitch of their instruments rose with the heat until they were playing a semitone or more above standard pitch.

Finally *The Star-Spangled Banner* was played and the string of electric lights was doused. The bandsmen took their instruments apart, drained the water from the brass instruments, and swabbed out the woodwinds. Empty instrument cases and green flannel bags were hauled out from under their chairs or from under the bandstand, and the instruments were hurriedly put away. Small boys stood by and watched in envy and wonder. The bugs flew away to the few shopwindows still lighted, and the tired and happy audience began the homeward trek.

Teams were unhitched from the hitching racks, the children were rounded up and bedded down in the soft, clean straw, and the farm families started their slow passage through dark roads and winding lanes to their homes. Young couples from town walked enchanted, hand in hand, along dark streets to the creaking porch swing. After a few last-minute games of tag small boys mounted their bicycles and wheeled madly for home, unworried by red lights and stop signs.

One or two evenings during the following week were devoted to band practice. On these evenings the men hurried home from their regular employment at the store, shop, or farm, gulped down a quick meal, snatched their instrument cases from off the floor of the parlor, where they have been practicing their individual parts, and congregated in shirt sleeves in the band room. There the professor waved them through several numbers with his baton, and the often discordant music drifted out through the open windows and filled the night air with the offerings for next week.

Periodically there was a special paid engagement, and the professor was faced with a dilemma. All the members of the band worked and he had to canvass the players to see if he would have enough musicians for the engagement. The banker, who played clarinet, said he could come, and the president of the local glove factory, who played baritone, said he was available. The first cornet player said he would have to see the boss and obtain permission to be absent for the day. The bass drummer said the weeds were very bad in the corn right then and he ought to cultivate, but he guessed he could spare a day if the other men could come. The first trombone player turned to the bass tuba, who owned the leading department store, and asked him if he could be spared from the ribbon counter for a day. The bass tuba nodded assent, and two more players were enrolled for the engagement. The county judge, who played "peck horn," said he had to hold court that day and could not come. A cigar maker, who played E♭ clarinet, said he nearly lost his job when the band played for the dedication of the new post-office building in the adjoining county the previous June, and he was sure he could not get away for the engagement. The professor said perhaps he could borrow a peck horn and an E♭ clarinet from a neighboring band. And so it went. Although four players short the band finally showed up for the special paid engagement, and the treasury was augmented by sixty dollars, which was quickly spent on the fifth installment for the new set of uniforms.

Music papers and business magazines published during this era told the story of the daily happenings of the amateur band in an eloquent and revealing way. As members of the band moved to other cities, died, or dropped out of the band for various reasons, their places had to be filled with other players. Sections of these publications were devoted to ads placed by players looking for a new playing position or by bands in search of players. In addition to stating musical qualifications these ads also stated the kind of work the player was accustomed to doing for a livelihood or the kind of work available for the prospective player if he should join the band.

Below are a few of these ads, gleaned from such publications. They are reprinted just as they appeared in 1896. No attempt at humor is meant by such ads as "A cornetist who is a glass blower," "A tuba player would like position at light work," or "A snare drummer would like position in barber shop." The incongruity of some of these qualifications happens to be a faithful reflection of the kind of men who made up the adult amateur bands of this bustling band era.

WANTS

PICCOLO, clarinet and saxophone players, who are coal miners, tailors or barbers, please address Geo. J. Pearson, Hillsboro, Ills.

WOULD like to hear from a band man who wishes to buy a grocery store. Will have support of band. Address Wm. C. Doyle, Bellmont, Wis.

A CORNETIST who is a glass blower can secure employment by addressing box 29, Swayzee, Ind.

A HARNESS MAKER who can play anything in brass would like to obtain employment. Address Phil Schmidt, North Branch, Minn.

SOLO CORNETIST, who can play first violin and wishes to start a cigar factory, address M. L. Reinhart, Ahnapee, Wis.

AN ALL ROUND PRINTER, who is a slide trombone player, wishes to locate in live town. Address lock box 210, Red Bank, N.J.

MUSICIANS, with trades, are wanted for the 1st Cav. Band. Opening for good barber who is a clarinetist; also tailor. Address Carl Leake, Gainesville, Texas.

A TUBA PLAYER would like position at light work. Address Wm. Seeman, Box 217, Charter Oak, Iowa.

AN EXPERIENCED CORNETIST would like work in meat market or at the harness trade. Address D. D. Buchy, Sugar Creek, Ohio.

WANTED—2 Slide Tenors, 2 B♭ Clarinets, 2 B♭ Cornets, 3 Altos, 4 Saxophones, 1 Piccolo and 1 B♭ Bass players who have worked in carriage factory and are experienced carriage trimmers. State wages and experience. Address W. H. Makutchan Cge. Co., Princeton, Ills.

CIGAR MAKERS, tailors or any tradesmen who play clarinet and trombone, address Wm. Polzin, Merrill, Wis.

GOOD CLARINETIST, who is a competent photographer, can hear of fine opening by addressing Rollin W. Bond, Ord, Neb.

A SNARE DRUMMER would like position in barber shop. Address Geo. Baldry, Hiawatha, Kans.

WANTED—For the 5th Batt. band, S. T., four musicians that are cigar makers, to play the following instruments: clarinet, cornet and trombone, valve or slide. Can get $14 per thousand and up for cigars. Spanish hand work. Address Will D. Hallowell, Tampa, Fla.

A GOOD STRONG TUBA or alto player, barber by trade, would like to locate in some good town; am strictly sober and reliable. Address H. G. Herb, 126 South 12th Street, Lincoln, Nebr.

A GOOD OPENING for a first-class cigar maker, who can play cornet, clarinet, solo alto or anything lacking in a band, to start a shop. No competition. Address Elmer Brown, Pickneyville, Ills.

WOULD LIKE to hear from barber who will open shop and buy outfit. Play anything in band but tuba. Address box 153, Sweetser, Ind.

SITUATION wanted by a good double bass player, well up in opera house and dance work. Capable of taking charge of paint department in carriage factory. Address C. D. Kniffin, Waterloo, Iowa.

GOOD MOULD CIGAR and a good mould stogie maker wanted. Must be good Bb cornetist and own their instrument. Address, R.C.Y., Box 396, Greenfield, Ohio.

WANTED—A cornet, clarinet or slide trombone player. Must be good coat maker. Address J. W. Strouse, Fostoria, Ohio.

Eb CORNET or Bb clarinet player wanted who is a machinist, to work in bicycle repair shop. Must know his business. Address E. H. Strong, 208 Front St., Oswego, N.Y.

A FINE OPPORTUNITY for a good barber who can play a piccolo, clarinet or Eb cornet, will be given by an amateur band in return for services in the band. Address Arion band, Box 373, Guilford, Conn.

WOULD LIKE to hear from a first class wagon maker, married, who is a number one solo cornetist and euphonium player. Good position to right man. Address Pat Reiley, Hamburg, Iowa.

The development of the professional business band cannot be understood properly without knowing something about these adult amateur bands which flourished around the turn of the century. The connection between the two is somewhat analogous to that between the sand-lot baseball teams and the big leagues. The greater the activity and interest in the sand lots, the greater are the ticket sales at the big-league stadiums. The amateur bands were comprised of thousands and thousands of men who became prime customers at the ticket windows when the "big-league" bands visited their city. Add to these the hundreds of thousands of persons who cultivated a liking for band music from listening to the local band, and you have a vast potential audience for the professional business bands, which began multiplying during this time and which soon crisscrossed the nation incessantly with their tours.

Sousa was fortunate in launching his New Marine Band at the beginning of this upsurge in band interest. The following year, in 1893, Liberati returned from his solo tour and made his third try at establishing his own business band. This time he succeeded. He called his new organization Liberati's Grand Military Band. He used special care in selecting his musicians, and some of them became distinguished performers under his baton. Among these were Oscar Ringwall, solo clarinet; Erminio Giannone, euphonium soloist; A. J. Campbell, cornet soloist; and Di Salli, bass tuba. For the following three or four years Liberati and his Grand Military Band were heard far and wide. He toured, he was the main attraction at the Dallas Exposition in 1894, and in 1895 and 1896 he was given big billing at Ringling Bros. Circus. This engagement was not as the regular circus band but as a special concert attraction, rated on a par with the trapeze acts, animal acts, and fancy horseback riding.

We will never know what happened to Liberati's short climb toward popularity in the business band field, but the following year he left the circus and abandoned his Grand Military Band. He then went to Cleveland and organized a band for the 5th Regiment of the Ohio National Guard. He continued to direct this band for about a year, and took it on a short tour in 1897. Among other engagements was the one at the horse racing held in Lexington, Kentucky.

Next year, however, Liberati was back in the big-time band business, stronger than ever. Whereas his former Grand Military Band had usually been comprised of forty players, his new Grand Military Band totaled eighty men. For two years he was especially prosperous, one of his principal engagements being the plum of band bookings, Washington Park on the Delaware, near Philadelphia, at that time said to be Philadelphia's greatest resort.

Washington Park was rivaled in Philadelphia only by Willow

Grove. Playing at the latter park at this time were Brooke and his Chicago Marine Band. Innes was also booked into Willow Grove and later Sousa was to make this a regular stop for a full month. In a few years Willow Grove was to outstrip Washington Park, but while Liberati was booked there it was rated as the best job in the country.

In September 1899, shortly after finishing his engagement at Washington Park, Liberati rose to what was probably the very pinnacle of his fame, when he led the parade of the Grand Army of the Republic through the streets of Philadelphia. Embodying in himself the multiple roles of conductor, soloist, composer, and field marshal, he rode to glory on the back of a black horse.

For this special occasion Liberati augmented his band to one hundred and twelve players. This large band he placed at the head of the G.A.R. procession, and at the head of the band he placed a big black stallion, and in the saddle he placed Signor Alessandro Liberati. Using his cornet as a field marshal's baton, he directed the line of march through Philadelphia streets. As the procession neared the reviewing stand, in which sat President McKinley and other notables, Liberati drew up his big band in a wide company front, with trombones extending across the first rank from curb to curb and the other instruments stretched out in succeeding ranks to form a huge company square.

Liberati rode out ahead of the band on his prancing black stallion. As he came abreast of the President, he made an elaborate salute, leaning far out of his saddle. Then he deftly used the reins in his left hand to direct his steed forward and with his right hand he lifted his cornet to his lips. Giving a signal by bobbing his cornet up and down, he started the band playing the strains of his *Kansas City Star* march. Above the boom of bass drums, the rattle of the snare drums, the blare of resounding brass, and the shrilling of piccolo and reeds Liberati played the martial strains of his march, adding embellishments as inspiration of the moment prompted.

Liberati's Grand Military Band marched like West Pointers and played as they had never played before. They swung with military precision past the reviewing stand and blared at the top of their lungs. Meanwhile Liberati reined in his excited black stallion and made him stand at attention on the side lines as the band swung past him. Like a commander watching his troops pass in review, Liberati sat astride his mount as his band marched by. Holding his cornet with his right hand, he continued to play the solo strains of his *Kansas City Star* march, his powerful tones riding above the whole band and giving President McKinley a close opportunity to hear how a real cornet virtuoso should sound.

As the G.A.R. veterans began filing past the reviewing stand, Liberati broke off his solo at an appropriate place, gathered the bridle reins tightly in his hands, and galloped off to take his position again at the front and center of his Grand Military Band.

Although Liberati continued for nearly a quarter of a century to conduct a band, play cornet solos, compose music, and march in parades, subsequent achievements were an anticlimax when compared to his spectacular performance at the head of the G.A.R. procession.

The year after Liberati established his Grand Military Band, Frederick N. Innes made a second attempt to launch his own business band, this time calling it Innes' Festival Band. If Sousa could make a success of a band of this kind, he could do it too, he reasoned. As he watched the successes of Liberati, he decided to hesitate no longer. The beginning of the upsurge in bands, which he had observed several years before, was now in full swing and the better days he had been waiting for had arrived.

Among the noted musicians he gathered together in this band were B. C. (Ben) Bent, cornet soloist, and his brother, Thomas C. Bent, also cornetist; W. Henning and Tom Clarke, both cornet soloists; Joe Wise, trombone soloist and J. Lavalle, trombonist; Harry Whittier, euphonium soloist; Luke Del Negro, bass tuba; and the saxophonists H. Morin on alto, E. Shaap on tenor, and V. Ragone on baritone. These men were all accomplished musicians, a number of them, such as Ben Bent, Tom Clarke, and Harry Whittier, being former members of Gilmore's 22nd Regiment Band.

The brightest star in the band was Innes. In addition to his duties of conductor and manager of the band he appeared regularly as principal soloist. Now in his early forties, he was playing better than ever. To facilitate his phenomenal technique, he developed a piston trill valve which was actuated by his left thumb and which lowered any tone a half step in pitch. Not only did he use this valve to embellish his florid solos with trills, but he relied on it for obtaining faster playing, especially of those tones in the seventh position.

On a standard slide trombone the tones in the seventh position are obtained by extending the hand slide to its full length. This requires maximum movement of the slide. In a descending chromatic run, the slide often must be whipped from its extreme extension back to closed position, a total distance of approximately tweny-four inches. Being able to obtain all notes for the seventh position with the thumb valve, Innes was able to reduce this extreme movement and thereby speed up his execution.

Since this valve eliminated about four inches of slide movement every time it was used, the mileage Innes saved during the next twenty years of his solo playing must have amounted to several hundred miles!

A number of manufacturers adopted this trill valve and some called it the Innes trill valve. As long as Innes performed before large audiences, there was a demand for an instrument similar to the one which, apparently, was the secret of Innes's superb playing, but when he passed from the public eye, the demand dwindled and finally the trill valve disappeared. After about 1920 American manufacturers discontinued such an instrument from their standard line.

During the first two years after launching his Festival Band, Innes played it safe by retaining his job as director of the 13th Regiment Band. By 1896, however, Innes was booked for a heavy schedule of concerts, and he resigned from the 13th. From March 15 to May 29 the band toured the West and Canada; from May 30 through September 20 it played daily concerts at Willow Grove; from September 21 to October 3 the band appeared at the Pittsburgh Exposition, and then moved to the St. Louis Exposition for three weeks.

The following year, after a long tour through Tennessee, Maryland, West Virginia, Pennsylvania, Ohio, and Kentucky, Innes arrived in Nashville on June 7 for an engagement of eight weeks at the Tennessee Centennial Exposition. The Innes band was the principal musical attraction at the exposition and scored a big hit, although other leading bands shared the engagement, including the 22nd Regiment Band (Gilmore's old band) under Victor Herbert, Conterno's Band, and the Bellstedt & Ballenberg Band from Cincinnati.

Innes the virtuoso was a thorough musician, because of talent, training, and experience. As conductor he was rated among the best. He was well acquainted with all types of band music but excelled in the interpretation of the German classics. He had a phenomenal memory, and he conducted literally hundreds of classical and semi-classical numbers without a score of any kind. His programs were built after the manner of Gilmore, alternating light and popular selections with solid, worth-while music from classic operas, oratorios, and symphonies.

As a man Innes was generally regarded as austere. Rarely did anyone refer to him as Fred Innes, and still more rarely did anyone address him as Fred. There was little comraderie between Innes and his players. Nobody referred to him as "governor" or "the old man," as Sousa's players were in the habit of referring to him. From slightly protruding eyes Innes looked out upon the world unsmilingly. But he was always highly respected, a man of his word in business, a staid and solid citizen.

Nevertheless he was not above using a bit of cheap showmanship if it would draw customers in at the box office. For his promotion at the Tennessee Centennial and subsequent tours Innes took a page from the book of Louis Antoine Jullien, who exploited a giant ophicleide for the good of ticket sales; Innes chose the modern descendant of the big ophicleide—the bass tuba.

Perhaps Innes never heard of the promotional stunt of Jullien and may have been incited to exploit a giant tuba by Adolph Kirchner, the man who followed him, in 1896, as director of the 13th Regiment Band. Almost immediately after taking charge of the 13th, Kirchner broke into print with a monster bass drum which was built for use in his band. This drum was said to be so large that two men were required to beat it. It was so heavy that even two men could not carry it, and it had to be mounted on a tricycle carriage and wheeled around the field when the band was marching.

As a further stimulant to this circus stunt Innes probably was affected by the efforts of Thomas Preston Brooke, who had become a leading contemporary bandmaster and director of the Chicago Marine Band. At the same time that Kirchner was having his giant drum built Brooke was having a giant tuba constructed. This big bass was to be the largest ever made. It was to have two hundred and eight inches of tubing and a bell that was thirty-two inches in diameter. Before it was finished, Innes placed his order for a bigger one—bigger by one inch in bell diameter! That would make it bigger than Brooke's tuba and enable Innes to put forth a super-claim to the biggest tuba ever constructed.

The Innes tuba was a large one, but it couldn't anywhere near

*From slightly protruding eyes
Innes looked out upon
the world unsmilingly.*

live up to the exaggerated newspaper stories which were written
about it. The less the writers knew about music and musical instruments, the wilder were their stories.

One writer of an article which appeared in the Nashville *American*
on July 18 did an especially outstanding job of inciting wonder—and
incredulity—about the monster tuba. "The giant tuba used by Innes
is a wonder," he wrote. "It is the largest ever made. It is triple B
flat. The instrument has such weight of tone that it takes the place of
four other basses which Mr. Innes formerly used.

"Therein lies the story of the great tuba. Innes is practically its
inventor. It was a business necessity for him to get the bass section of
his band down to the number of instruments used by his business
rivals. He had always enjoyed distinction of having a band of peculiar tone, which, aside from its unique instrumentation in the reed
section, was largely due to the bass effects made up of a number of
graded tubas and two bass violins. Other bands differently constituted could get away with less men."

Either this writer had an uninhibted imagination or (what is more probable) he was a young and gullible reporter who had the misfortune to fall into the hands of William Grett, the tuba player. Grett, with his tongue in his cheek, no doubt enjoyed talking about his big tuba and facetiously advanced the hypothesis that this one bass would take the place of four other basses, and that the reason for this was to save Innes money by requiring fewer players. The reporter thought Grett was leveling with him and wrote it up as the truth.

The facts about the tuba came out in the *Dominant,* a musical magazine of relatively small circulation, edited primarily for professional musicians by Arthur A. Clappé, who later wrote the authoritative book *The Wind-Band and Its Instruments.* Clappé gave the relatively prosaic but accurate specifications of the tuba as weighing sixty-three pounds and as having three piston valves and a bell thirty-three inches in diameter. Its range was the same as any other tuba of the time, going down to the B♭ which was in the third octave below middle C. Its principal distinction was its wide bore and sonorous tone quality.

Even Sousa became infected with the "bigger" virus, for in 1898 he placed an order with an instrument maker to build for his band a bass tuba, large in bore and surmounted with a big bell opening upward. Sousa did not claim that his instrument was bigger than others, but it was a spectacular instrument, both in performance and in appearance, especially when held and played by the military giant Herman Conrad. In time this instrument proved its merit as a musical instrument and became known as the sousaphone.

In 1907, Jesse Lasky, later of movie fame, and B. A. Rolfe, who made his name immortal later as director of the fast-tempo Lucky Strike orchestra, teamed together and had a monster horn constructed for their vaudeville syndicate. This was the monster horn to end all monster horns, and is probably the largest that was ever made for musical purposes or ever will be made. It was twelve feet in diameter at the bell and was thirty-five feet long! It was christened by the appropriate name of Immensaphone. Eight musicians with band instruments were located at the small end, and what came out of the bell was supposed to equal the volume of sound that issued from the entire band of Sousa.

Actually this was not a musical instrument but was in principle a megaphone, merely amplifying at the bell whatever sound was injected at the small end. However, it was a blood relative of the giant tubas, because size was its chief excuse for being and its purpose was to spellbind the gullible in P. T. Barnum fashion.

At the termination of the Tennessee Centennial Exposition concerts Innes loaded his band and his big tuba aboard his special railway coaches and made a twenty weeks' tour of the Middle West, Southwest, and Pacific coast, ending a strenuous but successful year on December 10.

The next few years were filled with tour after tour. The routine was a spring trek, followed by one or more big summer engagements and a tour in the fall and winter. The routing took Innes and his band into practically every state in the Union and province in Canada. He crossed and recrossed the continent from coast to coast and from north to south. He carried a big band of sixty picked players, and his specially painted railway cars were a familiar sight on hundreds of railroad sidings, where they were shunted during his playing engagements. In one of these he and his soloists and first-chair men rode, and in the other rode the balance of his men. The instruments, music stands, music library, and personal belongings of the players took up most of a baggage car.

It is generally conjectured that T. P. Brooke established his Chicago Marine Band in 1893, but there is evidence that he formed and conducted other bands before this time. In an article published in 1903, it is stated that Brooke began his band activities "fourteen years ago," which would place the beginning in 1889. The 1893 date is taken from a review of Brooke's concerts at the Chicago Coliseum Garden in 1904, in which it is stated that Brooke was "in his eleventh year of activity"; but this reference was probably only to his winter concerts, which he had been conducting annually since 1893.

In these winter concerts Brooke "found himself." For two seasons, 1893–94 and 1894–95, Brooke and his Chicago Marine Band played a concert every Sunday afternoon throughout the winter. These were held in the old Shiller Theatre, and Brooke played to "standing room only." The following season the concerts were moved to the Columbia Theatre, and the season after that they were held in the Great Northern Theatre. Finally, for the 1898–99 season, the band moved to the Grand Opera House.

The printed program for these Grand Opera House concerts carried an ad in which it was stated: "Brooke and his Chicago Marine Band, The Greatest Popular Music Band in the World. Engaged for twenty weeks, playing every Sunday afternoon at three o'clock. Prices 25¢ and 50¢—no higher."

Brooke himself was now known as "The Popular Music King." He had found a place for himself in the band world, and his selection was a good one, for he enjoyed a meteoric rise to the very top. Let Sousa, Brooke's friend and esteemed contemporary, be known as "The March King." Brooke as "The Popular Music King" would be as well known.

The kind of music Brooke presented on his programs ranged widely, including Wagnerian and other classic operas, symphonies, semi-classics, American compositions of various kinds, popular songs, patriotic numbers, dance numbers, coon songs, and cakewalks, plus almost anything requested by the audience. He once stated his rules for program building this way: "I always follow a heavy 'classical' piece, such as *Tannhäuser* or the *Leonore Overture,* with a sweet, simple little song. I always visualize two persons sitting side by side in the audience, one liking the former and the other liking the latter. I am interested only in giving the public the music they enjoy, and I am not interested in 'educating' them."

In his stand for popular music Brooke went even beyond Sousa. Sousa entertained his audience with lighter music so that they would be in their seats while he played some of the more solid music from the classics. Brooke made no pretense of sugar coating a few classic numbers on his program. He was an out-and-out player of light and popular music, but because he recognized that there were those who liked the classics, he included some of the classics on his programs.

Not only did Brooke have his own peculiar knack of building programs of music to suit the public taste, but he knew how to interpret these pieces with the most telling effect. His musicians were all masters on their instruments and he knew how to get the utmost out of them. As one critic wrote of Brooke about this time, "Mr. Brooke is the one great conductor in the country today who knows how to get those astonishing, sweeping crescendos, explosions, crashes and terrific displays of brilliant execution which create sensations and make people declare that the life and spirit in his concerts are not equalled."

Just when Brooke hit the road with his band is not known, but he was well launched on road tours by 1896. Following his winter concerts at the Columbia Theatre, he set out on his summer concert tour, which took him a total distance of nine thousand miles. It was on this tour that Brooke unveiled for the public his "biggest tuba ever made," only to discover shortly afterwards that Innes had a "biggest tuba" also. Since very few persons knew the specifications of the two tubas, both Brooke and Innes each advertised his own as biggest. When Brooke found out that the bell of the Innes tuba was thirty-three inches in diameter, he discontinued advertising that the bell of his was thirty-two inches in diameter. He continued, however, to say that his tuba contained "208 inches of tubing," and this remained its chief claim to fame, since Innes apparently never got around to measuring the length of tubing in his tuba. If he had, he would have found that the tubing in his tuba also was 208 inches long, for both were of the same pitch and bore. This discovery could have put Brooke out of the running in the tuba tournament. The amount of publicity Brooke obtained from his giant did not compare with the volumes of fantastic stories Innes secured. The reason probably was because William Grett, Innes's bass player, could spin more and better yarns than Hod Seavy, Brooke's bass player.

Two summers later Brooke was booked for twenty-eight weeks in the larger cities of the East. These included Philadelphia, where the famous Willow Grove Park was located. Here Brooke hung up a record on August 6, when he played to over one hundred thousand persons, "the largest crowd ever drawn by a military band," according to Howard Pew, Brooke's manager. This was praise indeed, coming from Howard Pew, who became booking agent for Sousa's New Marine Band in 1892 and was associated with Sousa and his exploits for a number of years. At this time Pew was managing, in addition to Brooke, such bands as Banda Rosa, Bellstedt's, and the Carlisle Indians Band.

Returning from this tour late in the fall, Brooke's Chicago Marine Band went to the Grand Opera House for twenty weeks of winter concerts. Here was a stiff schedule for any band: twenty-eight weeks of tour followed by twenty weeks of winter concerts. Such solid booking around the calendar was rare for any band at any time, but it was the lot of the Brooke band for several years. Only a band of tremendous popularity can find such solid bookings. When such a band becomes "hot," the managers and bookers pile on the engagements and try to cash in while they can. If the bandmaster and his players can stand the pace, they go along with these mankilling plans.

And so, at the turn of the century, the trail blazers of the business band were well on their way. Riding the crest of the upsurge of interest in bands, Sousa, Liberati, Innes, and Brooke—all four—finally learned the formula which made Gilmore so successful with his band, but during this band craze era they met with success which Gilmore only dreamed of in his most optimistic moments.

After 1900 it is difficult enough to follow the intense activity of these few leaders, for they were shuttling back and forth across the continent at a dizzy pace. Sousa was especially difficult to keep track of because he was periodically darting across the Atlantic for engagements of from four to seven months.

But to make matters worse, important new bands began to pop out onto the stage from year to year, and the pattern of activity became an almost impossible tangle of events. The Italian bands descended upon the American scene like an invasion of locusts. Billboards and newspapers broke out in a plethora of unpronounceable Italian names. In 1903, Arthur Pryor and Patrick Conway jumped in with both feet. In 1906, Bohumir Kryl added his band to the ever-increasing din, and the following year Al Sweet opened the floodgates of chautauqua bands.

The business band had become such an alluring prospect that more and more bandmasters wanted to give it a whirl. As Jimmy Durante would say, everybody wanted to get into the act. By 1910 these business bands were so numerous that they were trampling over each other. The "demand for high class military music," which Sousa in 1892 regretted was not being met "in any sort of satisfactory manner," was not only being satisfied but surfeited.

In such a situation the narrator of business-band activities becomes almost hopelessly lost if he attempts to tell what goes on from year to year. Only by limiting the number of bands to a few of the most important and following one band at a time, over a period of years, can he make sense to the reader.

Nine

SOUSA MAKES
FOUR TOURS OF EUROPE

First European Tour

≫ SOUSA ≪

and His Band

Mr. JOHN PHILIP SOUSA, Conductor

THE OFFICIAL AMERICAN BAND AT THE PARIS EXPOSITION OF 1900.

Saturday, May 5, to Tuesday, May 15	Universal Exposition of 1900, France	PARIS
Wednesday, May 16 Thursday, May 17	Théâtre de l'Alhambra, Bruxelles, Belgium	BRUXELLES
Friday, May 18	Jardin d'Acclimatation	LIEGE
Saturday, May 19	En route to Berlin	
Sunday, May 20, to Sunday, May 27	New Royal Opera Theatre, Berlin, Germany	BERLIN
Monday, May 28, to Monday, June 4	Concerthaus Ludwig, Hamburg, Germany	HAMBURG
Tuesday, June 5 Wednesday, June 6	Burgerpark, Bremen, Germany	BREMEN
Thursday, June 7 Friday, June 8	Tivoli, Hanover, Germany	HANOVER
Saturday, June 9	Wintergarten, Halle, Germany	HALLE
Sunday, June 10, to Wednesday, June 13	Palm Garden, Leipzig. Germany	LEIPZIG
Thursday, June 14, to Sunday, June 17	Bergkeller, Dresden, Germany	DRESDEN
Monday, June 18	Stadtpark, Nurnberg, Germany	NURNBERG
Tuesday, June 19, to Friday, June 22	Kindl Brau, Munich, Germany	MUNICH
Saturday, June 23	Huttenscher Garten, Wunzburg, Germany	WUNZBURG
Sunday, June 24	Kurtpark, Bad Nauheim, Germany	BAD NAUHEIM
Monday, June 25, to Wednesday, June 27	Rosen Ausstellung, Frankfurt, Germany	FRANKFURT
Thursday, June 28	Kurtpark, Wiesbaden, Germany	WIESBADEN
Friday, June 29, to Sunday, July 1	Flora, Cologne, Germany	COLOGNE
Monday, July 2	En route to Paris	
Tuesday, July 3, to Sunday, July 15	Universal Exposition of 1900 GRAND AMERICAN CONCERT AT PALAIS DU TROCADERO, JULY 4.	

MR. GEORGE FREDERICK HINTON, *Manager European Tour.*

TYP. P. SYMONDS, PARIS

*In 1900, Sousa made his first European tour,
of six months, with a band of sixty-five players.*

Early in the spring of 1900, Sousa announced that he would make a six months' tour of Europe with a picked band of sixty-two players. This was the first of four tours of Europe made by Sousa from 1900 through 1905. During these six years Sousa spent nearly two years, or one third of the time, in taking his band to audiences across the Atlantic.

Details were given out about the tour. Sousa and His Band had been appointed official American band at the Paris Exposition, where they were to play a total of five weeks. For nearly five months the band would give concerts throughout Belgium, Holland, and Germany.

The fates seemed to conspire against this tour, and most bandmasters, lacking the determination and sterling qualities of Sousa, would have given up; but not Sousa. While the band was still on its regular spring tour, with about two weeks left before it was scheduled to leave on April 25 for Europe, Sousa's European manager suddenly dropped dead, nullifying all contracts for engagements in Europe except those at the Paris Exposition. Sousa promptly sent to Europe an American agent, with instructions to rebook the band and renew all contracts if possible.

Another blow awaited Sousa just as he was about to sail. The baggage and instruments had been placed aboard the American liner *St. Paul,* on which passage had been secured, and the players, some with their wives, were beginning to come aboard. At this critical moment Sousa's manager, Everett Reynolds, accosted him with the demand that Sousa renew his contract before he sailed. The contract had a year to run, and Sousa refused to sign a new contract.

Reynolds probably was getting cold feet concerning the European tour. At best the long European tour was a gamble. Twenty-two years before, Gilmore had made a tour of five months with sixty-five players, and he returned to America broke if not in debt. The expenses for Sousa's tour were estimated to aggregate a half million dollars. With the cancellation of contracts brought about by the sudden death of the European manager it didn't appear to Reynolds that the tour could be anything but a financial nightmare. When Sousa refused to sign the new contract, Reynolds threatened to resign. If it appeared to Reynolds that he had Sousa in a pocket and that Sousa would not dare accept his resignation at such a critical time, he, like David Blakely during Sousa's first tour, had failed to take proper measure of the man Sousa. The resignation was accepted, and Reynolds walked down the gangplank just a moment before it was raised and the *St. Paul* cast off.

Actually the situation was worse than stated, for although the Sousa band had been engaged for a total of five weeks at the Paris Exposition, the band was slated for only eleven days in Paris, from May 5 to May 15, before it shoved off for the German tour of nearly six weeks, returning to Paris on July 3 for further concerts. He faced the prospect of carrying the entire expenses of the nearly five months of touring Europe on his own shoulders. But he was undaunted, and declared he would make the entire tour as planned, regardless of what happened.

When Sousa arrived in Southampton, he was met by Colonel George Frederick Hinton, his European publicity agent, and Sousa appointed Hinton as his manager. Sousa opened on May 5 at the Paris Exposition. The band played at various exhibition buildings and at the dedication of the Washington and Lafayette statue, and paraded with the American Guards through the Rue de Rivoli. Not since Gilmore and his band had played at the Trocadéro twenty-two years before had Parisians heard an American band, and Sousa was a big hit. The band was feted and praised.

A group of exposition and government officials took the band for a trip on the Seine River. Two boats were required, the officials in one boat and the band in another, both boats being lashed together with hemp cables. A brash young man came up to Sousa while the boats were floating down the river and asked Sousa if he might direct the band in a number. Sousa was a guest in the country and disliked appearing unfriendly, so he gave his consent, against his better judgment. The boat carrying the band was very crowded, and Sousa suggested that the young man stand in the boat carrying the officials. The would-be director stepped to the other boat and started the band, but hardly had a half-dozen bars of music been played when the cables holding the boats together parted, and the two boats drifted apart. As the boats drifted, the distance between them became greater and greater, but the band played on, much to the delight of the bandsmen, Sousa, and the officials but to the growing consternation of the brash young director. As the piece finally ended, the chagrined upstart was frantically waving his arms from the stern of the official boat, fully fifty feet away.

This ludicrous incident recalls a somewhat similar experience which happened to Liberati a few years later. Liberati and his band were scheduled for an evening concert in a Middle Western town. Sponsors of the concert inveigled Liberati into touring the town aboard two streetcars, the purpose being to advertise the band and drum up ticket sales. The front car was motorized, and in this car Liberati placed the treble instruments. The second car was a trailer, pulled by the first car. In the front of the trailer Liberati placed the percussion section, the harmony and bass instruments being seated back of the drums. Liberati took up his position near the percussion section so he could control the tempo, which the drums would pass out to the rest of the band, fore and aft.

Everything went according to plan until the two cars suddenly came to the end of the line. There it was necessary to detach the motorized car, turn it around, bring it back on a siding alongside the trailer, and switch it over so it could be coupled to the other end of the trailer for the return trip. The uncoupling incident happened just after the Liberati band had started a piece. As the motorized car set out on its switching journey, the treble instruments played along without the prompting beat of the drums. By the time it came alongside the trailer on the parallel siding, this section of the band was playing a whole measure ahead of the section on the trailer, and the disharmony was excruciating. Liberati shouted Italian expletives at the treble section, but to no avail. Mercifully the piece ran out soon and the harmony of silence settled over the band.

The motorized car was finally hooked onto the trailer, and the band set out again, playing another piece. This performance was not much better, for now the percussion section was at the rear of the caravan and could scarcely be heard by the treble section above the rumble and rattle of wheels.

While in Paris, Sousa had a good opportunity to listen to French bands and especially to the famous Garde Républicaine Band, and although he was impressed with their artistic performance, he disliked some of their instrumentation. He expressed these convictions in a letter, which he mailed to the Paris office of the New York *Herald* and which appeared in the foreign edition a few days later. This letter was answered by some American living in Paris, who evidently hoped to curry favor with the Frenchmen. He rebuked Sousa for daring to criticize French bands while living in France as a guest. Sousa answered this epistle by asking why the expatriated American felt he was qualified to speak for the French on any subject, and particularly on bands, about which he apparently knew nothing. This interchange of remarks in the columns of the *Herald* caused considerable interest, and probably helped attendance at Sousa's concerts.

The points Sousa made regarding instrumentation in French bands have become classic with American bandmasters, and have been followed generally. He said, "I do not care for the use of string contra-bass in a military band. If a string-bass, why not a 'cello? And once grant the 'cello, why not the viola and divided violins? In fact, why not become a symphony orchestra at once? There is no room in a military band for stringed instruments, except the harp which has no simulating voice. The bass tuba does all and more than a string contra-bass can do, is richer, gives fuller and rounder harmonic basis for the volume of tone, and can be played on the march—which a string bass cannot.

"I think, too, that French military bands would be improved if the alto-horn and valve trombone were abandoned. They are only poor concessions to the laziness of instrumentalists, and are a poor substitute for the warm, effective and beautiful tone of the French horn and slide trombone. Another thing: I fancy musicians still entertain a vague idea that a military band is inferior to the symphony orchestra; inferior it is not. It is simply different. There is no hierarchy in art. The artistic effect is the sole criterion of values."

Fortunately for Sousa he had in his own band players who could back him in his statements. The French horn section was headed by Anton Horner, who later was solo horn for many years with the Philadelphia Orchestra. On slide trombone Sousa had a performer who was probably the greatest who ever lived: Arthur Pryor. As for bass tubas the section was comprised of August Helleberg, Herman Conrad, Luke Del Negro, and Hod Seavy. It is claimed by some who heard this section that it was the greatest ever assembled, in Sousa's or any other band. Conrad had for many years been Gilmore's prize performer and was still in his prime. Del Negro distinguished himself in later years as recording star and as principal bass at the Capitol Theatre in New York. Seavy formerly played with T. P. Brooke and his Chicago Marine Band as principal bass. Helleberg is known for his long association with the Metropolitan Opera Orchestra and the New York Philharmonic as principal bass tuba.

The six weeks spent in Germany were especially gratifying. The reviews were generally favorable and some of them were enthusiastic.

The Germans liked the way the band played and were sufficiently discriminating to notice the unusual effects Sousa obtained. They were struck particularly by the manner in which Sousa used the entire brass section in pianissimo passages. These muted strains produced unusual tints and shades of tone not heard before. It is said by members of the band that in Berlin Richard Strauss not only attended the Sousa concerts but was present at rehearsals. He was intrigued by the unique tonal effects produced by the band, and later he wrote some of these effects into his compositions, an artistic tribute to Sousa by one of the world's greatest creators of tone tints.

Not only in Germany but all over Europe the band made a big hit with the Sousa marches. Sousa found to his great satisfaction that the march *The Washington Post* was one of the most popular tunes in Europe. Over there it was used for dancing the two-step, and it was credited with reviving this dance. In fact the two-step had actually lost its original identity and was known as a "Washington Post." As an encore this piece was most often called for. On one particular program the audience demanded that Sousa play *The Washington Post* six times before they were satisfied.

Having played in the principal cities of France, Belgium, Germany, and Holland for nearly five months, the band returned to New York in September. Contrary to the opinions of Everett Reynolds, the tour was a financial success. Sousa had succeeded where even the great Gilmore had failed. Sousa's convictions had again been vindicated, and he immediately started plans for another tour in Europe for the following year.

In 1901 Sousa and his band dropped into their regular routine of a spring tour, followed by a month at Willow Grove, Philadelphia, and a month at Manhattan Beach, N.Y. This year, however, between Willow Grove and Manhattan Beach Sousa sandwiched in a month at the Pan-American Exposition in Buffalo, opening on June 10.

After Manhattan Beach, Sousa moved on to the annual Pittsburgh Exposition, where he played for two weeks, beginning September 3. When he arrived in Pittsburgh, Thomas Preston Brooke and his Chicago Marine Band were finishing their engagement on the same bandstand Sousa was to occupy. A few days after Brooke had left, Sousa received a unique letter from him. It seems that the attractions at the exposition were regularly advertised in the local papers, but the typesetters did not properly separate the different items, with the result that the copy ran together and created some incongruous sequences.

Brooke's letter consisted of his letterhead, with some clippings from the newspaper ads pasted on it, and some humorous comments, as follows:

Hello, John, how about this?

EVERY RESIDENT OF THE CITY SHOULD HEAR SOUSA
THE WONDERFUL EDUCATED HORSE

It is almost as good as this, eh?

BROOKE AND HIS CHICAGO MARINE BAND AT THE EXPOSITION
A WONDERFUL TROUPE OF TRAINED ANIMALS

> *Faithfully yours,*
> *Tom Brooke*

Late in September, Sousa and his band embarked for their second European tour, and opened in London in Albert Hall. In two concerts the band pulled twenty-seven thousand paid admissions. Sousa was engaged for a month at the Glasgow International Exhibition, and the final concert there attracted over 152,000 people, the second largest of the exhibition. After a tour of the provinces the band returned to London, where six afternoon concerts were given at the Empire and six evening concerts were given at Covent Garden. This tour was the first taste English audiences had had of the Sousa music, and they became his most enthusiastic admirers.

On the first day of December, Sousa experienced one of his greatest triumphs, a command performance before King Edward VII and his Queen, Alexandra. The King had made his request through a confidential emissary, and the arrangements were kept in the strictest secrecy. This was the Queen's birthday, and the King had planned to have Sousa's Band play as a surprise. The players were told that the engagement was to be played at another location, and only after the troupe had entrained did Sousa reveal that they were journeying to Sandringham, residence of the King and Queen.

Six of the eleven numbers requested by the King were Sousa compositions, including *El Capitan, The Washington Post,* and *Stars and Stripes Forever.* Two other numbers were compositions of Sousa's bandsmen, a trombone solo by Pryor and a cornet solo by Herbert

PROGRAMME.

JOHN PHILIP SOUSA AND HIS BAND

1. SUITE - "Three Quotations" - - Sousa

2. MARCH - - "El Capitan" - - - Sousa

3. SOLO—Trombone "Love Thoughts" - - Pryor
   Mr. ARTHUR PRYOR.

4. a. "A Collection of Hymn Tunes of the American Churches"
   b. MARCH "The Washington Post" - - Sousa

5. SOLO Soprano
   "Will you love me when the lilies are dead?" Sousa
   Miss MAUD REESE-DAVIES.

6. a. CAPRICE "The Water Sprites" - - Kunkel
   b. MARCH "The Stars and Stripes Forever" Sousa
   c. COON SONG "The Honeysuckle and the Bee" Penn

7. SOLO—Violin "Rêverie Nymphalin" - - Sousa
   Miss DOROTHY HOYLE.

3. PLANTATION SONGS AND DANCES - - - Clarke

SANDRINGHAM.   DECEMBER 1, 1901.

Six of the eleven numbers requested by the King were Sousa compositions.

Clarke. In addition to the programed numbers seven encores were requested, most of them specifically selected by the King. The royal audience was most gracious and behaved like any other music-loving human beings, ready with enthusiastic applause and revealing their delight in simple and genuine praise. At the close of the unusual concert the King came forward with the medal of the Victorian Order. Scanning the swelling breast of Sousa, the King asked where he should pin the decoration. "Over my heart," promptly replied the proud bandmaster. "How like an American," commented the amused Queen.

A little over a year later Sousa and his band were back in England to begin their third European tour. They opened in London on January 8, 1903, and gave a second command performance three weeks later. Apparently the royal family were not much different from other Englishmen, for they found that one Sousa concert only created the desire for more of the same. A special feature of this command performance was the premiere of Sousa's newest march *Imperial Edward* and the presentation of the original score to the King, for whom the march was written and to whom it was dedicated.

During this tour Sousa's Band played a total of fifty-two concerts in London. The band then proceeded through France, Germany, Austria, Russia, Denmark, Holland, and other countries, playing a total of three hundred and sixty-two concerts in one hundred and thirty-three cities located in thirteen different countries, during the thirty weeks of touring.

The great band was accorded a most enthusiastic reception everywhere it appeared. The music reviews were especially lavish in their praise. Below is a typical account which appeared in the London *Daily Mail* on February 23:

"Sousa is here! Mark the blackness of his hair, save for that circular spot in the rear of his head. Mark the close-cropped beard, the eye-glasses, the white-gloved hands, the little white baton. . . .

" 'That's fetched 'em,' I could see Sousa remarking to himself. 'They want an encore.' There is no nonsense about Sousa. He recognizes an encore at the first sound. Up goes his baton. The men are ready. In a moment the splendid rhythm of his own *El Capitan* march is pulling every one from their seats. I firmly believe that if the band had risen and marched out of the hall playing, they would have been followed by the entire audience marching after them, keeping time with their left foot first. A pretty Saturday night scene in Pros-

pect street it would have been—a thousand people in evening dress and many hundreds more in their ordinary attire, following Sousa as the rats followed the Pied Piper!

"Sousa gave us many more marches after this. He proved himself to be a very generous King. The March King flung his pieces about as freely as the King in the fairy tale flings his pieces—of money. He gave us a *Suite,* in three sections, called *Looking Upward*—a fine piece of music for a band constituted as this is, with plenty of work for the glockenspiel, and if I mistake not, for the xylophone. Encored! Of course. Double-encored; treble-encored. The audience went wild with joy when the band struck up *The Coon Band Contest* and shouted hilariously as they recognized the opening passages of *The Washington Post.*

"Sousa presented quite a novelty in arrangements after this. He submitted an orchestrated version of Liszt's *Second Hungarian Rhapsody* for piano. Here was another musical 'outrage' to be condoned.

The correct thing, I know, would be to denounce Sousa as they denounced Tausig when he orchestrated Weber's *Invitation to the Dance;* but, as I have said, my scruples had all been swept away—I might say blown away, to vary the idea. I went to denounce but remained to applaud. 'Ha!' Sousa said to himself, 'there's another encore. Let's give 'em *The Rose, Shamrock and Thistle.'* Before the audience knew where they were the band dashed into an ollapodrida of British and national airs, winding up with glorious blatancy in *Rule Britannia.*

"Four encores came in rapid succession after Mascagni's *Danse Erotica.* Encored, too, was Sousa's *Imperial Edward* march. Towards the end of this march, as first played, after the theme of the English National Anthem had been sounded, all the cornets came to the front of the stage in line, and blazed away. Played a second time, the cornets were reinforced by the trombones, all blowing in unison. The blare was tremendous beyond the telling—and still the roof of the Assembly Room remained intact.

"Through all his long programme Sousa comported himself with great calmness. Many people had, no doubt, expected to witness an exhibition of eccentricities such as the caricatures of the music hall imitators have accustomed them to. They would be disappointed, for though Sousa has mannerism, he has no extravaganzes. With such a highly-trained body of men under him as he has, there is not much need for 'conducting' in the ordinary sense. All that is needed is a characteristic indication, a reminder, here and there; the details have all been mastered at rehearsal."

Arthur Pryor on this tour was playing his twelfth season with Sousa, and although few knew it this was to be his final season, for in November of this year he launched his own band. During these twelve seasons with Sousa, Pryor played an estimated ten thousand solos, and Sousa is authority for the statement that "I do not believe there was a man in the world his equal while he was with me."

In London, Pryor received special mention for his extraordinary virtuosity. The music critic in the *Daily Mail* wrote:

"Opulent as was the programme from the point of view of the band, it was very markedly enriched by the introduction of certain individual contributions. Mr. Arthur Pryor revealed himself as a man who has carried the art of playing a trombone to the point of virtuosity. His solo was a revelation of what the trombone can be in the hands of one who has investigated its mysteries and solved its difficulties. He played his own composition *Love's Enchantment,* with

Pryor's "cadenza was remarkable for extraordinary agility."

such tenderness that one began to suspect that the trombone has possibilities as a serenading instrument. His cadenza was remarkable for extraordinary agility."

Said the Birmingham *Post:* "A trombone solo *Love Thoughts* contributed by Mr. Arthur Pryor was an achievement quite unique. The player realized a tone quality which no other soloist on that instrument has ever produced, and yet in the way of rapid scale passages, his performance was especially astonishing."

Said the Dublin *Mail:* "His [Pryor's] execution . . . savors of the marvelous. It was almost too much to believe that such a pure and exquisitely beautiful tone could be produced on an instrument, whose usual characteristics are aggressive."

At a concert before a great audience of twenty-five thousand in Leipzig, Germany, after Pryor had played one of his most difficult solos in his usually superb manner, the entire audience arose and gave him one of the greatest ovations ever known in that city. At the intermission members of the Gewandhaus Symphony Orchestra came to the stage and examined Pryor's trombone. They took the slides apart and looked at the mouthpiece and bell. They thought it must be some kind of new instrument, for they could not believe that any soloist, however accomplished, could play as Pryor did on a trombone such as they were acquainted with. However, they found it a conventional instrument, except for the small bore—only .458 of one inch.

In a sense Pryor was similar to Jules Levy, for each of them used a small-bore instrument. This made their instruments easy to "fill," but nobody else could produce such a big and beautiful tone on a small-bore instrument. The bell of Pryor's trombone was also small —six and one-quarter inches in diameter, whereas the regulation size for such a small bore was seven inches.

Pryor learned to play on a trombone with a nine-inch bell, but about the time he joined Sousa he adopted a bell six and three-quarters inches in diameter. He kept reducing the diameter until he determined that the six-and-one-quarter-inch diameter suited him best. Ralph Corey and Gardelle Simons, later trombone soloists with Sousa, were two of the very few who were able to use such a small trombone. Small-bore trombones were discontinued by manufacturers thirty-five years or more ago.

Simone Mantia, who as a euphonium soloist ranked with Pryor as a trombone soloist, was also a star attraction with Sousa on this tour. When the great Signor Raffayolo died in 1896, Sousa selected Mantia as the euphoniumist most able to take his place. Raffayolo had been imported from Italy by Gilmore, and for many years was a great attraction of the Gilmore band. When Gilmore died, Raffayolo was among the first to join Sousa. It is understood that Mantia was for a time a pupil of Raffayolo, and it is certain that Mantia was equal if not superior to his great predecessor.

Mantia was a master technician and made a specialty of playing the most difficult cornet solo arrangements on his big instrument, a feat that few have ever attempted. His solo cadenzas were brilliant exhibitions of the amazing technique of the great virtuoso. He used a five-valve euphonium with two bells, one the regular bell for the euphonium and the other a trombone or echo bell, which was used for novel effects. Contrary to some opinions, Mantia was not the first to adopt the five-valve euphonium. Harry Whittier, while soloist with Gilmore in 1888, first used such an instrument, and Raffayolo adopted it a year later.

Mantia's solo cadenzas were brilliant exhibitions of his amazing technique.

At the same Leipzig concert in which Pryor so amazed his listeners Mantia created a sensation only a little less spectacular. Mantia's instrument was also inspected by the Gewandhaus players. Someone had passed the word around that Mantia was able to perform his rapid triple tonguing by means of a special invention consisting of three little balls in each of his five valves. The Gewandhaus musicians took out all the valve pistons and peered into the valve casings and slide tubing, but they looked in vain for the secret. They found that Mantia's instrument, like Pryor's, was conventional in every respect, and that the phenomenal performance of Mantia was achieved by his superb ability as a musician.

Herbert Clarke, the cornet soloist, also amazed his listeners, not only by his artistic playing of the cornet but by his endurance, a quality commented upon by Gilmore when he hired him in 1892. He had a full-tone range of six C's and could play a chromatic scale of three octaves four times through with one breath. Said one of the writers during this European tour:

Clarke could play a chromatic scale of three octaves four times through with one breath.

"Suddenly Herbert L. Clarke seizes a note, but such a note! Stupendication causes complete silence around this note. It prolongs itself, it loses itself, it becomes eternal. It is not possible that Clarke can have accumulated so much breath in his lungs. Someone is injecting air into him. Or is it by some unexplained psychological phenomenon the substance of Clarke is being transformed into breath with which to feed his cornet? One expects to see Herbert L. Clarke melt into sonorous ripples. Finally the note stops. And yet Clarke has not thinned sensibly. What a man!"

When Pryor left Sousa and formed his own band, he took Mantia with him as assistant conductor. Many stars came and went from the Sousa band during the forty years of its existence, but it is doubtful if Sousa ever felt any loss as he did when these two great stars departed. Leo Zimmerman became solo trombone, to be followed by such other greats as Ralph Corey, Gardelle Simons, and John Schuler, but Sousa never had another Arthur Pryor. John Perfetto filled the solo-euphonium chair with honor for many years, and was followed by Funaro and DeLuca, but there was never an equal of Mantia.

Sousa and his band arrived home from Europe just in time to fill the regular Willow Grove engagement in August, after which followed the Cincinnati Fall Festival and the Indianapolis Fair. Important engagements kept the band in America in 1904, the Louisiana Purchase Exposition, better known as the St. Louis World's Fair, being the most important.

Before going to the St. Louis Fair, Sousa took his band on a sort of shakedown cruise or trial run through the East. If we can believe the music critic of the Boston *Herald,* the Sousa band was in exceptionally fine fettle. Of a concert in April at Symphony Hall the critic unburdened himself, in part, as follows:

"No little part of the pleasure of the listeners was to hear Symphony Hall—vast, hollow, defier of squeaky violins and dainty female voices—get a thorough melodic trouncing from a battalion of well ordered brass. With thunderous blast and blare, from Wagner's *Parsifal* to the popular swing of the popular *Bedelia,* the musicians satisfied the varied preferences of the audience, and then sailed out to pummel the walls with volumes of sound that seemed like colliding thunder clouds. It was a great victory for the brass instruments. Sousa's band is made up of musicians who find the distance of the surrounding walls with the accuracy of ship gunners taking range, and then they bombard melodically until the most exacting umpire is satisfied where the victory rests."

Sousa was also in fine fettle, according to another Boston newspaper writer. "As always, he was John Philip Sousa, the urbane, the non-chalant, the be-gloved, the Beau Brummel of the baton. . . . The persuasive side glance of the head, the comely beckoning of white kid finger tips or the picturesque, low cut aslant of the baton, brought answering crash of cymbals or the booming of bass-drum thunder."

Sousa opened the Louisiana Purchase Exposition on April 30 by playing the *Louisiana* march, written by Sousa especially for the occasion, but this march was soon forgotten by those who heard Sousa play *Smoky Mokes* and *Hunky Dory, At a Georgia Campmeeting* and *Creole Belle.* As at the Chicago World's Fair a decade earlier, Sousa made musical history by playing the tunes which were popular at that time, *After the Ball* and *Ta-ra-ra-boom-deay* being replaced in St. Louis by the cakewalk and ragtime tunes.

Although Arthur Pryor had left the Sousa band a few months before, he was to considerable extent responsible for Sousa's success with these tunes. Pryor was born and reared in St. Joseph, Mo., not too far from Sedalia, the home town of Scott Joplin, who composed the *Maple Leaf Rag,* one of the first great ragtime tunes and still a perennial favorite. Pryor understood the coon song and the cakewalk and ragtime, and when these tunes began to take the public fancy, Sousa soon learned that Pryor had a special knack of making arrangements of this music, and he turned most of such work over to him.

Pryor did more than arrange the music. After his arrangement was set on the music stands, Pryor, in his capacity as assistant conductor, showed the band how to play it. The oldsters in the band and the classicists did not know how to play syncopation. This was a new kind of music. Players had to feel it or they couldn't play it. As Duke Ellington was to put it so well during a later stage of syncopation, "It don't mean a thing, if you ain't got that swing." Pryor had the coon song and the cakewalk and ragtime in his system. His trombone "smears" (the classicist likes *glissandi* better) were right out of the cakewalk shuffle. In his compositions *Trombonium* and *Lasses Trombone* he has expressed his feeling for this sort of thing. *Southern Hospitality,* another of his compositions, is a typical ragtime cakewalk of the times. And so Pryor not only made the arrangements but demonstrated how they should be played. The result was the best syncopation playing by a band until Pryor formed his own band.

This in no way detracts from Sousa's fame. He was one of the first bandmasters to play the cakewalk and ragtime. Whatever the people liked, that he would try to give them. As early as 1899 we find Sousa picking up cakewalk tunes. Once when he was on tour and played in Kansas City, the J. W. Jenkins Music Company arranged for him to perform *Doc Brown's Cakewalk,* written by Charles Johnson, a local tune writer. By the time he brought his band to the St. Louis World's Fair in 1904, he had quite a library of cakewalk and ragtime band arrangements.

One of the multitude of events at the fair was the National Ragtime Contest. This brought ragtime enthusiasts from all over the country, but these were the professionals mostly. This event was not in any important degree responsible for Sousa's success in playing ragtime, but the fact that such a contest could be held shows that this was the age of ragtime and that Sousa hit the bull's-eye when he presented this kind of music to the paying customers.

For several weeks Sousa and his band played twice a day, moving from plaza to plaza and from building to building. At the beginning Sousa's Band was the only band engaged, except Weil's band, a local organization which played the entire fair. Later other American bands began to filter in. Innes began to alternate with Sousa, and after Sousa left the fair, still other bands came and went. Among these were Conterno's Band, Banda Rosa, Weber's Band from Cincinnati, and the Boston Band.

The last-mentioned band was an especially fine organization of sixty-five players, and it was conducted by two members of the Boston Symphony Orchestra, Emil Mollenhauer (violin) and Max Zach (viola), the two men alternating as conductors. It so happened that the St. Louis Symphony Orchestra was not entirely happy with Alfred Ernst, conductor at the time, and various men were being scouted and appraised as a possible successor to him. Zach made such a favorable impression during his ten weeks of conducting at the fair that he was later appointed as permanent conductor of the St. Louis Symphony Orchestra, a position he held until his death in 1921.

There were also five bands imported from foreign countries, which generally furnished music and entertainment for their exhibits. These were the Grenadier Guards Band of England, the Garde Républicaine Band of France, the Kaiser's Band of Berlin, The Philippine Constabulary Band, and the President's Band of Mexico.

For fear that all these would not be sufficient to furnish the fair patrons with an adequate quantity of band music a national band contest was held the week of September 12. The rules of the contest required that competing bands participate each evening during the contest in a massed band performance and that each band also play a special concert for fairgoers. By these devices the management of the fair was able to present a lot of band concerts without cost.

Published rules of the contest classified entrants by instrumentation, and these rules furnish a bench mark on the progress of bands. The instruments specified for the three classes show that slight progress had been made by the average band during the previous fifteen years. There is relatively minor difference between the band Leon Mead describes as typical in 1889 and the bands that came to the St. Louis Fair in 1904. Below the three classes are specified.

	Class A	Class B	Class C
Conductor	1	1	1
Piccolo			1
Flute	1	1	1
Oboe		1	1
E♭ Clarinet	1	1	1
B♭ Clarinet	4	7	8
Bassoon		1	1
Saxophone		1	2
Total Woodwinds	6	12	15

French Horn (Alto)	3	3	4
Cornet	3	4	4
Trombone	2	3	3
Tenor (Barit.)	1	1	1
Euphonium			1
Tuba	2	2	3
Total Brass	11	13	16
Snare Drum	1	1	1
Bass Drum			1
Cymbal	1	1	1
Total Membership	20	28	35

The "slight progress" referred to consists in shifting the proportion of reeds to brass from one for two to one for one, at least in Classes B and C. French horns are recognized, even though altos are still optional. Trombones have achieved independent standing and are no longer interchangeable with tenor horns. Tenors, unfortunately, are still preferred to baritones. And happily absent are the E♭ cornets, although the E♭ clarinets still hang on.

Following his engagement at the St. Louis Fair, Sousa was the big attraction at the Corn Palace Exposition in Mitchell, S.D. On the bill with the Sousa band was a vaudeville company in whose act two hundred assorted hats were used. These were held in a big net, secured above the stage and hidden by the flies. At the psychological moment during the act the net was released and the hats spilled out. This always brought a good laugh for the vaudeville company. This laugh, however, was nothing compared to the uproarious laughter which occurred one afternoon while the Sousa band was playing a concert.

Right in the middle of a big number, and at a point in the music which was serious and somber and where all the musicians were putting forth their utmost, the overhead net accidently became unhooked and two hundred hats came spilling down on the band. This stopped the music! Some of the players thought the scenery was falling on them, and they jumped from their chairs and started for cover, bumping into each other and creating general havoc.

This ludicrous anticlimax to the serious music struck the audience as hilariously funny, and they exploded into loud laughter. Waves of mirth swept the listeners for a period. A clarinet player pointed out to the audience how one of the hats had done a "Ted Lewis" over the bell of his clarinet. Attention then shifted to a sousaphone player who was gravely and methodically fishing hats out of the big upright bell of his instrument. As each hat was retrieved, the audience broke out in a new gale of laughter, until a total of four hats had been recovered. Then the player uttered a low snort on his instrument to show that the air passage was unobstructed.

As the last of the hats were carried off stage, Sousa ascended the podium to continue the concert. He knew better, however, than try to finish the number that had been so unceremoniously interrupted. He quickly passed the word and the concert was resumed by taking up the next number on the program.

On more than one occasion various objects fell on the band, especially when the band was playing on stage. In a Middle Western town, the band was playing the Sousa *Field Artillery March,* and had come to the staccato passage where the firing of pistol shots is called for in the score. The tympanist raised his pistol and three shots rang out. A split second later, from the flies overhead, a dead duck plummeted to the stage floor and came to rest near the podium. The duck was followed by a cloud of feathers, which settled gently over the front rows of the band. This bit of comedy was perpetrated by the local stagehand, who had learned that Sousa was an ardent hunter and champion clay-pigeon shot. Sousa thoroughly enjoyed the joke and laughed heartily along with the audience.

On another tour the violin *Concerto* by Mendelssohn was programed. This number always gave the bass drummer, Gus Helmecke, an opportunity to stretch his legs backstage. One time, as he wandered at the rear of the stage, he spied a hole in the scenery, and he put his eye to the hole and watched the soloist performing the heroic pyrotechnics of this celebrated composition. As Gus did so, he noticed that the bassoon player was sitting just to one side of the hole. Gus reached through the hole with a feather and tickled the bassoonist's ear. The bassonist swung his hand vigorously backward and hit the scenery. It hadn't been cleaned for years, and a great cloud of dust and dirt came down on the band and for a moment or two practically hid the rear ranks of the band from the audience. The imperturbable Sousa and the very busy soloist scarcely noticed the exploding scenery, but the performance of some sections in the back of the band was rather ragged for several bars.

During a tour of the Southern states one summer the band played in a town remembered by the bandsmen for the numerous dogs lying asleep in the sun and for the large bluebottle flies which flew in and out of the open windows of the auditorium. During the concert one of these big flies settled on the bald spot of Sousa's head and refused to be dislodged, although Sousa shook his head vigorously several times. Finally Sousa, who knew there was something up there but didn't know what it was, stopped directing for a moment and scraped it off with his baton.

In Harlingen, Texas, a large hatching of big black beetles nearly stopped the concert, but nothing short of a major catastrophe could force Sousa to postpone a performance, and the program was eventually carried out without any casualties. The musicianship that day, however, was not up to par, for all during the program these huge and menacing black beetles crawled all over the stage and up the pant legs of the perspiring players.

In Salt Lake City the Sousa band played one afternoon in the choir loft of the Mormon Tabernacle. The kids in the balcony above made life miserable for the players by sailing down over the band dozens of airplanes improvised from programs.

The fourth European tour by Sousa and his band opened in Liverpool on January 6, 1905, and ended over seven months later. Touring Europe had become commonplace for Sousa, but new heights in popularity were reached in Vienna, where the band played as an encore *The Blue Danube* by native son Johann Strauss, and in Prague, where the band played the *Largo* from the *New World Symphony* by Dvořák, former professor of music in the Prague Conservatory.

On this tour Sousa invaded Russia, opening on May 16 for a series of nine concerts at the Cisnicelli in St. Petersburg. Imagine Sousa's consternation when he arrived in the city to see that a rival band called "Cyza and His Band" had monopolized the billboards and had plastered them with announcements about a series of concerts on the same dates.

Sousa remonstrated with his European publicity manager and asked him how such a boner could have been made. Before the manager could answer, Sousa shifted his wrath to his rival. "Who is this C-y-z-a anyway, whose name is plastered all over the city? Who ever heard of this C-y-z-a bandmaster?" When the amused manager could get an opening in the flow of remonstrances, he explained that Cyza was simply the local Russian spelling of Sousa!

Seldom has a name been kicked around as has the name Sousa. Those who have searched the records about Sousa's ancestors have been puzzled and frustrated by the various spellings of the name. These variations include Sauza, Sowsa, Soussa, Souzza, and Sioussa.

During Sousa's first European tour a fiction arose which made one of Sousa's ancestors a native of practically every country in Europe, and these stories persisted for many years. All of them turned on the last three letters of his ancestor's name—USA—and all of them started with his immigration to the U.S.A. This ancestor was illiterate, and all he could write on his baggage tag was his initials, which were S.O., and his destination. which was U.S.A.

Said one version, this ancestor came from Yorkshire, England, and his name was Sam Ogden. Said another version, he came from Germany and his name was Sigismund Ochs. A slightly different version managed to explain also how the name John originated. Said this version, the ancestor came from Greece and his name was John So.

In his autobiography *Marching Along,* published in 1928, Sousa clears up this confusion by stating that his father was a Portuguese named Antonio Sousa, who was born in Spain and came to the U.S.A. by way of England. Before he published this explanation, however, Sousa only smiled when he was asked about these stories. He knew they were the creation of his resourceful European publicity agent, Colonel George Frederick Hinton. He confessed to friends that he could not bring himself to refute these stories because he didn't like to kill a good story. Besides, being a native of whatever European country he happened to be playing in was good for the box office.

Not long after returning from his fourth successful visit to Europe, Sousa was off on an almost continuous tour of the United States and Canada, which took him through thirty-three states and lasted nearly a year. When the band pulled up for a breather in the summer of 1906, Sousa revealed to Herbert L. Clarke, his premier cornet soloist and assistant conductor, that he had been negotiating with various foreign agents to take his band on a trip around the world. This world tour would take about two years.

Clarke, the overworked wheel horse in the band, decided he had better take a vacation and rest before starting out on such a journey. He bought an old farm of twenty-two acres near Reading, Mass. This was not only a good spot for resting, but it would provide a home for his wife, away from New York City, during the two years he would be on tour.

While Sousa was waiting for the world-tour arrangements to be consummated, he took advantage of the interim to fire his opening shot against recorded music. This was an article which appeared in *Appleton's* magazine and was entitled "The Menace of Mechanical Music." For the next twenty years Sousa was to keep blazing away at the "menace," which he believed stole employment from players and royalties from composers.

The phonograph was invented by Edison in 1877. At first it was regarded merely as a curious gadget but by 1889 it had become a popular toy. On Broadway in New York it appeared in the penny arcades as the gramophone, a coin machine with listening tubes. Eugene Rose, who became flutist with the Sousa band in 1900, earned some of his first money, after coming to America from Germany, by making recordings on wax cylinders for Thomas Edison. These recordings were made in 1889 and are regarded as the first recordings of instrumental music.

In 1903, Columbia and Victor were making recordings of such stars as Sembrich, soprano; Scotti, baritone; J. Reszke and Caruso, tenors. In this same year Edvard Grieg recorded some of his own piano music, and the following year Claude Debussy played the accompaniments in a recording session for Mary Garden. By this time, also, Pryor's Band had begun to make recordings of band music for Victor. The phonograph was attracting the interest of serious musicians, and Sousa could read the handwriting on the wall.

In the meantime Eugene Rose had joined the Sousa band and had made two European tours with Sousa in 1900 and 1901. He was an accomplished flutist, and Sousa was just beginning to consider him one of his principal musicians when Rose quit—to make recordings again for Edison! He became flutist with the Edison Concert Band and with the Edison Venetian Trio, comprised of harp, violin, and flute.

Besides being a virtuoso on the flute Rose was a wizard on the ocarina, and he made many recordings using this little instrument. One of his solos on the ocarina was entitled *The Genevieve Waltz Medley*. When it was released in 1906, it became a hit and best-seller. We do not know if this event was what triggered Sousa's blast at recorded music, but it could well have been. He had lost Rose to the recording business, and now the ocarina recording had made Rose more famous than he could have become if he had remained to play flute with the Sousa band.

In the *Appleton's* article Sousa coined a phrase which stuck with recorded music for many years and was a term of ridicule which was used with devastating effect by those attacking the phonograph. Sousa referred to recorded music as "canned music" in the sentence: "Canned music is as incongruous by a campfire as canned salmon by a trout stream."

Sousa's principal argument, however, was that mechanical music threatened the livelihood of all those associated with creating and performing music. He pictured the recording process as a dreadful robot which took the music produced originally by live musicians and multiplied it "by means of wheels and pulleys." If this robot were permitted to go on, Sousa could see a few recording sessions replacing a season of touring, and one copy of his marches supplanting thousands of copies then being sold. In time Sousa's arguments, repeated interminably, brought about better conditions, especially for composers.

Meanwhile Herbert Clarke was enjoying his rest on his newly purchased farm. The summer and fall months went blissfully by, but Clarke heard nothing from Sousa. Late in the year, however, Sousa gave him the startling information that the world tour had been abandoned! Sousa had torn up all the newly-drawn contracts because of unforeseen difficulties with the foreign manager of concerts in Australia. This left Clarke in debt for the farm, a debt he had been confident he could pay off when he returned from the long two-year tour around the world. It also left him without a job, and for several months he had to resort to teaching cornet pupils.

The world tour by Sousa and His Band was postponed from year to year, but eventually, late in 1910, it began, and Clarke went along as originally planned. Both Sousa and Clarke probably would have been better off if the world tour had been postponed indefinitely.

Ten

CREATORE STARTS
ITALIAN-BAND VOGUE

*Viewed from any angle,
Giuseppe Creatore
was a sad spectacle.*

The Italian Band, comprised of fifty-five Italian musicians, arrived in New York City from Naples in 1899. Apparently this was the complete name of the band and was believed to be a sufficient designation. In those days Italian bands were not as common as they were to become a few years later.

The Banda Rosa, under Eugenio Sorrentino, had been traveling here and there over the United States for about ten years, but was not too well known. Just about the same time the Italian Band arrived in New York the Banda Rosa was giving a series of concerts in Chicago at the Grand Opera House. The band followed Brooke's Chicago Marine Band at this spot. This could mean that the Banda Rosa was of similar caliber with Brooke's band were it not for the fact that Howard Pew of Chicago was agent for both bands, and he may have sold the two bands on a package deal, such as "If you'll take the Banda Rosa, I'll give you Brooke."

About the only other Italian band of note at this time was Cassassa's Cornet Band, attached to the 1st Regiment of the California National Guard. Charles H. Cassassa had made a name for himself as early as 1895, and was a great favorite at Golden Gate Park in San Francisco. However, Cassassa's was essentially a local band.

And so the new Italian band was billed simply as the Italian Band, as if it were the only Italian one in America, which was very nearly the truth. The band played a few concerts in New York and then quietly journeyed to the Atlantic City Steel Pier. Nobody was paying very much attention to the Italian Band. The manager, the conductor, and the musicians were not happy over the reception they were receiving. And the most unhappy man of all was the trombone player named Giuseppe Creatore.

Even if Giuseppe was not unhappy, he appeared so. He had large, black, sad eyes which were sunk in a lean and sallow face. A long black mustache drooped over his mouth, which also seemed to droop at the corners. Long black sideburns led upward into a great head of straight black hair, which was combed backward on each side of his head and cascaded over his uniform coat collar at the rear. Viewed from any angle, Giuseppe was a sad spectacle, but when seen front on, his large, liquid black eyes fairly cried out from their depths with melancholy and anguish.

Giuseppe Creatore wanted most of all to be a conductor. He studied music in the Naples Conservatory and learned to be a good player of the trombone. He also studied conducting, and he was so talented that when he was only seventeen years old he was selected to direct the Naples Municipal Band. This honor was bestowed on him in 1887, and he held the position with success for eight years. Now, at the age of twenty-nine, he was back playing trombone in the Italian Band, and he was discouraged.

The Italian Band finished the engagement at Atlantic City and went on to Willow Grove. Creatore's mustache seemed to droop lower and his eyes seemed to become more sad with each concert. Suddenly, one night just before the concert, the conductor became ill. It was almost time for the band to walk out on the bandstand. Whom could the management get to lead the band? Creatore knew a man who could do it! But would he be the man selected?

The audience had no idea of the dramatic situation backstage as the musicians began taking their seats. They watched this man or that, as he adjusted his instrument or leafed perfunctorily through the music on the stand. Finally all was quiet. It was time for the conductor to make his appearance. At this moment, if those in the audience could have seen the trombone section clearly, they would have noted that there was a vacant chair there, and that the band would be short one player for the concert.

Between the time when Creatore broke out from the wings backstage and when he reached the podium and lifted his baton the audience had scant time to note that a new conductor had come upon the scene. It is doubtful if many noticed this fact, and it is probable that no one cared much, for the unnamed conductor who usually directed the band was nothing to get excited about and would scarcely be missed.

If the dash to the podium by the young man with the wild and flying hair signaled nothing to the audience, they were not long in feeling that something electrifying was taking place. The baton quickly came down for the beginning of the overture, and a stir went through the thousands of listeners. They were not sure whether it was the music or the extraordinary conductor who held them so enthralled. Certainly they had never witnessed a conductor who took his work so seriously and who resorted to such desperate gymnastics in directing. They sat fascinated until the last note was played, and then they broke out into applause such as the members of the Italian Band had not heard during the entire tour so far.

Number followed number. Some of the regular patrons at Willow Grove looked at their programs to see if they were mistaken about this being the Italian Band. It certainly sounded as if a new band had been substituted, but the program said it was the Italian Band. Even some of the players in the band began to feel there was something a bit unreal about the whole performance. Was this really the Italian Band? This band sounded unlike the band they had been playing in for all these weeks. Individual musicians sensed that they were playing "away above their heads." How come they were playing so much better than they ever played before?

The applause was a great tonic. The conductor had them all inspired. The program got better and better with each number. It was the greatest concert they had ever given. Creatore had performed a musical miracle.

When it was all over and the musicians in the band had time to think and exchange views with each other, they realized more fully what Creatore had accomplished. They went singly and in groups to congratulate him on his splendid performance. Creatore sat in a small room called the conductor's dressing room and mopped his face and neck, hands and arms with a towel. His uniform, hanging over the back of a chair, was soaking wet with perspiration, caused by the strenuous physical exercise he had undergone for nearly two hours. His long hair hung down over his face, and he was near the point of complete exhaustion. He accepted the praise of his fellow musicians, but he scarcely changed expression. His melancholy and sadness were too deep to be removed by one triumph on the podium.

Fortunately for Creatore the regular conductor was ill for several days. This gave the substitute conductor an opportunity to prove to one and all that the first concert was not a fluke of some kind. He showed them that he could turn in one fine performance after another. When the regular conductor did show up, the audience and the musicians in the band were sorry that Creatore could not take his place permanently.

The performances thereafter reverted to their former character. They were well played and directed, but they lacked something which Creatore had imparted to them. The applause died down to a polite and moderate amount of hand clapping. There were no more shouts of "Bravo! Bravo!" Factions in the band talked over the pros and cons of throwing out the old conductor and installing Creatore as permanent conductor. Creatore refused to plead his own cause and merely sat and brooded. Before the end of the season there was open dissension, and the band split. Some stayed with the old conductor, but others cast their lot with Creatore, who formed a new band.

During the following season Creatore and His Band made headlines wherever they appeared. They played at the Atlantic City Steel Pier from February through July. They then went to Willow Grove, after which they made a tour of five thousand miles. The chief trouble Creatore experienced during these early days with his band was the inadequacy of many of his players. He was like a great violin virtuoso trying to play on a cheap fiddle. Work as he might, he could not make the performances come up to what he had in his mind.

Accordingly, in the fall of 1901, Creatore returned to Naples for the purpose of recruiting musicians of the caliber he needed. As he auditioned and selected musicians, he talked about his triumphs in

America. He told of the great audiences and the long tours and the favorable reviews—and about his new contract. Money and fame awaited the Italian musician in the New World. Creatore's visit in Italy resulted a few years later in a great influx of Italian bands in America.

In the spring of 1902, Creatore returned to New York with his new band of sixty picked men. He now felt he had the musicians who were more capable of carrying out his musical conceptions. His first concert was at Hammerstein's Roof Garden and it was a sensation such as seldom occurs in music. Creatore took New York City by storm. Sensational reviews in the newspapers built up the name of Creatore until there was standing room only at his concerts.

After the opening concert one newspaper headline shouted: "A SVENGALI TO HIS BAND." The story which followed described in vivid language the hypnotic effect which Creatore seemed to create in his musicians. He first cast them under a spell. Then he did with them as he desired. He handled them as slaves of his will, causing them to play the most exalted music, music which they were able to play only while under Creatore's spell.

Another newspaper was even more extreme. It screamed: "WOMEN ON TABLES IN HYPNOTIC FRENZY. Broadway Pleased By Exhibition of Athletic Leadership." The story under these headlines related how Creatore hypnotized not only his musicians but the people in the audience, especially the women. Creatore possessed some strange power over women, executed through the wild music he directed. Women at the Hammerstein Roof Garden were said to be under such a strange spell that they jumped to the top of the tables and writhed and "emoted"as in a frenzy.

The physical contortions of Creatore were also dealt with at length. He ran all over the stage, he jumped and gyrated, he shadow-boxed and skipped the rope, he put the shot and hurled the discus, he ran the hurdles and pole-vaulted. He was portrayed as a great athlete who could perform the feats of track and field and gymnasium with a skill and endurance seldom witnessed.

The New York *Journal* devoted space to some doggerel written by G. Schlotterbeck, which went as follows:

Creatore! Creatore! There's a fury in your form
That can lash the tamest music to a shrill and shrieking storm;
To every order telegraphed from that hypnotic eye
Reverberating kettledrums respectfully reply,

While swaying like a wind-swept reed your body cleaves the air,
Inciting boom, and clash, and crash, and bray, and blow, and blare.

You frown upon the oboe, and it grievously makes moan,
You draw from the euphonium a grumbling undertone;
You throw a double duck fit, just as if you liked to work,
To get results from yonder where the queer tympani lurk;
Meanwhile the evolutions that you set yourself to do
Resemble macaroni when it bubbles in the stew.

Old Patsy Gilmore, bless him, was a leader who could show
Contortionists and gymnasts things they really ought to know,
While our Philip Sousa, with his short but gifted arms,
And his limber neck, possesses many captivating charms;
But as spectacles, we own it neither one of them would do
For an instant in competing with a whalebone man like you.

Blessings on you, Creatore: if we all could work like that
We would not get results that seem trifling, tame and flat.
If we could but hurl ourselves at what is given us to do
And keep that whirlwind up until we get completely through,
We'd make a noise perhaps ourselves to echo through the land
And get as much good out of life as you do from that band.

Not since Jullien did newspaper and magazine writers have so much fun as they did writing about Creatore. He was good copy and he received columns and columns of space. He had little need for a press agent: writers from town to town vied with each other in praising, ridiculing, describing, and evaluating Creatore. From these various eyewitness accounts we can obtain a good picture of the fabulous bandmaster.

After New York, Creatore took his band on a cross-country tour. When he played in Kansas City, the music critic of the *Journal* wrote a piece which is particularly vivid and amusing. The story carried the caption "THE POETRY OF PROSE," and continued as follows:

"Creatore starts the band in a mild, entreating way. A simple up-lifting of the arms. Then suddenly, with a wild shake of his shaggy head, he springs across the stage with the ferocity of a wounded lion. Crash! Bang! And a grand volume of sound chokes the hall from pit to dome.

"Then he doubles up like a question mark and, with glaring eyes and gritting teeth, with outstretched prompting finger, creeps stealthily around, the very picture of hate and malice personified. Suddenly a wild leap into the air, and with his long hair standing straight up, he lands like a bucking bronco.

"Now he leans over the row of music stands, he smiles the smile of a lover—pleading, supplicating, entreating, caressing—with outstretched hand, piercing the air with his baton, like a fencing master. Almost on his knees, he begs, he demands, he whirls around with waving arms. He laughs, he cries, he sings, he hisses through his clinched teeth.

"He feels the music with every fibre. Now it is the rushing winds; now the mad plunging of galloping horses; now the booming of the surf on bleak rocks; and now the birds singing in the treetops, the sound of angels' wings.

"He throws up his hands lik an Aztec in prayer, there is a wild burst of melody and it is over. He bows and smiles, then goes behind the scenes and combs his hair."

And the writer in the Kansas City *Journal* was not exaggerating! This is probably one of the best descriptions of Creatore in action that have come down to us, even it fails to do full justice to this overemotional, wildly imaginative, and uninhibited Italian maestro.

One would think Creatore would burn himself out, performing at such an exhausting pace, but these concerts went on for years. Only an unusual man, supremely well endowed with nervous energy and tireless tissues, could have stood up under the strain.

During the tour the following year the Creatore band hit Cleveland in September and brought forth this comment in the Cleveland *Leader:* "One minute he seemed a monarch as he pompously gloated over a sweet strain well executed, and the next he seemed a groveling subject, beseeching grace from the powers before him. Again, he would dart among the musicians, shouting, yelling imprecations in terse Italian monosyllables, or singing his mightiest in an attempt to swell the volume, or merely to express his ecstasy in the work. Fervor was personified by him in some selections and in others he characterized the fiery spirit."

On to Chicago in October, and this more restrained appraisal of the mad Italian appeared in the *Tribune:*

"The audiences that crowded the Studebaker yesterday afternoon and evening, when Creatore and his band gave their first concert in Chicago, had their nerves twitched and tingled as if they were in connection with an electric battery. It is claimed that Creatore hypnotizes both his band and his hearers. He gets them in his control to give them a succession of electric shocks that make them gasp. . . . Tone is the wireless medium he uses to reach you, but the current he sends to you is his own intense individuality, and you feel it and obey it just as unresistingly as do his men. . . .

"There is about all Creatore does a sincerity and earnestness that disarms criticism. It is so clearly an expression of personal musical conviction, and so clear an expression that it stands in a class by itself, and has to be so judged. There is never for an instant any suggestion of posing about him. The whole being of the man is engrossed in his work, and the wonderful positions that he takes and the movements he makes are but the outcome of the intensity he feels, and his overpowering desire to compel his men to play exactly as he wishes."

Not all reviewers were as sympathetic and charitable as the foregoing writers. Some looked upon Creatore's antics as extreme exhibitionism and excessive sentimentality of the most flagrant kind. They were repelled by what they regarded as an emotional orgy of the most revolting nature. Even when they were constrained to admit his sincerity, they felt that Creator allowed this sincerity to lead him to extremes. Their artistic sensibilities were offended by the indecent public parade of his private feelings and impulses. No true artist would so openly "wear his heart upon his sleeve," they concluded. Such conduct was a gross insult to good taste.

Creatore returned again and again to Chicago. It was generally a stop on his cross-country tours. In 1904 he accepted an engagement in Sans Souci Park, where he uncorked another of his extravaganzas. The following day the newspaper critics wrote fluently about how Creatore had started the *Tannhäuser* overture more slowly than customarily, and had built it up to a tremendously climactic crescendo that had everybody's hair standing on end—and left some of the musicians prostrate on the floor, so fast and strenuous was the pace. The following year Bismark Garden bid him in as a summer attraction, and he enjoyed a tremendous season in the evening open-air concerts; so tremendous, in fact, that he returned in 1906.

These were prosperous days for Creatore. He had started a vogue which caught on. Everywhere resorts and amusement parks were clamoring for Creatore and His Band. He was booked solid for months at a time. His fee rose until it reputedly reached five thousand dollars per performance. This was more than other bands could

All of these Italian bandmasters wore fierce mustaches.

Marco Vessella

Don Philippini

Stanislao Gallo

Alfredo Tommasino

demand, even the great and popular Sousa. Somewhat later, in the early twenties, Sousa boasted that he was taking in an average of thirty-five hundred dollars per concert; and in 1924 he advertised that he had reached the highest guarantee in the history of bands, when he received a guarantee of twenty thousand dollars for six concerts, at Regina, Canada. Probably the five thousand dollars' fee was a figment of a press agent's imagination, but Creatore unquestionably was receiving top money.

Creatore probably did not realize, any more than a dozen other bandmasters at this time, that the band business couldn't "go on like this forever." But Creatore was especially hard hit by competition from his own kind of band, when the influx of Italian bands commenced. He had "spilled the beans" in the winter of 1901–02, when he visited Naples for the purpose of recruiting his new band. His loose talk started the formation and the emigration of Italian bands which brought disaster to Creatore.

One of the first Italian bandmasters to take the bait was Marco Vessella, who made his debut in America in 1903, one year after Creatore opened at Hammerstein's Roof Garden in New York. Other bands comprised of Italian musicians followed in rapid order. By 1909 the billboards were filled with Italian names, such as Gregory's Italian Band, Corrado's Italian Band, Don Philippini and His Band, Alfredo Tommasino and His Band, Verdi's Italian Band, directed by Francesco Creatore, Ernesto Natiello and His Band, Gallo's Primary Italian Band, Ferulla, Gargiulo, and Satriano. On the West Coast, Cassassa was confronted by Chiaffarelli, Donatelli, Rivela, and Ruzzi.

Practically all of these Italian bandmasters wore fierce mustaches and most of them, with the outstanding exception of Don Philippini, who was getting bald, cultivated a luxuriant head of hair. Notable among these were Vessella, Tommasino, and Francesco Creatore. The last sported a head of long, black curly hair that was the envy of a host of women.

For a time these newcomers were in clover. If bookers at fairs, resorts, and amusement parks did not have Creatore, they at least could furnish an Italian band of some sort, and that was what every spot was crying for. The word spread to Germany and at least one band of German musicians came to America in 1907. This was Luedtka's Band, comprised principally of musicians from the Conservatory of Music in Berlin. But this German band fared no better than the Germania Society, Gungl's Band, and the Saxonians, who came to America fifty to sixty years before.

With all these Italian bands fighting for engagements Creatore began to find the going tough. The public became surfeited with the sights and sounds of long-haired and mustached maestros. The emotional binge of American audiences which lifted Creatore to the height of popularity began to subside. In time a reaction set in, and listeners stayed away from concerts that featured such parading of the emotions and extreme romanticism.

Eleven

*Thomas Preston Brooke
inherited a fortune
of $800,000
from an uncle
in London.*

By the spring of 1900, Thomas Preston Brooke and his Chicago Marine Band had completed seven seasons of winter concerts in Chicago and four seasons of road tours. They were now involved in what was probably the longest and toughest series of concerts of any band on record, including Sousa's. For six solid years, from 1898 into 1904, Brooke and his band played almost constantly. The general pattern of Brooke's activities during this time was fifteen to twenty weeks of winter concerts in Chicago, followed by twenty-five to thirty weeks or more on tour during the spring, summer, and fall months.

After the 1899–1900 winter season at the Grand Opera House, Brooke left Chicago on April 14 for the tour and arrived back in Chicago on December 23, completing a long, hard trek of about thirty-six weeks. The first engagement on this tour was the Louisiana Exposition in New Orleans, and it was during this engagement that Bohumir Kryl made his first appearance with Brooke's band. Kryl accepted a contract with Brooke when Sousa embarked on his first European tour, probably expecting to rejoin Sousa after his return. For some reason, however, Kryl never again played with Sousa.

In the spring of 1902, after the winter concerts in Chicago, held now in Coliseum Garden, Brooke took his band on tour as far as New Orleans. The return tour began in September and ended in Kansas City on December 22. The tour didn't land the band back home in time for Christmas this year, but it was headed in the right direction, and the players reached the Windy City in time for the holidays, about the only off time throughout the entire year.

It was on the tour to New Orleans that Brooke played at the Zoological Gardens in Cincinnati for several weeks. The first Wednesday there he thumbed his nose at the fates and devoted the entire evening concert to ragtime. Did the cultured and musical people of Cincinnati stay away in droves from Brooke's ragtime concert? They did not. To the surprise of almost everyone this concert made a big hit; and every Wednesday evening afterward Brooke played a ragtime concert. Brooke drew from twelve to fifteen thousand at each Wednesday evening concert. This was more than twice the attendance at the concerts that included Wagner and symphonies and other classical music.

Brooke immediately became even more of a celebrity. He was not only a well-known authority on popular music, but he now became an authority on ragtime. Music writers and reporters sought to interview him about the secret of his success with ragtime and to find out just what ragtime really was. In an article which appeared in the Chicago *Tribune,* Brooke expounded his ideas on the new kind of music.

He said, "Ragtime is now the most generally mooted theme among musicians. During the last year there have been published countless articles on ragtime, written by prominent musicians, teachers and critics, many of them having something to say about who discovered or invented it. Ragtime was not discovered or invented by anyone. It is the 'juber,' buck and wing dance of the old plantation darkey, and no more inspiring ragtime was ever played than that which he patted with his hands, shuffled with his feet, or plunked on his rudely constructed banjo.

"All the oldtime fiddlers were ragtime players. The backwoods player who sat perched on a barrel in the corner, at a 'husking bee,' who held his fiddle at his elbow and his bow at half-mast, played the *Arkansas Traveler* and *Up Duck Creek* in a style that would put to shame many of the fellows who claim to have originated what they are pleased to call 'Ragtime.' "

Here again Brooke demonstrated his pioneering in band music and his keen understanding of what the people wanted to hear. This was two whole years before Sousa risked playing ragtime at the St. Louis World's Fair, although Sousa is reputed to have played some ragtime in 1900 in Paris. Brooke started playing coon songs and the cakewalk almost from the day he started his Chicago Marine Band, and he is probably the first bandmaster who had the temerity to devote a whole evening's concert to ragtime tunes.

Brooke also made some sort of record by hiring a woman cornet soloist for his band. When Kryl left, Brooke signed up Alice Raymond and for two years advertised her as the "World's Greatest Lady Cornetist." There was nothing wrong with a woman's being a vocalist, and it was permissible for one to be a violinist or harpist, but it was hardly acceptable for "a lady" to blow any instrument, especially a cornet, and "doubly especially" with a band! But Brooke and Alice Raymond changed many people's mind about this, for she was an accomplished soloist and won approval and respect by her stage presence and her artistry.

The stars in Brooke's horoscope were conspiring together to make 1903 a fabulous year. He started out in January on a twenty-four-week tour which eventually took him through twenty-seven states and into Canada. He followed this up with a return swing of twenty-four weeks which led him through sixteen states and fifteen thousand triumphant miles. As if this were not enough for even so favored a man as Thomas Preston Brooke, he inherited an $800,000 fortune from an uncle in London!

Already under contract to put on his winter concerts at the Coliseum Garden in Chicago, he averted his gaze from the pile of pounds sterling and proceeded with the concerts. Soon after this, however, he began making plans which were to lead rapidly to his undoing.

Brooke was a handsome man, large and powerful of stature, with a head of thick, dark hair, and a stiff brush of a mustache. His features were classic, his eyes were friendly, and he wore an expression of smiling affability. But the past five or six years had taken their toll. He was exhausted. Howard Pew, his manager, and the applause of his audiences had driven him beyond his strength. Although only forty-seven years of age he was already an old man, and he began to plan an escape from the treadmill in which he had been caught. This large fortune which dropped into his lap had come just in time, he thought. He would use it to enable him to continue his band under conditions less exhausting.

He set about organizing what he called Brooke's Casino and Exposition Company, capitalized at $150,000. He accepted as stockholders in the venture a half-dozen of Chicago's prominent citizens, among them Mayor-Elect Busse. He was contented to hold the office of vice-president and general manager. He set up offices at 260 South Wabash, where he could lean back in a soft leather chair and put his feet on top of a richly carved executive's desk.

He called in architects and began drawing plans for his Brooke's Casino, the summer home for his band. This edifice he had constructed on the northeast corner of South Wabash Avenue and Peck Court, only a few blocks south of his suite of offices. As it neared completion, he issued an announcement that this was to be the summer home of his Chicago Marine Band for five months of each year. During the other months it was to be made available for "various kinds of bazaars, dog, cat and flower shows."

Brooke had often played in New Orleans, at Athletic Park and at West End, and he liked the climate there during the winter months. He was exhausted by bucking the icy winds off Lake Michigan and he craved the sunshine of New Orleans. Accordingly he erected in this southern paradise his Brooke's Winter Garden. After five months of playing in the cooling breezes off the lake in Chicago he planned to move his band south for the winter. For five months during the coldest weather in the north he would present his popular music in the Mississippi Delta. He didn't say what he intended to do during the other two months of the year.

He opened on May 31, 1905, in his Brooke's Casino, sometimes known as Brooke's Summer Garden, in contrast to his Brooke's Winter Garden in New Orleans. An ad in Chicago newspapers announced: "Brooke's Chicago Marine Band. Fourteen soloists, plus T. P. Brooke, Jr., cornet soloist. Ragtime music Tuesday and Thursday. Many good things to eat."

When the leaves began to fall and the winds began to blow cold off Lake Michigan, Brooke left his Casino to the "various bazaars, dog, cat and flower shows," and headed south for a repeat performance in his Winter Garden in New Orleans. Chicagoans bid him good-by and contented themselves as best they could until Brooke would return to Chicago with the bluebirds and daffodils and again make Brooke's Casino ring with popular music and ragtime.

Chicagoans waited. A regular procession of traveling bands came to Chicago that summer. They came by twos and threes, and opened in this amusement park and that. After their engagements they were followed by other bands. All summer the parks were filled with band music. But Brooke never opened.

Why? Chicagoans could only speculate. Perhaps the "various bazaars, dog, cat and flower shows" did not produce sufficient revenue during the winter months to carry the venture. Perhaps there was internal trouble among the stockholders. Perhaps competition took the play away from Brooke, but this was difficult to accept, for Brooke had been a favorite son for many years and had a tremendous following. Perhaps Brooke was simply tired of it all.

After some months went by and the Casino didn't open, William Morris, prominent booker of vaudeville and variety shows, took over. He changed the name to Concert Garden and filled it with dog and pony shows, soft-shoe dancers, and blackface comedians.

Today the building still stands, not much changed in outward appearances. It is now known as the Eighth Street Theatre and has been occupied for many years by the radio troupe known all over America as the WLS Barn Dance.

The curtain was rung down the following year on Brooke's mysterious fading from the band picture, with a brief statement: "On April 11, 1907, Thomas Preston Brooke filed bankruptcy papers in the United States District Court of New Orleans, listing liabilities of $82,583 and assets of $18,864, including his music library, valued at $15,000."

Fourteen years later came the anticlimactic announcement: "Thomas Preston Brooke died on September 20, 1921, in his home at 4160 Drexel Boulevard, Chicago, after an illness of two years."

During the years while Brooke was knocking himself out with

solid bookings around the calendar, Innes was also making hay all over the United States and Canada. Such solid bookings provided steady jobs for his musicians, and many of the men he selected in 1894 for his Festival Band were still with him. Outstanding veterans were the celebrated saxophone trio of Morin, Shaap, and Ragone. Ben Bent had died in 1897, and after several replacements Innes secured the services of Bohumir Kryl as cornet soloist.

After two years with Brooke, Kryl had played a short engagement with the Duss Band at Madison Square Garden in New York. This was an excellent organization of fifty men, among them being such stars as Gardelle Simons, soloist on trombone, and P. C. Funaro, soloist on euphonium; but Duss didn't rate with Sousa or Brooke, and when Innes offered him a job Kryl took it. This turned out to be a fortunate choice, for it was with Innes that Kryl made his greatest fame as a cornet virtuoso.

The first taste Kryl had of life with Innes was a four months' transcontinental tour early in 1902, during which he faced over one hundred and fifty audiences, for each of which he played an average of two programed solos plus several encores, an estimated total of over six hundred solos for the tour. To the uninitiated this heavy schedule would have come as a blow, but Kryl had played two years with Brooke, during which he had come to regard such a man-killing schedule as only normal.

Kryl's spectacular solos on the cornet became the talk of the country and helped increase the drawing power of the Innes band. In 1903, to appease Kryl's mounting ego, Innes made him assistant conductor as well as premier soloist, and Kryl's name was carried in the advertising only a little smaller than the name of Innes.

About this time Innes hit upon an idea for further increasing the ticket sales at his engagements. Not content with bringing his band and great music to a community, he began stirring up local participation in music by organizing home talent of various kinds into choruses and bands. This aroused interest in the appearance of Innes more widely than would otherwise have been possible, and it turned out to be a good promotional scheme.

But such efforts were difficult to carry on and some of them were failures or backfired. One such was the engagement in Indianapolis in the summer of 1904. Innes was booked in the Fairbanks Resort, and he set about organizing a children's chorus which was to sing with the band. Just when the project was about to bear fruit, it occurred to some members of the Women's Christian Temperance Union that liquor was sold on the premises of the Fairbanks Resort. A campaign of boycott and reprisals was started. The churches of the city got behind the campaign and fought Innes so hotly that after one week Innes pulled stakes.

Kryl continued to be the most sensational single attraction in the band. Innes' Band was at its peak, and afforded Kryl the opportunity of playing before the greatest audiences of the times. Although he continued to solo with his own band for another twenty-five years, for sheer virtuosity Kryl probably never excelled or equaled his phenomenal performances of this period.

When Innes' Band appeared in Lincoln, Nebraska, in September 1904, the *Evening News* carried a story which shows how Kryl's audiences reacted. The writer commented on the performance of the band and then continued: "It remained for Bohumir Kryl, in his rendition of *Dudu* with variations, to arouse the audience to the highest pitch of enthusiasm. He has marvelous command of the instrument and, notwithstanding his display of technique, managed to preserve the lacelike delicacy of tone in the finer lifting passages. In response to the continued applause, he rendered *Psyche* and took the house by storm, and then the *Carnival of Venice,* in which he once more demonstrated his complete mastery of the instrument."

In May of the following year, when the Innes band played in Los Angeles, the papers were full of comments on Kryl. The *Examiner* critic said, "About Kryl there is no question—even without his wonderful mass of tangled flaxen hair he would be a musical wonder. He is both artist and magician. Caruso of the golden voice might almost envy Kryl his artifical golden throat, for Kryl sings through his cornet with a rich, clean-cut tone that carries no suggestion of metal with it."

The critic on the Los Angeles *Daily Times* was even more impressed with Kryl's performance. "Kryl is a wonder—an instrumental freak," the critic said. "He played a lot of things on his cornet. He began with *Kryl's King Carnival* . . . winding up with a skyrocketing note of a minute duration in *Kilarney,* the ever popular.

"In triple tongueing, in attainment of very high notes and in terrific coloratura work, Kryl is probably unexcelled in the world. When he had shown off high notes, the people were startled at a tremendous low tone coming from somewhere—down, down, down it went, all the time coming, as you finally knew, from Kryl's

*In 1902, when Kryl
first joined Innes
he wore his wavy locks
close-pruned.*

magical cornet, until the notes would have registered bass on the scale, absolutely of deep trombone character. How Kryl effects these notes, he himself does not know—they are of startling quality to anyone understanding the nature and limitations of a brass instrument."

While Kryl was not the only cornetist who could play below the fundamental range of the instrument, this trick was limited to a very few with exceptional embouchures. These low tones, which Kryl himself couldn't expalin, were what the physicist calls "difference tones." A man with sufficient control of his lips, or embouchure, can produce two tones on his instrument at the same time. The difference in frequency between these two tones becomes the "difference tone" sounded.

For simplification, let us say he produces the frequency of B♭ (first partial, or fundamental), which is 233 cycles per second, and the frequency of F, a fifth above, which is 349 cycles per second. The difference between the two is 116 cycles per second. This is the frequency of the B♭ which is one octave below the fundamental of the cornet and is the fundamental of the trombone.

An important part of the trick is to shape the oral cavity so that the resonance favors the difference frequency over the frequencies of the two tones; otherwise, the two-tone chord is heard and not the difference tone.

A number of soloists have exploited their ability to play these chords. Joseph DeLuca, euphonium soloist with Sousa in the twenties, featured three-note chords in his solos. August Helleberg, bass-tuba artist with Sousa, became noted because of his ability to play four-note chords.

Kryl attracted a lot of attention, not only by his superb solo playing but also by his new hair-do, referred to above by the Los Angeles *Examiner* critic. In 1902, when Kryl first joined Innes, he wore his wavy locks close-pruned. In 1903 he continued his Spartan hair-do. But after watching and hearing Creatore for several years, and noting the growing success of Marco Vessella and other new Italian maestros, all of whom sported long and flowing heads of hair, Kryl decided he was overlooking an open door to immortality. Early in 1904 he began boycotting the barbers, until his hair became a massive tangle of kinky, tawny tresses. From that day on, this leonine mane was a Kryl trademark.

After four years with Innes' Band, Kryl decided he was too big for the job, and early in 1906 he launched his own band. His first tour took him to Riverview Park in Chicago. Here he played in direct competition with Innes' Band and became one of the principal competitors of Innes for as long as Innes remained in the band business.

Solo-cornet duties in the Innes band were delegated to Herman Bellstedt, great German soloist. Bellstedt was a prominent musical figure in Cincinnati, associated with the best in band, symphony, and opera of this great musical city. Although he was an acknowl-

edged virtuoso on the cornet, he lacked the flair for the spectacular which Kryl possessed, and at the box office Innes felt Kryl's absence.

About this time Innes was interviewed concerning bands and the future of the band business. In this interview he spoke of "new bands that are good but will have to battle for a place for themselves." Here was the experienced and wise and successful bandmaster peering into the future. Innes went on to mention the most notable of these as "Pryor's, Weil's, Morin's Kilties and one or two bands of exclusively Italian membership." He did not mention Kryl's band, and this interview took place in August, following the tough summer during which Innes had to buck Kryl in Chicago. It is felt that Innes was not entirely candid in this interview.

Not only did Innes fail to pick Kryl as one of the "most notable" of the new bands, but he picked only one winner: Pryor. None of the others came even close to making the big time. Innes may have had Creatore in mind when he spoke of the Italian bands, but also he may have had in mind Vessella, Ferulla, Gargiulo, Philippini, Rosati, or Tommasino; and only the Creatore band, out of a score of Italian bands, achieved national prominence. Furthermore, looking back today, one wonders why he didn't include Conway in his list, to say nothing of Phinney and Weldon and Duss and Weber and Short and Nevers and Sweet and several others, all of whom rated either on a par with Weil or certainly above the Kilties.

Even though Innes proved to be a poor prognosticator, he did throw an interesting light on the growth of the band business during the previous twenty years or so. "When I first went into the business as a band director," reminisced Innes, "there were just two summer places employing bands of the first class. Today it is safe to say there are two hundred."

Innes could have done a good turn for posterity if he had made a list of these two hundred places, for a mere reading of the list today would fill many an oldster with nostalgic memories. In the absence of such a list, below are about fifty of the names, gleaned from extensive reading about bands of this era. These are arranged very roughly by state or city and from east to west.

New Hampshire   Hampton Beach Casino
Massachusetts   Nantasket Beach; Point of Pines (near Boston)
Providence, R.I.   Crescent Park
New York   Manhattan Beach; Hamilton Fish Park; Madison Square Garden; Luna Park (Coney Island); Golden City (Long Island)
New Jersey   Asbury Park; Atlantic City Steel Pier; Lincoln Park; Young's Pier
Washington, D.C.   Luna Park
Philadelphia   Willow Grove; Washington Park on the Delaware; Lincoln Park
Pittsburgh   Luna Park
Cleveland   Luna Park
Cincinnati   Zoological Gardens
Detroit   Electric Park; Boulevard Park
Chicago   White City; Riverview Park; Sans Souci Park; Bismark Garden; Coliseum Garden; The Shutes
Milwaukee   Schlitz Park; Pabst Park
St. Louis   Delmar Gardens; Forest Park Highlands; Lemp's Park; White City; Suburban Park
Kansas City, Mo.   Electric Park
Indianapolis   Fairbanks Resort
Lincoln, Ill.   Sunnyside Park

Herman Bellstedt was advertised as "Germany's Greatest Cornet Soloist."

Kentucky   Ludlow Lagoon
Memphis   East End Park
Nashville   Centennial Park
Waco, Tex.   Cotton Palace
New Orleans   West End; Athletic Park
Omaha   Krug's Park
Atchison, Kans.   Turn Garden
San Diego   Redondo Beach
San Francisco   Golden Gate Park
Oakland   Idora Park
Portland   Oak Park
Spokane   Natatorium Park

As related a few pages back, Kryl left Innes and formed his own band in 1906. On April 15 he opened in Kansas City, went on to St. Louis and Louisville, and finally to Chicago. Awaiting him in the Windy City was a great array of business bands, probably without parallel before or since. For a new band, just starting out, this was enough to defeat any except the most hardy, but Bohumir was most hardy.

He opened in Chicago in May, for twenty weeks at Riverview Park. This was not one of the better amusement parks, but it probably was the best Kryl could do for a starter. Admission to the park was ten cents and opened to the visitor all the wonders of a group of Igorote savages (left over from the St. Louis World's Fair of 1904), a two-headed monster from the tropical jungles—and Bohumir Kryl and his band of fifty players. Kryl advertised that he carried ten soloists with the band. Outstanding were H. Benne Henton, one of the all-time greats on saxophone, and Jaroslav (Jerry) Cimera, trombone virtuoso. The biggest attraction of all, of course, was Kryl and his cornet.

Innes opened on the South Side at White City amusement park and advertised "60 players and 12 soloists." Thus Innes topped Kryl by ten players and two soloists. Featured cornet soloist, who replaced Kryl when he left, was Herman Bellstedt, advertised by Innes as "Germany's Greatest Cornet Soloist" in an effort to offset Kryl's popularity.

The sensational Giuseppe Creatore, at the highest pinnacle of his fame, opened at Bismark Garden. Another popular Italian band, directed by Marco Vessella, held forth at Sans Souci Park. Even the Weil Band of St. Louis, which achieved some national fame by playing for the St. Louis World's Fair in 1904, came north this summer and took over Coliseum Garden. Innes battled it out for the weeks he was engaged, but when he left, the Banda Rosa under Eugenio Sorrentino moved into White City, only to be followed a few weeks later by the veteran Liberati and His Grand Military Band.

Thus was Kryl's band initiated into the company of business bands by a baptism of fire. As previously pointed out, T. P. Brooke, a successful veteran of more than a decade, failed to open his Brooke's Casino that summer. Although not fully realized at the time, competition among the numerous business bands was becoming so fierce that the years of Innes' Band were numbered, as were those also of Creatore and Vessella and Sorrentino and Weil. But in spite of the fact that he launched his new band during an era of the toughest competition Kryl survived while others perished, and he was destined to go on and on to greater and greater successes, for more than twenty-five years.

Twelve

PRYOR, CONWAY
AND SWEET LAUNCH
BANDS

*After 1910, Pryor abandoned the regulation tour and
devoted most of his time to recording for the phonograph.*
CULVER SERVICE

After returning from his third European tour with Sousa in the summer of 1903, Arthur Pryor resigned and began forming his own band.

From Sousa's Band he took Simone Mantia, wizard on the euphonium and also an accomplished trombone soloist. It is said that on more than one occasion, when Pryor was ill or unable for other reasons to play his solo with Sousa, Mantia would lay down his euphonium, pick up his trombone and substitute for his friend, playing the same solo which Pryor was scheduled to play, and playing it nearly as well, if not equally well. Pryor and Mantia had grown up together in the Sousa band and had become close friends. Pryor appointed Mantia assistant conductor of his new band, and these two great musicians worked together in Pryor's Band for twenty years or more.

Pryor also raided his father's band, the 4th Regiment Band of Missouri, which his father had directed since 1897. Pryor knew the caliber of the men in this band and valued the sound musical training they had received from his father. Among the players he enticed away were his two brothers, Walter and Sam.

Pryor was a product of this same school. He was born in St. Joseph, Missouri, in 1870, one year before his father organized Pryor's Band. Throughout his seventy-two years of life he was never out of sight and sound of a band. When he was six, he studied piano with a local teacher and he learned violin and cornet from his father. By the time he was eleven he had mastered the valve trombone and was playing in Pryor's Band, along with his two brothers, Walter on cornet and Sam on drums. After he had spent five years on valve trombone, some good fate influenced him to take up the slide trombone, the instrument he was born to play.

When he was eighteen he became trombone soloist with Liberati, and when he was twenty-two he became a member of Sousa's New Marine Band. Pryor's best solo-playing days were spent with Sousa's Band, from 1892 to 1903. Sousa "made" Pryor, presenting him to the greatest audiences in America and Europe for more than a decade, supporting his solo performances with the superb Sousa band and assisting with his own sympathetic and skillful conducting. During his last few years with Sousa, Pryor's experience as assistant conductor convinced him that he was qualified to conduct a similar band of his own.

Pryor's Band played its first concert on November 15 at the Majestic

Theatre in New York, and the following year Pryor took it on a coast-to-coast tour. This was the practice of the Sousa band, and Pryor naturally thought it was the thing to do. But being a success-ful bandmaster was not as easy as it appeared to be while he was a member of the Sousa band. The tour was a financial flop, leaving Pryor three thousand dollars in debt to his musicians for salaries.

In 1905, while Sousa was making his fourth tour of Europe and while Innes and Brooke were making money hand over fist, Pryor led his band on its second coast-to-coast tour. This year he made a little money, a good part of which he paid over to his musicians for back salaries.

The following year, while Kryl's new band was receiving its "baptism of fire" in Chicago, Pryor made a third coast-to-coast tour. From it he managed to salvage a small net again, and made another payment to his musicians on his 1904 deficit. Finally, in 1907, after three hard years, he squared accounts with his musicians, paying them the last cent he owed them.

During the following two years Pryor made his regular coast-to-coast tours, a total of six by 1909. By this time he had convinced himself that touring was not for him. Everywhere he went during these six years he ran into Liberati, Sousa, Innes, Creatore, Vessella, Sor-rentino, and a lot of other business bands. Brooke had dropped out after the first year, but he was replaced by Kryl. Competition was becoming stiffer and stiffer, not only because more and more bands entered the business, but because the attendance everywhere was beginning to dwindle. After 1910, Pryor abandoned the regulation tour and devoted most of his time to recording for the phonograph.

Unlike Sousa, Pryor early espoused the phonograph, and for many years the name of Pryor's Band appeared on more phonograph rec-ords than probably the names of all other bands combined. He was a pioneer in recording band music. Various authorities set 1906 as the date of the first commercial recordings of instrumental music and 1912 as the date of the first commercial recordings of symphony orchestras, but Pryor began making recordings of his band for Victor as early as 1903, using the old amplifying horn and the mechanically actuated diaphragm cutting needle.

Operatic numbers by such artists as Caruso and the Reszke brothers were still being made at this time with only piano accompaniment. Pryor was one of the first to make special arrangements of instru-mental music expressly for recording purposes. These special arrangements made concessions to the crude recording mechanism of the time by eliminating the more delicate nuances and sticking to the bolder outlines of the music. It was not until six or eight years later that the original compositions were used in recording, and it was twenty years later before electrical recordings were made, using the microphone.

There are thousands of oldsters who can still remember the thrill which Pryor's early records gave them, when played on the old Victrola. This was a square box, surmounted by a tin horn which was shaped like a morning-glory blossom. The record turntable was driven by a spring mechanism which was wound by a hand crank. One winding was sufficient to play one record. Although much of the tone coloring of Pryor's Band was lost, at least the rhythm and the melody and the main harmony lines came through with spine-tingling effect.

For approximately a quarter of a century Pryor's Band made recordings for Victor, and the number of sides cut ran into the high hundreds, if not into the thousands. He recorded not only the favorite band pieces of the times but hundreds of special arrangements of operatic numbers. In the *Victor Book of the Opera,* published in 1912, Pryor's Band is listed as recording overtures, finales, marches, selections, and fantasias from approximately fifty operas. The well-known aria *Celeste Aïda* he recorded as a trombone solo. Pryor on trombone and Emil Kenecke, former cornet soloist with Innes, recorded *The Fatal Stone* from *Aïda* as a duet, with Pryor's Band accompaniment. The famous soprano and tenor duet in *Miserere* from *Il Trovatore* was recorded by Pryor on trombone and Walter Rogers, former cornet soloist with Cappa and Sousa.

In the recording of operatic numbers can be seen the fine hand of Simone Mantia. In addition to playing and conducting with Pryor, Mantia was for twenty-five years first trombone and orchestra manager with the Metropolitan Opera, and knew opera literature "wrong side out and hind side before," to use one of Pryor's Missouri expressions. Pryor and Mantia, who usually saw eye to eye on everything, were an unbeatable team in this type of work.

After Pryor had thoroughly demonstrated the merits of recording band music, many musicians from the great business bands forsook the rigors of traveling and joined the ranks of the various recording studios, Sousa's protests against the deficiencies of "canned music" notwithstanding. In addition to the cornetists Kenecke and Rogers other early deserters from the business concert bands were Leo Zim-

Mantia,
euphonium and
trombone virtuoso,
joined Pryor's Band
as assistant conductor.

merman, who succeeded Pryor in Sousa's Band; Leroy Haines, trombone soloist with Innes, and Bert Smith, who formerly trouped as trombone soloist with Pryor. Even Herbert L. Clarke, during the years when he was Sousa's right-hand man, was under contract with both Victor and Edison to record cornet solos, and he took time out from Sousa's Band to make numerous recordings during 1908 and 1909. This exodus from the business concert bands increased in tempo from year to year, and not only told in plain words the increasing popularity of recorded music but also the dwindling popularity of the business band.

In spite of Sousa's outspoken opposition to the phonograph and recorded music even he made a number of recordings. By 1912, Sousa had made fifteen or twenty sides for Victor. Notable among these are the *Der Freischütz* overture, the *Grand March* from Verdi's *Don Carlos,* the *Rakoczy March* from Berlioz's *Damnation of Faust,* the *Fest March* from *Tannhäuser,* selections from *Lohengrin, Meistersinger,* and *Siegfried,* and even his own *El Capitan!*

During the summer of 1904, Pryor began an engagement at Asbury Park, N.J., and for seventeen consecutive summers he played a month there. Several years later he accepted an engagement for a month at Willow Grove Park, going there in the spring, preceding his summer engagement at Asbury Park. His band became a regular attraction there for ten consecutive years.

He generally vacated Willow Grove just before Sousa came on, and often it was possible during the transition to stage a baseball game between the Sousa and Pryor players. Both bandmasters were baseball fans and close friends, and they enjoyed this form of relaxation and fun. No records of the scores or batting averages of this long series were kept, but in 1916 an exciting game was played, the startling results of which have come down to us. Sousa pitched for his team, and the score was: Sousa, 16; Pryor, 29. Apparently musicians are strong on offense but weak on defense.

The same year that Pryor launched his band and started slugging it out with competition over the band-touring routes, Patrick Conway started his own band in a quiet way. Conway was born in Troy, N.Y., and he spent almost his entire life within a small realm of central New York State. In 1895, at the age of thirty, he went to Cornell University to teach music. Within a few months he established the Cornell Cadet Band, which he directed until 1908. In 1897 he also became conductor of the town band of Ithaca. The latter band became the starting point for his famous career.

In 1903 he accepted an invitation to take his Ithaca band to Willow Grove for a concert, and his performance so pleased the audience that he became an annual attraction there for twenty years. In 1906 he cautiously journeyed a few miles farther from home and took his Ithaca band to Young's Million Dollar Steel Pier, Atlantic City, where he staked out a second claim, to which he returned year after year.

In 1908 he changed the name of the Ithaca band to Patrick Conway and His Band. It was at this stage of his band career that he began bringing in the best musicians he could find, to take over the first and solo chairs. He found that there were many top-notch players who were willing and glad to sign up with Conway for the summer months. Many of these musicians toured with Sousa, Kryl, Liberati, and other national business bands during the fall, winter, and spring seasons but welcomed a permanent and fixed engagement for the summer months. This was what Conway offered, and if the musicians could arrange it, they took a breather from the strenuous touring and settled down for the summer at Willow Grove and Young's Pier.

Not every conductor could attract such men. Conway not only paid top scale, but he made it a pleasure to play under his baton. On the podium he was every inch a gentleman. He was quiet, considerate, appreciative, and extremely competent. Although he was strict and insisted on the highest musical performance from his men, he

On the podium
Pat Conway was every
inch a gentleman.

was a conscientious and thorough musician who commanded everyone's respect.

Patrick Conway was remarkable for making such a deep and lasting impression on the American public with "low pressure" methods and with what was essentially either a local or a "pickup" band. He did not tour regularly with his band, as did Sousa, Innes, and Liberati. He did not enlarge or extend the reputation of his local band by composing, as did Reeves, Missud, and Downing. He played the cornet well, but he was not a soloist with his band, as were Pryor, Innes, and Liberati with theirs. He resorted to none of the extravagances of Innes and Brooke, each with his "largest tuba ever built," nor did he cultivate eccentricities on which to build notoriety, as did Creatore and Kryl.

Pat Conway was a musicians' musician, and he built his firm reputation on the high standard of his musical performances. In the beginning he was a teacher, and he remained essentially a teacher to the end, but he knew musicians, he knew good music, and he had a genius for quickly molding a group of talented players into a highly skilled performing band. He did not have at any time a permanent band, and his bookings were short and intermittent. But he could attract the finest musicians for a brief engagement, and through his kindly manner and phenomenal grasp of music he could make them play so well that his bands were widely celebrated for their musical excellence.

A couple of years after Pryor and Conway launched their new bands, Al Sweet and His White Hussars opened a whole new market for bands, as the modern merchandise manager would say. As has been pointed out several times in recent chapters, the regular band market was being oversupplied, and at the same time, the demand for band music was beginning to dwindle. By 1910 a number of the weaker bands were on the point of discontinuing operation, when this new market was opened up and they were given a few more years of life. This was the chautauqua market, and for fifteen or twenty years Al Sweet was known in music circles from coast to coast as Mr. Chautauqua, leader of Al Sweet and His White Hussars.

Around the turn of the century Al Sweet began to make a name for himself as cornet soloist and conductor of Sweet's Band and Orchestra. His engagements were mostly fairs during the summer, lyceum and vaudeville during the winter. He then drifted into circus

For twenty years
Al Sweet and His White Hussars
were chautauqua headliners.

work, and for several years he was band director and cornet soloist with Ringling Bros. Circus. He finally hit upon a combination which clicked in a big way with the public when he formed his White Hussars and featured his singing band.

Sweet was a handsome man, with wavy blond hair and a million-dollar personality. He liked flashy uniforms, and he created one which became a sort of trademark. He dressed himself and his men in gleaming white uniforms, liberally festooned with gold braid. White capes lined with white silk were rakishly draped over their shoulders. On their feet they wore knee-length, white kid boots tooled with gold, and on their heads was an elaborate busby or shako, sur-mounted by a flowing white plume.

His act opened with the *Poet and Peasant Overture,* which was followed by a sentimental ballad entitled *The Boys of the Old Brigade.* Sweet often joked about how "corny" the song was, but his audiences ate it up. Sung in close harmony by male voices, this song stirred the emotions and often brought tears to eyes of his listeners.

Where are the boys of the old brigade
Who fought with us, side by side?
Shoulder to shoulder and blade to blade,
They fought till they fell and died.

The men then took up their instruments and played a Sousa march, during the playing of which they marched and counter-marched in their resplendent uniforms. Another instrumental number would be Beethoven's *Minuet in G,* Dvořák's *Humoresque* or the *Pilgrims' Chorus* from *Tannhäuser.* Somewhere in every program the White Hussars sang *Asleep in the Deep* or the *Winter Song,* to the "zum, zum, zum" of the bass voices.

Ralph Dunbar, impresario who created such chautauqua favorites as the Swiss Yodlers and Dunbar's Bell Ringers, heard the act and decided it was just what chautauqua audiences had been waiting for. Al Sweet's career from then on was made, and he left the Ring-ling Bros. Circus. For several months the White Hussars were dis-patched with lightning speed all over the chautauqua circuit, and they became one of the most popular musical attractions chautauqua audiences had ever known.

There was only one Al Sweet and His White Hussars, and they could not cover all the circuits that were then in existence. It seemed a shame to Ralph Dunbar that there would be thousands of people who could never hear this ensemble, and he decided to do something about it. He corralled a lot of good-looking young men who could sing and play band instruments, and formed other groups of White Hussars. These groups were turned out as from a production line, and it wasn't long before there were White Hussars everywhere.

Naturally this led to some confusion. How could the White Hus-sars be appearing simultaneously in Ohio, Missouri, Nebraska, New York, and Oregon? The resourceful Dunbar thought up other names. There then began to appear the Black Hussars, the Red Hussars, the Imperial Hussars, the Grenadier Guards, the Imperial Grenadiers, the Royal Dragoons, and others.

Chautauqua grew up around the idea of "packaged self-improve-ment" and "courses in culture." It started at Lake Chautauqua, N.Y., in 1874 and by 1900 there were about two hundred copies of the original, spread across the United States through Ohio, Iowa, and Michigan to Oregon and California. These were permanent chautauquas, established in a grove of trees and beside some body of water, with the typical open pavilion where the culture was dispensed.

The real boom in chautauqua began about 1903, when the idea occurred to someone that culture could be disseminated more rapidly by a flying squad of talent who would go from town to town over a set circuit. Pioneers in this movement were Keith Vawter, who staked out his claim through the Middle West, and J. Roy Ellison, who covered the territory west of the Rocky Mountains and in Canada with the Ellison-White circuits.

Brown tents began springing up everywhere. Beneath them were a plain wood platform and rows of green painted boards for seats, later to be replaced with the luxury of folding chairs. For five days or seven days each of these tents would be visited by a succession of lecturers on current topics, "readers" of the best literature, humorists, magicians, Negro quartets and jubilee singers, Swiss Yodlers, Bell Ringers, light opera companies (*Pinafore* and *Mikado*), and eventually by bands of various kinds. When all units of this troupe had come and gone, the brown tent would be taken down and moved to a town farther along the circuit, where it would be visited again by the same procession of talent.

This was the chautauqua idea, which grew to amazing proportions during the next twenty years and temporarily rescued many of the faltering concert bands. All chautauquas were cut from the same pattern. Always there was the brown tent, the platform and rows of seats, the smell of fresh-cut grass and weeds which gradually withered and decayed on the ground, the clouds of dust, the heat, the palm-leaf fans always in motion, the teams of horses, and later the automobiles, parked all over town, and the crowds of people from miles around, come to get their dose of culture for the year.

William Jennings Bryan was one of the headliners for many years, with his lectures entitled "The Price of a Soul," "Value of an Ideal," and "Prince of Peace," the last being delivered to chautauqua audiences over two thousand times. Also, there was Russell H. Conwell, whose "Acres of Diamonds" lecture was delivered over six thousand times, at one hundred to five hundred dollars per delivery.

Besides Al Sweet and the many Hussars other bands began to

travel the circuits. These included Liberati, Creatore, Vessella, Philippini and other Italian bands. Toward the end of his career Innes found it expedient to take his band on the chautauqua circuits, and Kryl became a headliner for about ten years.

Sousa disdained this sort of engagement, after one irritating experience. His booker was finding it difficult to obtain engagements on the West Coast. Even at bargain prices there was a disappointing number of takers. In desperation Sousa accepted an offer by J. Roy Ellison, who promised him a full schedule in this territory, which he knew so well. Ellison apparently drove a hard bargain with Sousa and then went out and sold the Sousa band on the Ellison-White circuit at a high price, clearing a reputed fourteen thousand dollars in a few weeks. This so angered Sousa that he vowed he would never again turn the booking of his band over to a chautauqua or travel one of their circuits.

Other bandmasters with less determination and less demand for their bands, especially when the concert-band business began to dwindle after 1910, were glad to accept the sure schedule guaranteed by the chautauquas, even though it meant less money.

Sweet was mostly tied up with Redpath, which had a big territory and operated out of four offices, in Chicago, Columbus, Cedar Rapids, and Kansas City. Redpath had five-day and seven-day circuits, and year after year, for nearly two decades, Sweet took his White Hussars over the various circuits, until he had covered practically every sizable town in twenty or more states.

At the height of the chautauqua movement there was hardly a nook or corner in the United States that wasn't blanketed by one of the many circuits. Swathmore covered the North Atlantic states, Alkahest the South Atlantic, Radcliffe, with offices in Washington, covered the South, and Ellison-White the Pacific coast. The central states were the happy hunting grounds of the chautauqua, and besides Redpath there were Louis Alber working out of Cleveland, Whiteside out of Indianapolis, Mutual and Lincoln both out of Chicago, and the Britt System out of Lincoln, Nebraska.

The chautauqua season for Sweet usually opened about the middle of April and lasted for twenty weeks or more, ending in early September. Practically every day during this time Sweet put on two programs, one in the afternoon and one in the evening, a total for the season of two hundred and seventy or more. For the afternoon appearance the White Hussars usually wore a more subdued costume, consisting of a blue coat, white flannel trousers, and white shoes. This device saved a lot of cleaning bills on the all-white uniforms, which were used only for the night performance.

Sweet once recalled a crisis when the white flannels were sent out to be dry-cleaned. Through some mishandling they found their way to a steam laundry and were not returned in time for the afternoon concert. The audience sat for three quarters of an hour under the hot tent, fanning themselves, waiting for the White Hussars to begin. Eventually a truck rolled up to the dressing quarters and dumped the trousers out. The men pulled them on with all speed. There was considerable confusion even in this simple operation, for the trousers had shrunk and nobody was sure he had his own.

When the troupe lined up on the platform and began the overture, they looked more like a bunch of comedians than a concert group, for the bottoms of their trousers struck them anywhere from their shoe tops to just below their knees, and some of the trousers were so tight the men had difficulty marching.

The White Hussar uniforms were expensive and the men were cautioned about taking good care of them. They were to be donned only shortly before the evening concert and were to be removed immediately afterward. Sweet had special difficulty in preventing some of his men from wearing their uniforms after the concert, for the men had found that in their flashy uniforms they were irresistible to the local girls, whereas they got nowhere when they changed to civilian clothes.

Being a headliner, Al Sweet and His White Hussars usually appeared on the last day of the chautauqua. This arrangement was more than a recognition of Sweet's top billing: it was a bit of fiscal strategy. On the last day of the chautauqua the superintendent and the local guarantors put on a season-ticket sale for the next year, and it was important that everybody be made to feel well entertained and uplifted and full of culture on this day. The fate of the ticket sale sometimes decided whether or not the chautauqua would return the next year.

This position on the flying squad of talent carried with it much of the responsibility felt by the man in the cleanup position in the batting order of a baseball team. With the fate of next year's chautauqua resting in a large degree on him, Sweet and his men must always be in the pink. Such a responsibility would have worn down any ordinary man, but Sweet carried this load lightly for many years and he seemed to thrive on it.

The chautauqua remained one of the principal markets for business bands until the twenties. But eventually it, too, failed—suddenly and with little warning. This debacle occurred near the end of the business-band era, leaving only a few important bandmasters in the field, such as Sousa, Pryor, and Conway, who had never put their trust in chautauquas.

Thirteen

SOUSA
WORLD TOUR
AND
WORLD WAR I

The Navy granted Sousa special leave to complete the summer tour in 1917, during which he wore his Navy uniform.
CULVER SERVICE

Sousa had planned to follow his fourth European tour, in 1905, with a two-year tour of the world, but contractual difficulties in the Australian sector of the tour caused the whole project to be canceled late in 1906.

Sousa had found his European tours a welcome escape from the dog-eat-dog competition in the United States among the increasing number of business bands. In 1906 he looked forward to escaping to greener pastures for two whole years. If this was a pleasing prospect in 1906, it became more so in the following three years, as competitive conditions grew progessively worse.

There could be no world tour in 1907, so Sousa filled the year with strenuous activity, as if he would drown his disappointment in work. Herbert Clarke left the sanctuary of his farm and joined Sousa in Atlantic City on July 1. There followed a continuous tour for the next nine months which took the band as far as San Francisco and led through twenty-four states. In the Middle West, Al Sweet and His White Hussars were beginning to create quite a sensation on the chautauqua circuits.

There was no world tour in sight in 1908, and Sousa busied himself with his Willow Grove engagement and a fall and winter tour. Liberati and Innes had defected from the regular ranks of the concert band and had accepted bookings on the chautauqua circuits.

By 1909 there was still no prospect of a world tour, so Sousa made another transcontinental tour to San Francisco and back, taking in a side trip through Quebec and Ontario in Canada. While on the West Coast, Sousa learned that Innes had been forced to give up his band. He had accepted a position as musical director in chief of the Alaska-Yukon-Pacific Exposition, held in Seattle from June 1 to October 15. In this position he was responsible for engaging all musical talent for the fair. Both Brooke and Innes, two of the most respected contemporary bandmasters and warm friends of Sousa, had fallen by the wayside.

The year 1910 opened, and still the world tour was questionable, although Sousa was continuing to work on arrangements. As he went through his regular routine, Sousa nursed a new apprehension about the future of the business concert band. Trouping along the various vaudeville circuits were an increasing number of saxophone ensembles: quartets, sextets, and octets. Most successful and famous of these were the Five Nosses and the Six Brown Brothers. Also, bands of six, eight, or ten players on assorted instruments were becoming popular as purveyors of ragtime, a type of music best played by small groups of musicians. While these small musical acts probably did not take a single engagement away from Sousa, he could see that tastes were changing, and that the traveling concert band was no longer the great and unique attraction it had been.

Sousa was greatly relieved at the end of his summer season to find that arrangements finally had been completed for the long-awaited world tour. Since the tour would not start until November, Sousa set out for one of his favorite sports, which was hunting in the swamps of the Patuxent River, off Chesapeake Bay. This was his way of obtaining recreation and of conditioning himself for the strenuous trip around the world. As it turned out, the exact opposite resulted, for he contracted malaria fever and nearly stopped the tour before it began.

The world tour eliminated the Sousa band for a year from competition with other bands in America, and they made the most of it. As for the Sousa band itself, seldom if ever has a band traveled so far, endured so many inconveniences, played so few concerts to such small audiences, and made so little net profit. Never again did Sousa take his band overseas, not even to England.

The band Sousa hired for the tour was comprised of sixty-six bandsmen, plus Miss Virginia Root, soprano, and Miss Nicoline Zedeler, eminent German violin virtuoso. Sousa and the band's physician, Dr. Lowe, made the entire personnel an even seventy persons.

The band assembled in New York on November 2 for rehearsals. When Miss Zedeler returned from a trip to Europe to join the band, she was met at the ship by Sousa. She coyly remarked that this was the first time she had ever been met by a king, and presented Mr. Sousa with fourteen trunk checks. Many of Miss Zedeler's friends had given her trunks as appropriate gifts for the tour. With a whimsical smile Mr. Sousa said, "Young Lady, you may select one of those trunks for the tour, but be sure to select one large enough to catnap on occasionally."

Sousa knew what he was talking about, for when all was ready there were one hundred and fourteen large trunks, labeled "Sousa and His Band."

The world-tour band was not the greatest of the many Sousa bands. Some of his regular musicians begged off. They gave various excuses, the favorite being that they were afraid of the water. It was an excellent band, however, counting in its ranks the following soloists and first-chair men:

Herbert L. Clarke, cornet
Ross Millhouse, cornet
Ralph Corey, trombone
John Perfetto, euphonium
August Helleberg, bass tuba
Ben Vereecken, alto saxophone
Joseph Norrito, clarinet
George Ahlborn, flute
Paul Senna, piccolo
A. J. Garing, euphonium

Other important members, some of them old-timers, included:

Marv Lyons, trombone and baggageman
Edwin Clarke, cornet and personnel manager
Clarence Russell, cornet and librarian
Edmund A. Wall, clarinet and mailman
Albert Knecht, tenor saxophone and historian
Stanley Lawton, baritone saxophone
Emil Mix, bass tuba

The tour officially started on November 6, Sousa's fifty-sixth birthday, with a farewell concert at the Metropolitan Opera House. The next day Sousa conducted a matinee in Danbury, Conn., after which he fell ill with malaria fever. He was too ill to conduct the evening concert in Waterbury, and Herbert Clarke, assistant conductor, took over. Clarke also conducted the next concert, a matinee at Middletown. For the evening concert that day, in the Concert Hall on Yale University campus, Sousa came up from Danbury and conducted. After finishing the concert, however, he had to be carried from the hall on a stretcher and was taken to the New Haven Hospital. He was desperately ill. To Herbert Clarke fell the double duty of conducting the band as well as playing his regular cornet solos. Not until the band reached Montreal about two weeks later was Sousa able to rejoin the band and take over the baton.

This incident shatters the popular fiction, widely circulated, that nobody but Sousa ever directed his band, and that if he were unable to direct, the band didn't play.

The day before Christmas, Sousa and His Band sailed on the *Baltic* from New York and arrived a week later in Liverpool, to begin the European part of the tour. Albert Knecht, who kept one of the most informative diaries of the tour and who alone kept track of the daily mileage, began making comments about the cold hotels and concert halls. In Hastings, on January 9, he wrote: "Tonight I became initiated into the 'candlelight circuit' hotels. I must say that it is not a bit pleasant to go to bed in a cold room by candlelight."

Later on Knecht avoided such understatements and told more fully what the band members had to endure. A few days later he wrote, "When I awoke, the room felt like an ice-box. This is positively the coldest proposition I was ever up against." Regarding the Portland Hall in Portsmouth, he lamented, "It was painful to work on our cold instruments, as the fingers would almost freeze." The band eventually arrived in Ireland, and in Limerick it played two concerts in the Royal Theatre "which is the most tumbled down affair that I have ever played in during my whole professional experience," said Knecht. "It has been condemned, and anyone would be doing the community a favor by touching a match to it. It is cold and damp in addition to lacking ordinary sanitary conditions. In spite of the vile surroundings, business was good and our audiences were very enthusiastic."

In Scotland conditions were no better. Mixing compliments with contumely, Knecht wrote what others were merely thinking. "Edinburgh is the most beautiful city we have visited so far. There is so much to it that any description I could give would be a joke. The Waverly Market Hall, where we played two concerts, was no joke. It is positively the coldest barn that I have ever sat in for two hours and a half. Furthermore, it is under the sidewalk of the Strand. It has no seats, so the audiences were made up of thousands of 'standees,' and we played to big houses at each concert."

In Wales the tour almost came to a tragic end. The evening concert in Merthyr-Tydfil was scheduled in the Drill Hall. The stage was too small to accommodate the entire band, so a local carpenter enlarged it by building an extension in front. It was a frail-looking affair but large enough to hold twenty-two men plus Sousa.

Everything held together until the *Fairest of the Fair* march. When the six trombones went to the front for one of those spectacular fanfares for which Sousa was famous, the entire structure split down the center. The half on which the woodwinds were seated wobbled but managed to stand; however, the right half, on which were seated the brass players, crashed five feet to the floor. Sousa went down with the brass section, landing on the floor on his back, the podium and music rack following him.

For a few moments there was pandemonium. On the floor were musicians, instruments, music, music stands, and loose boards all jumbled together. In the mix-up Sousa was most concerned about his glasses. When order was finally brought about and a canvass taken, it was found that nobody was seriously hurt. The concert was soon resumed, but in a unique fashion. As many players as possible were squeezed onto the platform, while the remainder were seated five feet below on the floor level.

This may have been the first time the Sousa band played a concert in this "unique fashion," but it was not the last. Many years later, in Gloucester, Mass., the band played in a movie theater with a stage too small to accommodate the entire band, at that time numbering eighty players. About half of them crowded onto the stage. The other half sat on the floor level, where several rows of seats had been removed.

Contrasting with this low estate, the band upon another occasion was elevated high overhead. In Minneapolis the band was asked to play in Foshay Tower. Everyone, including Mr. Sousa, was compelled to climb a long ladder to reach the bandstand, which was built high above the second-story setback. Regardless of the situation, Sousa was always equal to the occasion. In Longwood, Pa., the band once played a concert in Pierre Du Pont's greenhouse.

After two months in the British Isles the band started a sea voyage of approximately twenty thousand miles, broken by a month of engagements in South Africa and three months in Australia. On the jump from Cape Town, South Africa, to Hobart, Tasmania, the small *Ionia,* on which the band made the crossing, was caught in a bad storm and violently tossed about for a week. Food spilled on the deck, dishes and furniture were smashed, and Miss Root fell and cut a gash in her nose which required several stitches to close. Practically everybody on board became ill, including the ship's doctor, who was placed under the care of Dr. Lowe, the Sousa-band doctor. Amid rain and sleet and snow and ice and a violent wind the ship plowed on and finally reached port without serious casualties.

The stay in Australia, coming after the storm experience, was doubly welcome. The band played to large and enthusiastic audiences. When Sousa arrived in Sydney, relates Knecht, "the Sydney people gave us the biggest reception this band ever has had accorded it. An immense crowd escorted us in a parade from the depot to the Town Hall. It was headed by a great massed band composed of all the musicians of Sydney and surrounding towns. At the Town Hall, Mr. Sousa was welcomed by the Mayor. This afternoon the Sydney musicians gave us a reception. . . . Tonight we opened to a capacity crowd at the Town Hall." In Sydney alone fifty-six performances were given, and almost as many were played in Melbourne.

After a short tour of New Zealand the band left Auckland for Victoria, British Columbia, Canada, a passage of sixty-eight hundred miles, via the Fiji Islands and Honolulu. On Tuesday, September 5, Sousa and His Band crossed the meridian of 180°, popularly called the international date line. When some of the musicians learned that there were two Tuesdays during the twenty-four hours, they insisted that they be paid for an extra day. Sousa and Edwin Clarke, band manager, patiently tried to explain that this extra day, gained during the east-to-west course, merely made up for the day that had been lost as the tour progressed from west to east.

When the musicians would not accept this explanation, Sousa took them down to the captain's cabin and had the captain show them on the maps how the day had first been lost on the west-to-east course and was now restored to them on the east-to-west course. No deal! Four or five men held out for the extra day's pay, and threatened to take the matter up with the musicians' union when the band returned to the United States.

Another union controversy centered around the fact that in English countries the musicians were paid seven pounds per week. This made their pay eighty-five to ninety cents per week less than the scale of thirty-five dollars. When the band arrived in Los Angeles, C. L. Bagley, president of the Los Angeles musicians' union, was on hand to enforce these and other union demands. Bagley years later told about how he went to Edwin Clarke with the matter, who in turn referred him to Sousa.

"Clarke introduced me to Mr. Sousa as 'Mr. Bagley, president of the local union and a lawyer.' Mr. Sousa shook my hand and said, 'Ah, I see, you get them going and coming.' I replied, 'Yes, just like the band leaders.' Sousa smiled, as if he enjoyed the banter."

Albert Knecht made a tantalizing entry in his diary on October 21, while the band was playing in Los Angeles: "Lawton, Cunningham, Berry and Gulley terminated their engagement with the Band after tonight's concert." Were these the four men who had demanded double pay for Tuesday, September 5?

After landing at Victoria on September 19 the Sousa band started down the West Coast on the last lap of the world tour, which was also the twentieth annual tour of the United States. It was not one of the best of such tours, because of small attendance at many places. Both concerts at Los Angeles were poorly attended, but there was an explanation for this: President Taft was in town and took the play away from the band. But there was no such alibi in some other spots. At a matinee in Bakersfield, Calif., the great and renowned Sousa and His Band, just returned triumphant from an epoch-making trip around the world, played to an audience of less than one hundred people. At Des Moines, Iowa, a few days later, the band played a matinee and an evening concert in an auditorium with a seating capacity of seven thousand, but the attendance at the matinee was about three hundred and at the evening concert was about five hundred.

In Sheboygan, Wisc., the smells from a nearby tannery pervaded the concert hall, furnishing the musicians with a pun when they told about the Sheboygan concert: "a Sousa concert that really smelled."

In some places attendance was at capacity. In Chicago the band had an especially enjoyable time, not only because business was good but because of the visit paid to the band by Simone Mantia. At a matinee in the Auditorium Theatre, Mantia borrowed an extra uniform from Knecht, and when the trombones marched to the front of the stage in Sousa fashion, to play *Stars and Stripes Forever,* instead of the usual six trombones, there were seven. Sousa was not apprised of the stunt, but when he saw Mantia in the trombone ranks again, he smiled his appreciation and approval.

In Albany, after a matinee on December 6, Sousa called a rehearsal. In a neat little speech he thanked the men for their services on this tour. He confided that he had received a letter from Mr. Branscombe, the Australian manager of the tour, in which he said that while he lost sixteen hundred pounds sterling on the African, Australian, and New Zealand tours, he was not sorry, because "the Sousa band gave these countries such a musical treat as they had never had before."

On December 10 the final concert was given at the Hippodrome in New York, and the place was packed. Mr. Sousa was presented with a huge horseshoe of flowers which stood two feet higher than his head. After the concert everybody shook hands with everybody else, and the world tour ended very quietly.

Like Gilmore, when he returned from his disastrous tour of Europe in 1878, Sousa could honestly say that the band did not return with a lot of money, but, unlike Gilmore, he could not fully justify the tour on artistic grounds. Only in South Africa and in Australia did the band bring a revelation in good band music to worthy audiences. In the British Isles, Canada, and the United States, Sousa had merely been playing a return engagement.

But his press agents made the most of the impressive statistics. The band during thirteen months traveled 47,552 miles, according to the log maintained by Albert Knecht. The weekly pay roll was four thousand dollars. The expenses averaged twenty-five hundred dollars a day. The receipts averaged thirteen hundred dollars for every day the band played. No statistics were issued on the total number of days during which the band didn't play, but there must have been seventy-five or eighty of these idle days, during which the band merely sailed on and on.

Neither did press agents publish the facts about income versus outgo, but anyone could have figured that with salary and expenses amounting to approximately three thousand dollars a day and receipts averaging only thirteen hundred dollars a day, for the days played, there was a big deficit somewhere. This deficit, however, was spread over many guarantors, in many countries. Sousa, ever the good businessman, came out all right.

Herbert L. Clarke was one of the hardest-working men on the tour. He had some interesting statistics of his own. He found that on the tour he had played a total of four hundred and seventy-three programed solos, plus an equal number or more of encores.

Sousa bought a home in Port Washington, on Sands Point, Long Island, overlooking the Sound. This was to become, in later years, the rendezvous of musicians, composers, and other artists. Here, also, in his study on the second floor, Sousa wrote articles, pamphlets, and books, and composed music. One subject which immediately commanded his attention was the old one about the phonograph. During the world tour Sousa everywhere had heard recordings of his music for which he received no royalties and for which his musicians received no pay.

Once, in "Darkest Africa," he was introduced to some of the natives as Mr. John Philip Sousa. This didn't mean a thing to them. But when someone played a phonograph record of his *The Washington Post* march for them, they broke out in smiles of recognition. This incident naturally impressed Sousa with mixed feelings.

Another subject on which he labored was copyright. Foreign editions of his music were found in practically every country visited. Music dealers in some of these foreign countries thought John Philip Sousa was a native of their own country. Other men were reaping the fruits of Sousa's creative labors. Sousa was more than ever determined to do something about it, not only for himself but for all composers. Partly owing to Sousa's efforts during the following years, the American Society of Composers, Artists and Publishers was established, in February 1914. Sousa was one of the founders of ASCAP, along with Victor Herbert, George Maxwell, Nathan Burkan, and five other men.

The year 1915 marked several high points in Sousa's career. He was booked for fifty-two weeks and enjoyed the "greatest financial success of his career to date." His press agents added that it was also his greatest year artistically, but they offered no special evidence to support the claim. About half the year he was on a transcontinental tour, traveling twenty-one thousand miles and playing in two hundred and twenty cities. On July 23, in the Tacoma Stadium, Sousa played to the "largest audience in the history of the Sousa Band" up to that time.

Probably the most important engagement of the year was the ten weeks he spent at the Panama-Pacific International Exposition in San Francisco. He opened there on May 22, in the Court of the Universe, and at his first concert he was greeted by ten thousand cheering listeners.

As he had so often done for other special occasions, Sousa composed a march for the exposition, called *Pathfinder of Panama*. Although he played it often during the ten weeks, and other bands played it occasionally, it never struck the popular fancy, and quickly died after the fair.

Sousa consistently drew the biggest crowds, playing in competition with Patrick Conway and His Band, the U. S. Marine Band, the Philippine Constabulary Band, the Garde Républicaine Band, and Cassassa's Band, official band of the exposition.

The fair management conducted an experiment by placing first a band and then the official orchestra of the fair in the same playing spot, and noting the relative pulling power of each. Although the orchestra numbered eighty pieces and was unquestionably an excellent organization, the band—practically any band—outpulled it three to one. This merely proved that fairgoers prefer light entertain-

ment to serious music, as Theodore Thomas had so forcibly stated at
the Columbian Exposition in Chicago twenty years previously.

A few days before Sousa's engagement ended, Miss Louise Brehany
was scheduled to sing *The Last Rose of Summer* with the Sousa band. On
this occasion Sousa presented an almost unprecedented novelty. When
the soprano appeared on the platform, the audience were much puzzled to see Sousa lay down his baton, peel off his white calfskin
gloves, and start walking away from the podium. They soon saw that
Sousa was walking toward the piano, where he sat down and played
the accompaniment for Miss Brehany's solo.

The biggest novelty of all, however, was Sousa trying to out-Gil-
more Gilmore. This he tried to do on June 18, celebrated at the fair
as "Bunker Hill Day," the one hundred and fortieth anniversary of
the "shot heard round the world." For this big day Sousa had written a fantasia entitled *Dwellers in the Western World.* It called for a
massed band of one hundred and seventy-five players, a huge chorus,
an array of anvils, a regiment of soldiers from the U. S. Army, a
company of U. S. Marines, a squadron of U. S. Cavalry, and a de-
tachment of sailors from the U. S. Navy, the last being used to haul
through the Court of the Universe a golden chariot, in which was
seated a beautiful girl impersonating Columbia. The purpose of the
fantasia was to tell the story of the birth of the nation, its economic
and industrial development, its wars, and finally victory and peace.

The massed band, consisting of the three bands of Sousa, Conway,
and Cassassa, started the show. As the story began unfolding, the
vast pageantry was set in motion. When the chapter arrived de-
picting the industrial development of America, men began pounding
the anvils in true Gilmore fashion. Theme followed theme, the band
played, the chorus sang, and the armed forces paraded hither and
thither.

At the close the audience stood while the band played *The Star-
Spangled Banner.* During the last few bars of the music the great
United States battleship *Oregon,* anchored nearby in the San Fran-
cisco Bay, let loose with several broadsides from its great guns, which
rocked the fair buildings. The Sousa finale, at least, topped anything
Gilmore had been able to dream up.

Before Sousa left the San Francisco fair for the return tour to New
York, he signed a contract to appear regularly at the Hippodrome.
He had played there repeatedly, and the Sousa music had been a
favorite, but this was a long-time, permanent engagement. It called

for Sousa and His Band to appear daily from September through May. From Monday through Saturday of each week the band was to be a part of the shows, but on Sunday it was to furnish the entire program.

One day while the Sousa band was playing at the Hippodrome, Leopold Stokowski, the young, new conductor of the Philadelphia Orchestra, wandered in. He had never before heard such music as Sousa played, and he related, years later, the effect it had on him —an effect he never forgot. Said Stokowski: "The music swept me off my feet. The rhythm of Sousa stirred me, for it was unique. I tried to analyze my sensations. The music had such wonderful regularity. Someone else might have such regularity but he would not have the enormous drive and push. . . . They say that genius is doing something better than any other person does it. Sousa is such a genius. He is a genius whose music stands supreme as a symbol of the red-bloodedness of humanity."

Stokowski has given in these few words one of the most penetrating and accurate descriptions of Sousa's unique style of playing that we have. He put his finger immediately on the unique quality which made Sousa great and separated him from all others: the wonderful regularity which, at the same time, had such drive. Sousa did not speed up in the fortissimo passages nor slow down in the pianissimo. His tempo did not change: it was a steady, driving force.

Such sameness of tempo could become monotonous, but Sousa avoided any monotony by varying other elements in the music. Sousa's marches as published were considerably simpler than they were when played by Sousa's Band. He dressed them up for his own concerts. One of the devices used was varying the instruments. The first strain or melody was usually played as written, but the second received various treatments. Usually it would be played through first with the brass and piccolo subdued, then when replayed the cornets and trombones and flutes and piccolo would dominate. A similar contrast usually was given the playing of the trio. This came to be known as the Sousa style. Sometimes he would have players of these instruments march to the front of the stage and blaze away, but everything took place under the driving regularity of an unchanging tempo.

Probably even more important in the Sousa style of playing his marches were the dynamics. These were not indicated in the published music but were added by Sousa. The accents were generally conveyed through the percussion section, and Sousa became recognized as one of the very few bandmasters who thoroughly understood this section. No sloppy performance or faking would go with Sousa. He knew precisely what he wanted and he knew when the drummers delivered the goods.

Colonel Howard Bronson, Sousa musician from 1921 to 1929 and former president of the American Bandmasters Association, has said: "His own compositions were played with meticulous attention to dynamics, shading and tone coloring. The printed scores did not carry dynamic markings as actually played by the Sousa band. The wizard of the bass drum, Mr. August Helmecke, once asked Sousa why these markings were not indicated. Mr. Sousa asked Helmecke to do nothing about it until after his death."

Dr. Edwin Franko Goldman commented on this subject in an address in 1952. "Sousa did many tricks that he never wrote into the drum parts for his music," said Dr. Goldman. "He relied on Helmecke. All Sousa had to do was nod at Helmecke and he knew what Sousa wanted done. Since Sousa's death, Helmecke has been engaged in revising the drum scoring in a number of Sousa's compositions, adding the things which Sousa wanted."

Before "Gus" Helmecke died in March 1954, he had edited a number of Sousa's compositions, "adding the things which Sousa wanted." By January 1955 the Theodore Presser Company had printed the following, as edited by Helmecke:

> *Manhattan Beach*
> *Liberty Bell*
> *The Stars and Stripes Forever*
> *Hands Across the Seas*
> *King Cotton*
> *The Bride Elect*
> *Fairest of the Fair*
> *Invincible Eagle*
> *Directorate*
> *El Capitan*

"The present editions, based on Helmecke's memory, must, under the circumstances, stand as authentic," an executive of the publishing firm has declared.

Although it is true that Sousa never varied his tempo during one of his marches, it appears that he did increase his tempo steadily over the years. This observation has been verified by too many of Sousa's former players to be in doubt. Some of the men in his latest bands declare that he maintained a tempo of 136 cadence. While he was conductor of the U. S. Marine Band and for years later he stuck to 120 cadence, the "official" cadence of the United States armed forces. During the Gay Nineties, when Sousa's marches were danced to, as the two-step, he continued to hold down the tempo. But in later years he edged upward and upward until he was playing at 136 cadence, almost a galop.

Many interesting theories have been advanced to explain this speed-up, the most ingenious and believable being that by Emil Mix, bass tuba with Sousa from 1910 to 1912 and a long-time friend. Mix used to box with Sousa, and he found that Sousa had unusually short arms. Somewhat as a short pendulum on a clock tends to cause the clock to run faster, so the short arms of Sousa gradually accounted for the increase in tempo from 120 cadence to 136 cadence, over a long period of years.

This speed-up of the tempo was observed by his players before he was thrown from a spirited horse in 1922 at Willow Grove, but they claim that this tendency was more noticeable after the accident. As a result of the fall, Sousa seriously injured his right arm and shoulder, and it was quite painful for him to conduct. Gradually he lowered the point to which he raised his arm in beating time, invariably directing "below the waist." This foreshortening of his beat further increased the speed of the tempo, according to certain men who played with Sousa during the last few years of his life.

This increase in tempo over the years has nothing to do with what happened during an engagement by the Sousa Band in 1924, at Regina, Canada. Here was an instance when Sousa increased the tempo during the playing of a march—something everybody said he never did. Players in the band, however, declare that one day during the fair Sousa put some money on a horse in a race. The band played during the race, and Sousa watched his favorite over his shoulder. As the horses came around the last turn, Sousa's favorite started to pull ahead of the pack, and as it did so, Sousa unconsciously increased the beat until, as his horse crossed the finish line a winner, the band was playing a wild galop!

The United States declared war on Germany on April 6, 1917. About a month later word came to Sousa, through his friend, John Alden Carpenter, that Captain W. A. Moffett, Commandant of the

U. S. Naval Training Station at Great Lakes, would appreciate it if he would take over the training of Navy bands. Captain Moffett had been trying for a few weeks to set up a band school and had recruited about one hundred musicians, just enough to realize what a big job it was and that he needed a good man to take charge.

Sousa was sixty-three years old, but he immediately offered his services and accepted the rank of senior-grade lieutenant. He was under contract to fill his regular summer engagements, but after these were finished, he disbanded Sousa and His Band, on September 10, just a little more than two weeks before the twenty-fifth anniversary of its first concert. Sousa had intended to make an important event of the anniversary, but when the day arrived, he was busy with his new Navy duties.

For thirty-seven years Sousa had worn a full beard, ever since the time when, as a young man, he accepted the job of conducting the U. S. Marine Band. A few days before Sousa was to leave for his duties at Great Lakes, he attended the theater with Mrs. Sousa. Early in the show he left the Sousa box without explaining to his wife where he was going. She supposed some friend had called him out, and she paid no particular attention to the matter. Some time later Sousa returned—and Mrs. Sousa hardly recognized him. Somewhere he had located a barber and he had directed the barber to shave off his beard, leaving only a short, well-trimmed mustache. His feeble excuse to Mrs. Sousa was that he felt the war had to be won by young men. To the end of his life he remained clean-shaven except for the mustache.

With his enlistment in the Navy, Sousa won the distinction of serving with all three branches of the United States armed forces. His service with the Marines is well known. He served as a youthful music apprentice and as conductor of the Marine Band. When the Spanish-American War began, he offered his services to the Marines again, but there was no opening for him as bandmaster. He then applied to the Army and was accepted. Almost immediately after being accepted he became ill. Some authorities claim this illness prevented him from serving in the Army, but others say he was for a time musical director of the Sixth Army Corps.

Sousa remained in the Great Lakes Navy job for twenty-two months and turned out approximately one hundred band units comprised of three thousand trained musicians. The most spectacular part of his services was the formation of the famous Great Lakes

To the end of his life
Sousa remained clean-shaven,
except for the mustache.

Battalion Band, a giant organization comprised of nearly three hundred musicians. Its instrumentation and marching formation were novel, consisting of seventeen files of sixteen men each and one file of twelve drummers. Details are given below.

1st and 2nd files   32 trumpets in "F"
3rd and 4th files   32 slide trombones
5th, 6th, and 7th files   48 cornets
8th and 9th files   32 horns and altos
10th, 11th, and 12th files   24 euphoniums and 24 basses
13th file   10 small drums, 1 bass drum, 1 cymbal
14th file   16 saxophones
15th, 16th, and 17th files   48 "B" clarinets
18th file   flutes, piccolos, oboes, "E" clarinets

In the formation of the battalion the soprano brass instruments were placed on the right flank and the soprano reeds on the left flank. The drums came between the heaviest brass and the heaviest reeds.

This band became the Navy's "window dressing." It toured and paraded all over the country, assisting in recruiting for the Navy, in Liberty Loan drives, Red Cross drives, and Navy Relief drives. In June 1918 it made a special tour into Canada. Those hundreds of thousands who heard and saw this spectacular band marching down the avenue, with the incomparable "Peacock Kelly" strutting as drum major at the head of the band, can never forget the thrill they experienced.

During the summer of 1918 the Battalion Band was ordered to Kansas City to take part in "Old Glory Week" and gave a concert in Electric Park. In the audience Sousa noticed former President Theodore Roosevelt with his family. Sousa approached him and asked if there was anything special he would like to have the band play. Roosevelt replied: "It would make me very happy if you would play *Garry Owen.*" This piece was traditionally the one used by the cavalry when they were about to charge, and the Battalion Band played it for the old cavalryman, Colonel Roosevelt of the Rough Riders.

Directing the Navy-band school and conducting the Battalion Band were not enough for Sousa. During the first year in the Navy uniform he wrote and dedicated to his country's cause a group of new marches and songs, including the following:

> *The Boys in Navy Blue*
> *The Anchor and Star*
> *The Liberty Loan*
> *The Volunteers*
> *The Field Artillery*
> *Sabres and Spurs*
> *We Are Coming*
> *Blue Ridge*
> *Solid Men to the Front*
> *The Chantyman*
> *Bullets and Bayonets*
> *When the Boys Come Sailing Home*
> *In Flanders Field the Poppies Grow*

Some of these new compositions clicked with the public and were of great value as morale builders during the war.

Sousa came out of the Navy a lieutenant commander, and he wore the uniform of his rank for a time after his retirement from service. He could have obtained higher rank had he desired it, for twice during his term of service he turned down offers from Captain Moffett to upgrade him. Nevertheless low rank in the services always has been a sore spot with bandmasters and is often the subject of bitter jokes and banter among them.

During a tour after the war Sousa was sitting in the lobby of the Antlers Hotel in Colorado Springs, smoking his cigar, following a matinee concert. He was still wearing his lieutenant-commander uniform. Three elderly women approached him timidly, the most venturesome of the three finally mustering up enough courage to ask, "Pardon me, isn't this General Sousa?" Sousa slowly removed his chewed-up cigar from his mouth, smiled in his usual friendly manner, and replied, "No, madam, Major General; and by rights it should have been Field Marshall."

Fourteen

Liberati's medals
jingled and jangled
on his chest
when he bowed
to applause.

The business band reached its peak in 1910, or thereabout. It had been building up over a period of fifty years, ever since the day when Patrick Gilmore took over the Boston Brigade Band in 1859 and formed Gilmore's Band. For nearly thirty years Gilmore alone seemed able to manage this new kind of band.

Liberati was the first to launch a business band of his own, but he quickly failed. Innes formed Innes' Great Band in 1887 and was successful for a year or two but could not make a go of it. Liberati tried again but after two years gave it up. In 1892, Sousa demonstrated how to establish a business band, and in quick succession Brooke, Liberati, and Innes formed successful bands of their own.

Riding the crest of the upsurge of interest in adult amateur bands, these business bands prospered greatly, and new ones entered the field—Creatore, Pryor, Conway, Kryl, Sweet and many others. By 1910 there were the greatest number of nationally known business bands, the greatest number of amusement parks and fairs and "gardens" relying upon the business band for their main attraction, the greatest number of theaters and auditoriums and "opera houses" booking concert bands for winter entertainment—and the rosiest rose-colored glasses through which bandmasters and aspiring bandmasters looked into the future.

Ten years after this peak the business band was generally discredited and undone. This decade was the *Götterdämmerung*, "The Twilight of the Gods." Intense competition and price cutting took their toll. Audiences dwindled, siphoned off by the new attractions of the automobile, the phonograph, the movies, jazz, and vaudeville. Mediocrity set in, the newer and weaker bands hoping to cash in on the name of concert band without striving for the musical excellence which had made the concert band great.

Some bands were able to stave off collapse for a while by accepting chautauqua engagements. This meant smaller and less expensive bands, for chautauqua fees were low. When the chautauqua bubble burst in the middle twenties, these "minor league" bands promptly died off like flies, leaving only a few of the more hardy, such as Kryl and Sweet. In the "big league" by this time Sousa and Pryor stood almost alone.

Before 1910, Brooke had dropped out of the race, after a meteoric career. Before 1910, Innes had faltered, and was temporarily rescued only by recourse to chautauqua engagements. In 1913 he finally gave up and accepted a position as conductor of the Denver Municipal Band, a position he retained for five years.

In 1915 he broke out of Denver with his band and went to the Panama-Pacific International Exposition in San Francisco. The band was a favorite at the fair, which proved that Innes had not lost his touch. Two years later he took the Denver band on a short tour, which included engagements at the Canadian National Exposition, Toronto; the Corn Palace, Mitchell, S.D., and the Cotton Palace, Waco, Tex. The Denver band was subsidized by the city, and both of these trips were made to publicize the "mile high" city of Denver.

In 1916 he established the Innes School of Music in Denver, and this project was to occupy most of his time and energy for the remainder of his life. The school was of the correspondence type, and offered courses in a wide variety of music study. Seven years later, after the death of his wife, Innes moved operations to Chicago, where he established the National School of Music, in 1923. The primary purpose of this school was to train bandmasters. School bands were growing rapidly, and there was a great scarcity of bandmasters capable of directing them.

Several hundred students were graduated as full-fledged bandmasters from the Innes National School of Music. Today there are still some first-rate bandmasters at the head of good bands, whose only special preparation for the job was this correspondence course and whose proudest achievement is represented by their National School of Music "graduation diploma" posted on the wall of the band room.

After the death of Innes in 1926 several attempts by interested persons were made to continue the school, but without the magic name of Innes all such efforts failed. The final act in the liquidation of the Innes school took place in a basement of a factory building on the north side of Chicago in 1933, when the remaining books and literature were hauled off and sold as two tons of waste paper.

Creatore was driven from the regular concert-band field by his compatriots. By 1910, Italian bands in the United States were "a dime a dozen." Creatore followed the trend of the times for weak bands by turning to the chautauqua circuits, and from 1910 until 1916 was a chautauqua headliner. Other Italian bands followed him to chautauqua engagements, and soon Vessella, Tommasino, Philippini, and others were making it tough for him under the brown tents.

In 1917, World War I slowed Creatore and other Italian bands practically to a standstill. A wave of Americanism killed the fervor of the public for the kind of musical performances dispensed by the Italians. When Sousa disbanded his organization and went to Great Lakes, other bands offered their services in all kinds of patriotic activities, but this ingratiating gesture was denied the Italian bands because of the incongruity of aliens posing as American patriots.

Creatore accepted some chautauqua work for several seasons following the war, but he never again regained his prestige. He resumed regular concert-band touring by 1920, when he covered the Eastern states and parts of Canada, but he no longer found the warm reception he formerly enjoyed.

Following an especially disappointing summer tour by Creatore in 1924, manager Frank Gerts announced that in the future Creator would form a touring opera company. This venture was fairly successful for a few years, but it was abandoned in 1929. Creatore never went back to his band activity after that.

In 1935 he accepted a position as director of the New York City Symphony Orchestra, a Works Progress Administration project designed to furnish improvident New York musicians with some employment. When the WPA dole was abolished Creatore was again out of a job. During succeeding years he filled numerous engagements as guest conductor of various local bands.

In 1945, when Creatore was seventy-five years old, he formed a temporary "pickup" band and filled a few engagements. Two years later he made his last public appearance, when he was guest conductor of a Tri-Boro Pop Concert at Randall's Island. Five years later, at the age of eighty-two years, he died at his New York home.

Liberati's Grand Military Band had seen its best days by 1910. From a complement of eighty men in 1898 it shrank to fifty, then to forty, later to thirty, and finally to twenty, when he traveled the chautauqua circuit. But every band which played under the baton of Signor Liberati was, if not a great band, at least a good band, fully competent to entertain and give the patrons their money's worth, for there was always one constant: the dashing, dapper, colorful Liberati. Both as maestro of the baton and virtuoso of the cornet, Liberati could make almost any band sound like a first-rate organization.

In the many Liberati bands the euphonium soloist was always a strong feature. Starting with Erminio Giannone in his 1893 band, he successively headlined Philip Cincione, Pasquale Funaro, Joseph DeLuca, Salvatore Florio, and Armando Manzi, all outstanding artists. Other sections of his band were not as strong, but he seemed purposely to neglect the cornet soloist, and for good reason: Liberati himself was one of the all-time greats as cornet soloist and he could not brook a rival.

One time, when he hired R. E. Trognitz as saxophone soloist at the Kansas City Exposition, Trognitz played as his auditioning number Liberati's *Battle Cry of Freedom*. Liberati said, "You are engage, but I playa de solo me myself." Liberati was so jealous he reserved for his own performance even his own compositions.

Signor Liberati spent fifty-five years among English-speaking people, but up to the day he died his "fractured" English remained unchanged. He had no real need of changing, for he supplemented his amazing and rich dialect with eyes, facial expressions, and gestures which were most eloquent, even though often sidesplitting. If he hadn't been a big-time musician, he could have made an excellent living as a comedian or character actor.

When he became hopelessly entangled in the intricacies of spoken English, his merry eyes, mobile face, and expressive hands took it from there. His listeners sometimes did not get the full meaning of what Liberati was trying to convey, but they usually said they did. At the end of an involved exposition of some point Liberati would grimace and spread his hands in an open gesture, as if to say, "You see?" Most people would nod good-naturedly, but if they didn't, Liberati would merely repeat his gesture and go on to something else.

Liberati was an inveterate collector of medals. Nobody enjoyed more than the signor the thrill of having a new medal pinned to his dress coat. These medals held an Old World significance for him, and each one stood for achievement and a rise in the world of music. By the time he paraded across the chautauqua platforms, he was loaded down with medals of all shapes and kinds. They jingled and jangled on his chest when he bowed to applause, and were as much a part of his jaunty appearance as his well-trimmed and smartly twirled mustache.

In 1919, tiring of the constant traveling, Liberati, now seventy-two years old, decided he would take a job requiring less energy, and he accepted the position of bandmaster of the Dodge Brothers Concert Band in Detroit. After a year or two of this relative quiet the blood of the old trouper became restless, and he again took to the road, sometimes with his own band, sometimes as soloist.

In 1921 he visited Omaha and played in Krug's Park. A review of this program appeared in the Omaha *Bee,* and revealed that the magic showmanship for which he was always noted had not entirely left him, even in his seventy-fourth year.

"Several thousand people," the account read, "were on hand last Saturday night at Krug's Park to hear Signor Liberati, noted cornet virtuoso. It was estimated at the time when Sig. Liberati stepped to the front of the platform, erected in the center of the park, that fully 12,000 people were on the grounds, so anxious were they to hear this noted artist, who was last heard by Omahans at the Boyd Theater in 1907. Rendering a selection of his own composition, he held the audience spellbound until the last note was played, and the applause greeting the Signor was deafening."

Although Liberati was the composer of many pieces of music, none of them reached any great popularity. Toward the end of his life he hoped to supplement his income with royalties from his music. In 1921 he offered for sale the following compositions, complete with band arrangement: *Suffragette March, La Mia Speranza Valse, Belle of Manila Dance,* and *Pow Wow (Indian) March.* Royalties were meager, however, and in 1923 he resorted to teaching in New York, where he died in 1927.

In contrast to the business bands of Innes, Creatore, Liberati, and a host of others, whose best days occurred before 1910, the bands of five leaders enjoyed their greatest popularity and prosperity after 1910. These five bandmasters were Sweet, Kryl, Conway, Pryor, and Sousa, all but Sousa late starters in the business-band marathon.

Sweet and Kryl were the youngest of the lot, but survival was not a matter of age. In 1910, Innes and Sousa were both fifty-six years old, but Sousa's band survived Innes's band by more than twenty years. Creatore and Pryor were both born in 1870, while Conway was five years their senior; and yet Pryor's Band survived both Creatore's and Conway's bands by ten years.

Kryl and especially Sweet relied on chautauqua engagements during much of their careers, while Conway, Pryor, and Sousa had no truck with chautauqua operators. Sweet was one of the first to climb aboard the chautauqua band wagon, and he stayed aboard for nearly twenty years. As the chautauqua circuits grew in number and popularity, Sweet grew with the movement. By 1923 the chautauqua had grown until there were twelve thousand towns and villages visited by the various dispensers of culture, and the total number of culture communicants mounted to thirty millions annually. Such a booming business furnished summer work for a lot of bands. In addition to Sweet and others already mentioned, there sprang up the "kilties" bands, small groups of fifteen to twenty musicians dressed in native Scottish costumes.

There weren't as many "kilties" bands as there were "hussar" bands, but there were several. There were just plain The Kilties and the Kilties Concert Band, but there were also the Scotch Highlanders, under the direction of cornet soloist Turner Nearing, and Power's Kilties, under the direction of cornet soloist Murdock MacDonald, the latter being favorites on the Swathmore circuit in the early twenties.

There were other strangely appareled bands, such as Ewing's Zuave Band, dressed in Turkish costumes. William Maupin, a White Hussar alumnus, formed his own band and dressed the players in flashy hotel bellboy uniforms. Maupin's Band was popular on the Ellison-White circuit up to 1925. To be a hit on chautauqua, these small bands had to adopt showy or bizarre costumes.

Just when it appeared that this sort of entertainment could go on forever, the whole chautauqua movement collapsed like one of the brown tents in a windstorm. The automobile, the movies, and the radio had a great deal to do with it, but there were other reasons. Good talent ran out or switched to other fields. Cheap acts, more typical of the street carnival, were substituted. A quick and sudden revulsion developed, and within a few years the chautauqua under the brown tent was no more.

The bands that had escaped oblivion a few years before by accepting chautauqua engagements now had no place to go for succor, and they died on the spot. A few others, like Sweet's, managed to pick up enough work on the surviving circuits to last until the late twenties.

In 1933, at the Century of Progress Exposition in Chicago, Sweet revived his popular chautauqua act, calling it Al Sweet and His Military and Singing Band. This was the White Hussars act all over again, except for a slight change in uniform. While Al retained the all-white costume for himself as soloist and conductor, he cut down on cleaning bills by substituting for his men dark coats with white braid, dark shakos, and black boots.

For a year or more after 1933 he took his troupe on the road, advertising them as Al Sweet and His White Hussars, "direct from the Century of Progress." By this time Al's white costume was worn in spots, and he bought for himself a dark coat, dark shako, and black boots. The White Hussars were now black except for the trousers.

In 1910, when many bands were beginning to falter and fail, Kryl was forging ahead. Being young at the business, he was flexible and resourceful. He was an excellent businessman, and he managed to accumulate quite a lot of money along the way. He formed Kryl's Bohemian Band as a side line and made recordings for Victor and other record companies. By 1916 he had formed his own booking agency and music bureau, which managed a number of bands and other musical organizations. The magic name of Kryl was sufficient to gain acceptance for these new groups, and all of his ventures prospered.

When the war hit in 1917, Kryl would not be outdone by Sousa. Kryl followed suit, disbanded his band and was appointed director of all military band camps of the U. S. Army, accepting a commission of lieutenant. He also formed a monster Army band as his answer to Sousa's celebrated Great Lakes Battalion Band. This big

The White Hussars were now black, except for the trousers.

band was formed by combining three field-artillery bands, four infantry bands, and one band of regulars, a total of approximately two hundred and fifty players.

By 1919, Kryl was back in the band business. The Kryl music bureau began booking Kryl's talented daughters: Marie, concert pianist, and Josie, violin soloist. The following year Kryl started a neat arrangement for himself, directing his band on Redpath chautauquas during the summer and Kryl's Opera Company during the winter months.

Kryl was not overlooking any tricks which would bring him success, and he latched onto one of Gilmore's gimmicks—the anvil chorus. As he toured the chautauqua circuits, he carried along a set of anvils, which his men pounded in true Gilmore style. This was a novelty to Kryl's generation and established Kryl as a great innovator and showman.

From 1919 until the chautauqua folded along about 1925, Kryl was a headliner under the brown tents. After 1925 his music bureau managed to book Kryl's band at fairs, expositions, and other summer amusement spots. Kryl possessed tenacity and great survival instincts, and he managed to subsist for years on a meager fare which was not sufficient to sustain other bands.

Kryl continued to play his superb solos with the band, but they were not up to the standards of his earlier days. His interests were many and varied, and he had no time to keep in top playing condition. Besides his many music ventures he became an art collector and was said to have a fortune tied up in his paintings.

Musicians who played in the Kryl band during the twenties have many stories about his frugality. According to these players Kryl owned the uniforms of the band, and should a button be missing, Kryl took the replacement cost out of the man's weekly pay envelope. There were thirty men in the band, but only twenty railroad tickets would be purchased. The men were instructed that as soon as they boarded the train they were to "circulate" up and down the cars so the conductor could not count them. Whether this was Kryl's idea or whether he had a crooked manager who was "knocking down" on him the players were never able to figure out.

Kryl was a hard man to work for. The musician who made a mistake during a concert was in for trouble. One of Kryl's favorite forms of chastisement was to pillory the offending player by pointing him out to the audience with his left hand, while with his right hand he would continue to direct the band. This unusual pose attracted the attention of everyone in the audience and served to expose the player to the gaze of all.

Kryl continued his musical activities until he had some difficulty with the American Federation of Musicians union. Whether this difficulty placed a ban on his further playing or whether he had had enough, after nearly forty years before the public, is still a moot question.

After 1910 Patrick Conway continued his cautious course of assembling a "pickup" band of top artists and filling his summer engagements at Willow Grove and at Young's Pier. Such a unique arrangement enabled Conway to escape the competitive problems of the ordinary band which had to keep a roster of musicians happy throughout the year. Such a moderate course leveled out the peaks and valleys which marked the careers of most bands; but if Conway had a peak in his popularity, it was in 1915, when he accepted an engagement for ten weeks at the Panama-Pacific Exposition in San Francisco. For this engagement he formed a band of fifty men. Among the stars who made up this distinguished band were Johnny Dolan as solo cornet, Gardelle Simons as solo trombone, and H. Benne Henton as saxophone soloist.

Conway was in fast company at this exposition, but he easily held his own. Sousa was there with his band and so was Cassassa, official band of the exposition and one of the best on the West Coast. On several occasions the three bands combined to present massed band concerts for the fairgoers.

One afternoon, while Conway was directing this massed band of one hundred and seventy players, he became slightly annoyed by an aerial stunt flier named Art Smith, who was diving and barrel-rolling his frail biplane over the heads of the fair patrons, creating a roar whenever he made one of his perilous dips. Conway involuntarily looked up for a moment while directing. This caused many of his listeners to raise their eyes heavenward also. Conway smiled inwardly, but the audience began to titter when they realized that the piece the band was playing was *Nearer, My God, to Thee.*

At the final concert of Conway's engagement the massed band played, and Conway, Sousa, and Cassassa took turns in directing. At the close of the performance the exposition director presented Conway with a bronze medal. Conway was so affected by this gesture that he choked up and couldn't say a word. Sousa relieved the tension of the situation by leading the massed band in *Auld Lange Syne*.

For the next six or seven years Conway and His Band were rated among the top half-dozen bands of the country. Although the services of his band were much sought after, Conway generally declined all offers which would change his routine of appearances, until, beginning in 1919, he added a winter engagement in Florida.

Early each spring Conway was occupied with teaching, but as summer approached he could not resist the temptation of forming another of his pickup bands and filling his regular engagements. In March 1925 he seemed content to rehearse his student band at Ithaca, but a few weeks later he hastily assembled some of his veterans from the bands of Sousa, Pryor, and other national organizations, and he opened at Willow Grove on May 16 for a month, after which he played three weeks at Riverside Park in Springfield, Mass. This band included the following soloists: H. Benne Henton on saxophone, Leon Handzlik and Harold Rehrig on cornet, Joseph De-Luca on euphonium, Isadore Berv on French horn, Pedro Lazano on trombone, and Joseph La Monaca on flute.

A complete roster of the musicians who played with Conway would read like the honor roll of the great performers in the leading national concert bands and symphony orchestras. Below are a few of the many who joined Conway year after year, some of them playing as many as eight or more summers, notably H. Benne Henton. In order to show the caliber of these men some of their other playing engagements are given.

H. Benne Henton, saxophone soloist for several years with Sousa and rated as one of the most competent and artistic of all soloists on this instrument. Even after 1920, when he established a successful music store in Philadelphia with Albert Knecht, former tenor saxophone with Sousa, he broke away to play solo chair with Conway.

John Dolan, one of the great cornet soloists for many years with Sousa. Dolan was another who signed up with Conway year after year.

Ernest Pechin, cornet soloist with Sousa.
Albertus Meyers, cornet soloist with Sousa, Pryor, and Liberati, and at present conductor of the famous Allentown Band (Pa.).
William Bartow, cornet soloist with Sousa.
Leon Handzlik, cornet soloist with Innes and Pryor.
Harold Rehrig, trumpet soloist with the Philadelphia Orchestra.

Ernest Williams, cornet soloist with Sousa and trumpet soloist with Philadelphia Orchestra.

Gardelle Simons, trombone soloist with Sousa and the Philadelphia Orchestra.

Charles Randall, trombone soloist with the Russian Symphony Orchestra.

Mario Falcone, trombone soloist with the Philharmonic Society of New York.

Charles Cusimano, trombone soloist with Pryor and Sousa

Pedro Lazano, trombone and euphonium soloist of Mexico.

Joseph DeLuca, euphonium soloist with Creatore, Liberati, and Sousa.

Isadore Berv, French horn with Philadelphia Orchestra.

August Helleberg, Sr., principal tubaist with Sousa and for many years principal tubaist with the Metropolitan Opera Orchestra.

Emilio Bianco, principal tubaist with Pryor and Sousa.

James Borrelli, solo clarinet with Sousa and Pryor.

Arthur C. Davis, first clarinet with Sousa.

Arnold Mason, first clarinet with Syracuse Symphony.

On Conway's programs Henton was often called on to play a solo entitled *Eleven O'Clock*. One of the features of his rendition of this solo was an almost impossible cadenza which Henton created. This cadenza soars away above the conventional range of the instrument. Only his phenomenal embouchure enabled him to perform this flight into the saxophone stratosphere, for it ascends beyond the limits of the keys on the instrument. Below, this cadenza is transcribed in Henton's own hand.

Gardelle Simons made himself famous with the trombone solo *Lucy Long,* the cadenza being a blaze of notes that were thrown off like the sparkles of a Fourth-of-July pinwheel. Below, Simons has written this cadenza as he used to play it with Conway.

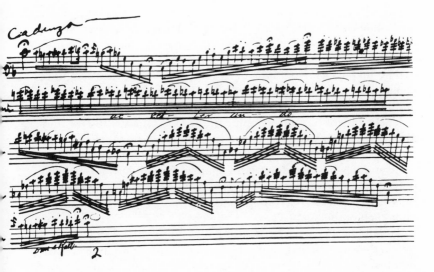

Conway's short stint of seven weeks in 1925 was his swan song. In 1924 he had established the Conway Military Band School in Ithaca and during the following three to four years he made it one of the outstanding schools of its kind in the country. Finally, in 1929 Patrick Conway laid down his magic baton for the last time.

By 1910, Arthur Pryor had established a routine for his band which he followed for many years: recording during the winter, followed by the summer engagements at Willow Grove and Asbury Park. This routine was altered in 1917, when Pryor allowed himself the luxury of wintering in Miami, and for nine winters Pryor's Band was a fixture at this popular resort town.

In 1919, after ten consecutive seasons at Willow Grove, Pryor was denied a return engagement, it is said, because some influential woman in the audience became offended by Pryor's profane language. This is believable, for profanity was one of Pryor's acknowledged weaknesses, and nothing could "rile" the famous bandmaster as could faulty playing by members of his band. He realized that this was not the proper attitude for a bandmaster, but he seemed to be unable to control himself.

Another incident happened at Asbury Park. A third-clarinet player, who acted as manager of the band and hired the musicians, sat directly below the podium in the pavilion. Some musician "hit a clinker," and Pryor, still waving his baton with a wild and erratic beat, shouted to his manager, "How in the hell did you ever come to hire that So-and-So? He's no musician. That So-and-So ought to be digging ditches. For Christ's sake, get rid of him."

The manager knew Pryor too well to take these instructions seriously. Soon the music had engrossed the conductor, and by the end of the concert he had completely forgotten about the matter.

This incident has some similarities to one told about Toscanini, another irascible conductor. In rehearsals, when things were not going well, Toscanini gave vent to his anger by breaking one baton after another by pounding them against his music stand. An oboe player, sitting directly beneath the podium, was supplied with a bundle of batons, and he would hand a new one up to the conductor after each outburst.

To a friend Pryor once commented on his foible. He said that bad playing not only irritated him but caused an actual physical revulsion he could not prevent. While he was directing the band, he lived the music being played. As someone once wrote of Pryor, "Music is his life; the correct interpretation of it, his life blood; tonal beauty, his life breath." Small wonder, then, that a sour note jarred violently on his nervous system and involuntarily loosed a flood of profane protest. He often lost good men because of this weakness. Even the best of musicians sometimes make mistakes, and after Pryor had "taken the hide off" one of these artists with his tirade, no apology could heal the wound.

At heart Pryor was one of the kindest of men. He was thoughtful and generous when away from the podium. Ollie May, euphonium soloist, who came to Pryor from the U. S. Marine Band in 1917 and played that one season, became critically injured in an automobile accident. May suffered for eight days in a hospital before he finally died, and although he was in no way involved, Pryor paid the total hospital bill and told hospital authorities to spare no expense to provide the finest specialists they could obtain to assist in May's recovery.

In spite of this known and feared fiery temper Pryor was able to engage the finest musicians for his band. Many of these players became closely attached to Pryor. He was the most democratic of all leaders in his attitude toward his men, often sharing their meals at hotels and restaurants and drinking with them at the bar. A favorite toast to Pryor by his men on such occasions was "More power to your elbow, Mr. Pryor."

In 1920, at the close of his seventeenth consecutive season at Asbury Park, Pryor voluntarily relinquished this engagement, saying he believed the audiences needed a change. Simone Mantia, his friend and associate, took over the engagement the following summer and continued for five years. Pryor replaced Asbury Park with Luna Park, Coney Island, N.Y., where he played until 1925.

In the 1930's, Arthur Pryor, now past sixty, lent his popular name to radio. His son Arthur, cornetist and radio producer with a big advertising agency, and his son Roger, trombonist, star of the screen and leader of his own dance band, were both in radio, and the father made it a threesome. Pryor's last role in radio was as conductor of a large band which presented the popular Cavalcade of Music, sponsored by Du Pont.

Besides being the greatest trombone virtuoso who ever lived, as well as one of the two or three most celebrated bandmasters, Pryor was a prolific composer, with approximately three hundred published works to his credit. He was so abundantly endowed with great musical talent that he would have been great in any musical endeavor he chose to undertake. Only time and energy limited his achievements.

He composed with great facility. In an informal circle of friends he would entertain at the piano for hours by improvising. Any three or four notes struck at random on the piano by a guest would be taken as a theme or motif, which he would proceed to embellish and work into an impressive composition. He also would use as a theme a person's name, improvising on the rhythm and sound of the vowels.

During the last few years, before his death in 1942, he lived at his farm in West Long Branch, N.J. But he continued for a time to journey to New York several days each week, where he gave lessons to a few advanced students, in a studio in Radio City. Giving lessons was mostly a pretext for the real purpose of mingling with musicians, young and old, who swarmed around this music center. Son of a bandmaster, player of ten thousand trombone solos with Sousa's Band, leader of his own band for more than thirty years, Pryor lived with music and musicians to the final days.

Fifteen

THE SOUSA
SAGA

Ted Lewis and other "jazz bands"
forced Sousa to play half hour
of syncopated music in 1924.

One bright winter day, early in 1920, an elderly man walked with firm step and military bearing into the Fifth Avenue shop of Centemeri's. He was clean-shaven except for a short brush of graying mustache, and he wore pince-nez eyeglasses.

"I'd like to see some of your white calfskin gloves," he said to the clerk. The young man looked slightly puzzled. "Yes, for me," the elderly gentleman answered his quizzical look.

After fumbling around for a moment the clerk came up with a pair. "These are too large," said the customer. "Have you any which are shorter in the fingers? No? Then let me try on a black pair for size."

Having established the right size, the customer asked, "Can you make up for me some gloves this size but in white calfskin? And how much will they cost?"

The clerk by this time had concluded that his customer was slightly daffy, but he answered guardedly, "If we make them up special they will be rather costly."

"But if I order a quantity, what kind of price can you make me?" countered the customer.

"About how many would you want?" asked the clerk.

"I'd want about one hundred dozen," said the customer.

The clerk choked and turned slightly purple in the face. Regaining his voice, he mumbled, "Please excuse me for a moment. I'll ask the proprietor."

To the proprietor, in the back of the store, the clerk blurted out, "There's a crazy old man up front who says he wants us to make up for him *one hundred dozen pairs of white calfskin gloves.*"

There was something so forthright about this quiet man that the proprietor set about seriously figuring costs and came up with a price of six dollars per pair. This was satisfactory. The proprietor then wrote out the order, amounting to seventy-two hundred dollars, and asked the customer to sign his name at the bottom.

The customer promptly wrote in a neat, clear hand: "John Philip Sousa."

Thus, dramatically, did Sousa announce the return of Sousa and His Band to the band business.

Although Sousa had been in the Navy service for twenty-two months, he had managed to keep himself before his public without serious interruption. He played up until September 1917. The following summer, having organized his Great Lakes Battalion Band, he set out again on numerous tours.

After he was placed on the inactive list of the Navy in March 1919, he recalled his musicians, reformed his band, and made a tour to the West Coast. Following an engagement in San Francisco, November 21–23, he made a return tour to New York. But this series of engagements was a sort of farewell tour for the Navy, since during this time he continued to wear his lieutenant-commander uniform. This was not the real Sousa and His Band, and he was anxious to resume his concerts on the original basis.

As shaving off his full beard in 1917 signalized the break with his civilian band, so the purchase of one hundred dozen pairs of white calfskin gloves signalized his return.

When Sousa opened in Willow Grove in the summer of 1920, he featured Richard Stross, cornet soloist, who possessed a freak embouchure which had earned for him the titles of "High Note King" and "Lip Trill King." "He produces a wonderful tone on the entire scale of the cornet," one critic wrote, "and ascends one octave higher than 'high C,' trilling a full tone on each of the intervals of this upper octave. He unquestionably has one of the most remarkable embouchures that musicians have ever known. His solos are rendered artistically and he never fails to create a sensation wherever he appears."

There is no question that Stross could perform spectacularly on the cornet, but apparently this was not the kind of cornet soloing the public wanted. John Dolan, the regular cornet soloist at this time, played in the musical style of Matthew Arbuckle, Albert Bode, and Herbert L. Clarke, and remained a fixture with Sousa for years, while Stross was dropped after this one season.

Sousa was entering a decade of his greatest successes. In 1921 he announced that he would tour the four countries of the North American continent: Mexico, Cuba, Canada, and the United States. On this tour he carried eighty-five persons, the largest regular band he had ever featured up to that time. He also announced he would premier three of his new marches: *Keeping Step with the Union, On the Campus,* and *Comrades of the Legion.*

His 1922 season set a new high mark in cash receipts. On a seventeen weeks' tour of the United States and Canada, during which he traveled over ten thousand miles and played in ninety-eight cities, he took in four hundred and thirteen thousand dollars, an average of approximately thirty-five hundred dollars a day. He also set a mark in the size of his band, carrying one hundred members, a number he did not maintain during subsequent tours.

In May of the following year, before his summer season began, Sousa took time off to visit the man whom, indirectly, he had been fighting for seventeen years: Thomas A. Edison, inventor of the phonograph. Dr. James Francis Cooke, for many years editor of *The Etude* music magazine, was a friend of both men, and he probably thought it was a shame that two such leaders in different fields should remain so at odds. If he harbored any thoughts that he could bring them together, they were an illusion.

When Dr. Cooke and Sousa arrived in West Orange, N.J., and entered the laboratory where the phonograph had been invented, they were cordially greeted by Edison. Although Edison was seventy-six years old, Sousa was sixty-nine, and Dr. Cooke was somewhat younger, it was difficult to tell from their animated conversation who was the youngest in the group. Dr. Cooke began to feel that the visit would be all he had hoped, until Edison made some derogatory remark about Mozart. Sousa immediately flew to the defense of Mozart, and the peaceful waters were muddied. A bit later Sousa expressed himself somewhat freely on the deficiencies of mechanical or "canned music," and Edison proceeded to uphold the merits of the phonograph in terms that took on a slight edge. After that the conversation slowed almost to a stop, and Dr. Cooke decided to end the visit before his two friends could get into further argument.

He afterward contended that his idea of bringing the two men together was a good one and would have been a great success if he could have kept Edison from talking about music and if he could have kept Sousa from talking about inventions.

Sousa's band in 1924 was comprised of seventy-five men, which was not remarkable; but what was remarkable was that he carried eight saxophones: four altos, two tenors, a baritone, and a bass. Another remarkable feature of his programs that year was the half hour devoted exclusively to syncopated music. The small dance bands called this type of music "jazz," but what Sousa and his men presented to the public was only a lame sort of jazz, and calling it syncopated music avoided a lot of controversy. This concert band, unquestionably an excellent one, could no more play authentic jazz than the Sousa band of 1904 could play true ragtime.

Sousa as usual had kept his ear to the ground. In former years he had noted the popularity of the coon song, and later of the cakewalk, which was followed by ragtime. Now he felt a ground swell of popular jazz. In an interview with the press he stated: "I believe syncopated music is here to stay and should be included as part of my programs, along with classical and semi-classical music." Accordingly, for thirty minutes on each program, Sousa did his best to furnish his audiences with jazz.

This decision of Sousa's came rather suddenly, just as the wide popularity of jazz came suddenly. Jazz was not new, having sprung up in New Orleans a quarter of a century before. Sousa, however, was hardly aware of it then or for many years afterward. He probably never heard of King Oliver or Nick La Rocca. Reports may have reached him about some of these early Dixieland bands that came up North and played in Chicago and New York, from 1915 to 1918, but this information held no special interest for him.

It is just possible that he heard about Paul Specht's "Georgians," along about 1920, for there was a concert-band angle involved. Frank Guarante was a cornet and trumpet player who had been a member of Creatore's and Don Philippini's bands. While traveling with these bands he became acquainted with jazz in New Orleans. Eventually this type of music so fascinated him that he left the concert band and played jazz in New Orleans from 1914 until 1918. In 1920 he joined Paul Specht's "Georgians" and became the spark plug of the group. They played an engagement at the Addison Hotel in Detroit, and made recordings under the Regal label for Columbia.

It is likely that after 1920 Sousa began to hear the names of Ted Lewis, Eddie Elkins, and Gene Goldkette. A year or so later he probably was aware that there were such names as Isham Jones, Paul Whiteman, Paul Biese, Coon-Sanders, Paul Ash, Mal Hallett, and Jan Garber. These bands were playing in hotels, cafés, theaters, and ballrooms all over the country. They also made a multitude of recordings for Victor, Columbia, Brunswick, Edison, Regal, Okeh, Clarion, Sterling, and Bell. But they were still no great shakes as far as Sousa was concerned.

What awakened Sousa as by a bombshell was what happened to all these struggling name bands when another of those "inventions" came along, this one being radio. Radio was not new in 1924. De Forest had developed the radio tube a long time before, and in 1916 had made the first commercially sponsored broadcast, using Columbia recordings for music; but Sousa probably knew no more about De Forest than he did about La Rocca. In September 1920, Paul Specht broadcast his band over WWJ, the Detroit *News* station, "the first radio broadcast" by a "live" dance band. Next year Specht's band went out over WJZ, New York, and KDKA (in Pittsburgh) established a studio orchestra for broadcast purposes. Vincent Lopez began broadcasting jazz in 1922 over WJZ and WEAF. Paul Whiteman entered radio broadcasting in 1923. From then on name dance bands, combined with radio broadcasting, fairly exploded into popularity and demand.

From a few hundred dollars a week the fee for a dance band jumped to twelve thousand dollars and more. Salaries for the musicians jumped from forty or fifty dollars a week to two hundred and more. New bands sprang up by the dozens and many of them achieved fabulous success in a matter of weeks. A band "with a wire" was sure to be a success.

The sudden popularity of radio broadcasting is revealed very graphically in the sales curve for radio receiving sets. By 1922 sales had climbed to sixty million dollars, and they more than doubled during each of the following two years, reaching one hundred and thirty-six millions in 1923, and three hundred and fifty-eight millions in 1924.

It was this combination of name dance bands and radio broadcasting which exploded with such a loud blast in Sousa's ears and caused him, in 1924, to carry eight saxophones and to devote thirty minutes on each program to "syncopated music."

In spite of jazz and name bands on the radio Sousa and His Band continued to climb the ladder of success. By this time the shrinking concert-band business was almost completely dominated by Sousa. The great bands of Innes, Brooke, and Liberati had dropped out of the race. Relatively ineffective and losing ground rapidly were Creatore and the few remaining Italian bands. Conway continued for two years his modest schedule of engagements but was not considered as competition for Sousa. Pryor was still going strong, but his activities were mostly confined to recording and he hardly conflicted with the Sousa interests. Sweet had never competed directly with Sousa, and now Kryl had dropped into a pattern similar to that of Sweet—chautauqua during the summer and odd jobs during the winter season. Sousa stood almost alone in the business-concert-band field.

In 1925, Sousa and His Band rounded out a third of a century. The thirty-third season for the band started on July 4 and continued for thirty-nine weeks. Harry Askins, manager of the band, stated that Sousa had a guarantee in excess of half a million dollars for the tour but that he expected the total receipts to reach a million dollars.

The guarantee usually ran about fifteen hundred to two thousand dollars a concert, but it was higher for some spots where business was normally big. The largest guarantee on this tour was twenty thousand dollars for six days at Regina, Canada. In addition to the guarantee Sousa received a percentage of the gate. In Chicago, two years before, Sousa played to an audience of over twenty thousand paid admissions, and two concerts brought a total of seventeen thousand dollars above the guarantee. Such good business often brought Sousa's take to two or three times the guarantee.

Sousa was seventy years old, but for thirty-nine weeks he never failed to start the matinee promptly at two-thirty and the evening concert promptly at eight o'clock. He made all the early trains and long night jumps, the same as his men. The younger musicians, who became completely exhausted toward the end of the tour, marveled at how Sousa could stand the pace.

At the close of this tour Sousa lost the last man who had been in his original band in 1892. Marv Lyons, second trombone and baggage manager for Sousa during all these years, handed in his resignation. Only Sousa, the indestructible, was left of all those fifty men who started the Sousa band.

Five years before, at a gala concert at the Hippodrome in celebration of Sousa's sixty-fifth birthday, Sousa had stated that there were in his band at that time only three members who had started out with him in 1892, and he added that these three men had traveled with the Sousa band approximately seven hundred thousand miles. We do not know who the third man was but the second man was Joseph Norrito, clarinetist, who resigned in 1924, after thirty-two seasons with the Sousa band. When he handed in his resignation, he jokingly told Sousa he didn't think he liked the work, and that he planned to go back to Naples and live the remainder of his life.

Of the fifty men who made up Sousa's first band probably forty were foreign-born. Among the principals there were Walter Smith of England, John Cox of Scotland, Staats and Jabon of France, Norrito of Italy, and Koch of Germany. Among the seventeen men Sousa recruited from Philadelphia and vicinity, most of them were from Germany. In Sousa's 1927 band of eighty-four men only one musician was foreign-born, and he was a naturalized citizen.

It is understood that Sousa never gave in to the phonograph, even though he did make some recordings of his band, but he finally gave in to radio, in 1928, appearing as conductor of a band of fifty-two men on an NBC chain broadcast sponsored by General Motors.

Time was passing for the seventy-four-year-old bandmaster, and in 1928 he wrote an autobiography, published under the title *Marching Along*. In this book he gives us a clear and concise picture of the general routine of the Sousa band. "General" is used advisedly, for this routine varied sometimes, with comic or tragic results.

"About July we start our tour," Sousa writes. "Contracts have been made from six months to a year ahead by my manager. . . . We assemble in New York (in June) from every part of the country—each man with his trunk and suitcase. The instruments are stowed in specially designed trunks under the care of the band baggage man. Arrived at our destination, the men go to their hotels, and the band luggage is sent to the hall where we are to appear. The band librarian lays out our music, the accumulation of which is, I believe, one of the greatest libraries of band music in the world. We carry our own music stands and my podium. The men arrive about three-quarters of an hour before the concert, to tune up, soften their lips, and make sure everything is in order. . . . When the concert is about to begin, the librarian calls out 'All on!' and they file on the stage. Each man is provided with a list of encores which, nine times out of ten, are Sousa marches. . . .

"There has been only one type of uniform for the men, and we have not changed it in more than thirty years. Salaries are from seventy-five dollars to two hundred dollars a week, according to proficiency and experience. . . . The Band is unique in the number of concerts given and the mileage covered. In the thirty-six years of its existence, it has visited every part of the United States and Canada, has made five tours of Europe and one of the world. We have traveled, in all, one million two hundred thousand miles."

To the summary in the final paragraph, Herbert L. Clarke has added some figures which he says Sousa gave him shortly before he died, in 1932. From 1892 to 1932, Sousa paid out thirteen million dollars in salaries and fifteen millions in transportation, and, comments Clarke, "he died a rich man—one of the very few bandmasters who did."

Dr. Peter Buys, well-known composer and bandmaster, who joined Sousa around 1912, has a slightly different version of the Sousa band routine. "In those days," says Dr. Buys, "train schedules were not strictly adhered to, especially in the Middle West. Trains would be from minutes to hours late at the slightest provocation. . . . When we struck a snag, it invariably was a good one. Imagine a heavy snow, the train several hours late, no transportation available from the station to the concert hall, the trunks (we had about thirty-five of them) piled in the snow on the station platform waiting to be hauled to the concert hall, and an audience which had been waiting for hours—patiently, we hoped. No matter how we hurried, Mr. Sousa always would be backstage to welcome us. No one knows how he managed to get there so soon, but there he was, waiting for us.

"Some of us would straggle in and take our places, and lo and behold, when about a dozen of the men who played the smaller instruments had taken their places on the stage, 'The Governor' would come from the wings, raise his baton, and we were off. . . . When the trunks arrived we would continue with the rest of the concert as usual. Afterwards we would boast jestingly about the many parts we had 'cued in' while performing the *Mignon Overture* without one of the horns, without basses, trombones, baritones, percussion and with but one or two men in each of the other sections."

James Borrelli, solo clarinet in the 1920's, tells about another of such fiascoes. "After playing a matinee in McAlester, Okla.," Mr. Borrelli relates, "we took autos to the next jump (I think it was Okmulgee). We arrived just in time to go directly to the theater. When we reached the theater we learned that the music trunks had not arrived, having been shipped by slow freight from McAlester. In order to relieve the tension and impatience of the audience, it was decided to raise the curtain and have the band seated on the platform, waiting for the trunks. The trunks finally arrived about nine-thirty, and to give the situation a further dramatic twist, the trunks were brought out onto the stage, near the drum and tuba sections. And good old 'Bus' [librarian], fretting and fuming as usual, proceeded to open the first trunk. The first thing that came out was a rat about as big as a rabbit. It made one leap in the direction of the 'Indian' [John Kuhn, tuba], jumped over his lap, and then got lost."

Not only were the trunks sometimes missing, but players failed to catch the train. Gus Helmecke, bass drummer, once told about the time he and Howard Goulden, tympanist from 1923 to 1927, missed the train on a jump from Albuquerque to Clovis, N.M. "I hired a small plane," Gus related, "to fly us to our next stop. It was only a two-passenger plane, and with three of us in it plus baggage, we hardly made it over some mountains. Besides, Howard couldn't sit still, and he continually rocked the plane. As luck would have it, Sousa's train hit a hand car at Vaughn, N.M., and stopped to ascertain the damage. This break enabled us to board the train there. As the train got under way, 'Buck' Weaver [clarinetist] stood up in the front end of the car and led 'three cheers for the Flying Dutchman.'"

Fred Bayers, who played with Sousa in 1923–24, once broke out in some doggerel about the grind of touring with Sousa. One verse puts it in a neat capsule, as follows:

First you play a concert, then you run and jump a train,
Stop to get a bite to eat, and then you play again.
Chase around and look for rooms; gee, but life is grand,
For there's always something doing in the Sousa band.

Finding something palatable to eat was a constant problem while touring. In the early days when dining cars were not always available the musicians had to rustle up something to eat en route. One of the "meanest men in the band" one day slipped off the train when it stopped at a station and called in a loud voice from the steps: "Fresh turkey sandwiches, five cents." There was a mad rush by the hungry musicians in the cars, but by the time they had piled out onto the station platform, the caller had disappeared.

In 1928 the band played a college town in Wisconsin. Between concerts the musicians went to town to eat and ran into a man, standing on a prominent corner, who asked them if they would like to know where they could get a good meal and where beer also was sold. This was during prohibition, and most of the hungry and thirsty men followed his directions. The food was good, and when the men asked for beer, the man who directed them to the place appeared behind an old-style bar and was the bartender. The next morning, when these musicians were walking down to the train, they met a man coming toward them. He was in uniform and the name on his cap read: "CHIEF OF POLICE." The musicians readily recognized him as the man on the corner and the bartender of the evening before.

Nearly every stop held some problem for the band. In Glendive, Mont., the concert was held in "the biggest garage in town." There were not enough hotel rooms to house the band, and the sheriff was kept busy most of the night, rounding up stray musicians and bedding them down in the Northern Pacific railroad station.

In many places the stage was either too long and shallow or too short and deep. Lighting in some places was so poor that the men couldn't see their music. In some places there was no light at all. In Tucson an electricians' strike left the hall in darkness, and the first half of the program had to be played by the light of candles, placed on the individual music racks of the players and around on the stage. In White Plains, N.Y., the band was playing in an armory when a severe electric storm came up and cut off the electricity, compelling the band to carry on for a time from memory.

One time in Calgary, Canada, where the band was playing the Canadian Fair, a stiff wind and gale came up, making it impossible to put the music on the stands. Since the band had been using the *William Tell Overture* as the regular traveling matinee number, it was suggested by some of the players that the band could fake the overture, then go on to play a goodly number of marches and call it a concert. The band felt under special obligation to play something, as a group of children from a blind school had traveled over one hundred miles to hear Sousa.

Rain was coming down pretty steadily by the time the band was ready to play, but "The Old Man" was determined to give a concert of some kind. He raised his baton, gave an encouraging look toward Schaeffer, the bass-clarinet player, and down went the beat. Schaeffer knew his part well and started his first-bar introductory solo. The two oboes gave their two-note answer, and after that there was silence. No one else could remember what came next. After what seemed like an eternity of waiting for something to happen, Sousa rang out with the command: "*Semper Fidelis,* gentlemen!" and the program was saved.

Nothing disturbed Sousa. He took emergencies of all kinds in his stride. Whether it was a catastrophe of the elements or a tussle of wits with players or audience, he always seemed to do and say just the right thing. His sense of humor hardly ever failed to carry him over any obstacle.

Sousa was often asked to audition a local aspirant to musical fame, and he seldom refused. Following a concert in a Western town, he was asked if he would come to the hall where a few of the cowboys and miners were trying to launch a town band. They had bought some music, among the pieces being one called *Hunting Scene.* This piece had them mystified, and Sousa went down after the concert to give them a tip or two, taking with him three of the men from the Sousa band.

It took Sousa but a moment to see that the town band had tackled something away over their heads. Sousa started them out several times, only to have some of the players lose their places or stop before some notes which were too difficult for them. Finally he told them: "Now, men, this is a hunting scene, and if any of you find you can't go on with your part, just shout Tallyho! Tallyho! or take out your revolver and fire a shot. This will furnish appropriate sound effects for such a musical theme as we have here before us. Now then, let us start again."

With that Sousa raised his baton and gave the down beat. The band played along for several bars, when one man lost his place and followed Sousa's instructions, shouting, "Tallyho! Tallyho!" and firing a blast from his six-shooter. Soon another joined in, and another. In a matter of seconds a regular fusillade was going on. At the height of the bombardment Sousa and his men slipped out of the hall unnoticed and walked to the train, which was waiting to take them to the next town.

Arthur Rosander, baritone saxophone with Sousa, recalls an instance when Sousa neatly turned an embarrassment into a laughing matter. "During the late twenties," Rosander relates, "when the band was in Philadelphia, my home town, Sousa pressed into service an old jalopy I owned, for transporting two ladies with the band to a swank dinner at the Country Club. Upon our arrival, the haughty doorman came up to the jalopy and tried to open the doors, only to find that they had no handles and could be opened only from the inside. I was embarrassed, but Sousa thought it was a wonderful joke on the doorman."

At an afternoon concert at a theater there were two boys "cuttin' up" in the front row. Sousa tried for a while not to notice the disturbance, but when it began to annoy some of the audience close by, he took action. After finishing a number Sousa turned to the boys and called out like a top sergeant, "Attention, you two boys!" The boys stood up. "Right face!" shouted Sousa, then followed with "Forward march!" Before the boys realized quite what had happened, they found themselves outside in the street.

William Carter White is the source of an amusing story which illustrates the tact and humor of Sousa. Following a concert at some society affair, an effusive lady came up to him and said: "Mr. Sousa, I just adore Fannie Hurst's *Humoresque* which you played."

"Yes, but it is by Dvořák," corrected Sousa.

Refusing to let Sousa realize how little she knew, she volunteered, "Oh, yes, he is from Iowa, isn't he?" [She probably had the composer confused with Ray Dvorak, the bandmaster.]

Not having the heart to unmask the pretender, Sousa gallantly replied, "I believe he summered there once but right now I believe he is in Czechoslovakia."

Gene Labarre, cornet soloist with Sousa in 1920, once asked Sousa's advice about having an E♭ clarinet in a band of which he was at that time conductor. "Young man," Sousa replied, "I have never had an E♭ clarinet player in my band who didn't foul up the introduction a little—in certain keys—so I decided that I would limit the use of an E♭ clarinet to just four measures, once every Leap Year."

After a concert at the prison at Atlanta some of the men were walking through the corridors, when one of the inmates behind bars shouted at Sousa's alto-saxophone player, "Hello, Schensley." Mr. Sousa, walking along, heard the salutation, turned to Schensley, and said, "I see you have friends everywhere."

A year or so after the 1929 stock-market crash the special Sousa train was pulling into Milwaukee, and all the engines in the railroad yards were blowing their whistles. Sousa asked someone, "What are they blowing their whistles for?" and received the reply: "They are saluting you on your birthday, Mr. Sousa." Sousa's comment was, "I wish they would save their coal and pay more dividends on their stock."

Bob Fuller tells about an amusing adventure of Sousa when the band was playing at the Chicago Theatre in 1928, just before Christmas. "The Chicago *Tribune* thought it would make a heart-warming, human interest item to have Sousa togged out as Santa Claus and have his picture taken beside the familiar Salvation Army pot while a little girl was dropping a coin to 'keep the pot boiling.' After Ralph Fulgum and others had applied the make-up and had dressed him in the Santa Claus suit, Sousa started across the stage. When he was about half way across, the drawstring in the pants gave away and the pants dropped to half mast, leaving an expanse of Mr. Sousa's long white underwear showing.

"Instead of reaching down and retrieving his pants, Mr. Sousa just stood there and began calling at the top of his voice, 'Ralph! Ralph! For Christ's sake, where are you, Ralph? My pants are falling down. Ralph! . . . Ralph!' Finally Ralph heard the cry of distress and ran to Sousa. He pulled up the pants and fastened the drawstring tightly. Then Sousa walked out and had his picture taken."

While the relationship between Sousa and his men was always congenial, rarely was it familiar, and hardly ever did Sousa kid a player. Howard Goulden overheard one of these exceptional instances. "We were playing daily matinees and evening concerts at Dominion Park in Montreal," Goulden recalls. "Mr. Sousa, as every player remembers, usually sat near the stage or in his dressing room before a matinee, smoking the proverbial Corona, Corona, Corona. On this particular day he was sitting in what 'Bus' Russell [librarian] called his music room. As I came in for the matinee concert, I saw Mr. Sousa and Joe DeLuca [euphonium soloist] together and could not help overhearing the conversation. Joe said, 'Mr. Sous', I am on the program this afternoon for a solo.'

" 'Yes, Mr. DeLuca,' Sousa said, encouragingly.

" 'My girl is in Montreal,' went on DeLuca with embarrassment, 'and is coming out tonight, so would you change my solo so I play him tonight instead of this afternoon? She wants to hear me playa the solo.'

"Mr. Sousa, waving his cigar with the flourish of his baton, replied, 'Well, Mr. DeLuca, I would think that if your girl really loved you, she would be here this afternoon.' Mr. Sousa tried to look serious but there was a merry twinkle in his eyes that he could not cover up. After seeming to study the matter over for awhile, during which time Joe was a picture of dejection, Sousa finally granted the request, and Joe went away as happy as a kid with a new toy."

Frank Simon, who later became famous as director of the Armco Band, joined Sousa along about 1913 and played solo cornet in the band for several years. He tells a story on himself which happened during his first season with Sousa, while playing at Willow Grove. Having just joined the cornet section, he was anxious to play a solo to show what he could do. Sousa kept putting him off, until one day he told Simon, "Tell Mr. Russell [librarian] to put out the parts next Monday afternoon."

Frank had prepared his solo carefully, and he knocked it off in great style. At the close of the solo he bowed to Mr. Sousa, and Mr. Sousa gravely bowed back. After the concert Mr. Sousa failed to make any comment about the solo.

The next day Frank arrived at the band shell early, and when he saw Mr. Sousa approach, he knew Mr. Sousa was going to congratulate him on his fine solo. When The Old Man saw Frank, he beckoned to him, and Frank walked toward Sousa eagerly, hoping to hear him praise his efforts. But Sousa said, "Mr. Simon, I wish you would dig a hole about eight feet deep and bury that solo at the bottom."

Notwithstanding this inauspicious start, Frank went on to become one of the great cornet soloists of the Sousa band.

Seldom did Mr. Sousa discharge a man. While he was extremely exacting, he was also very human. Furthermore all his men were carefully selected. In the early days he auditioned every applicant himself, but in later years he relied upon the recommendations of men who had played or were playing in the band. There were enough Sousa players scattered over the continent to vouch for a promising musician, and Sousa would take their word for it.

One of the rare instances in which Sousa decided to let a man go is told by Clarence Booth, bassoonist from 1927 to 1930. "After a concert, The Old Man told his manager to fire a certain clarinet player," Booth recalls, "and the manager promptly carried out the order. When the clarinet player asked the manager why he was fired, the manager told him to see Mr. Sousa and find out. The clarinet player went to Sousa, who told him he was lax and indifferent in his playing. 'I often see you using only one hand on your instrument,' Mr. Sousa said. The player protested that often these passages required only one hand to play. After a moment's hesitation, Mr. Sousa exclaimed, 'You may remain. I have an idea! I shall write a concerto for a one-armed clarinet player.' "

There was another instance during a rehearsal when every man in the band would have bet his last dollar that a certain cornet player would lose his job. The story can best be told by Dr. Peter Buys, who was doing arranging for Sousa at the time and who was involved. "The Governor wrote a sparkling bit of whimsey entitled *With Pleasure.* For the sake of brilliancy he wrote it in the key of D major. We played it once at Willow Grove Park, and all of us found it to be extremely difficult. In fact, it was found that the cornet parts could hardly be fingered fast enough. Since the first performance was anything but good, we had hopes that The Governor would put it on the shelf and forget about it.

"About a year later, all of a sudden and without warning, there it was, staring at us from our program covers. It happened that we had a new, but very capable, first cornetist with the band. We started the piece at a terrific speed. The first strain was very difficult, but we cleared that hurdle in rather good shape. At the second strain it happened. The new man laid his cornet in his lap and looked at Mr. Sousa, who in turn gazed at Mr. Cornetist in amazement. At the end of the strain, our cornetist joined in with the band. From that point on to the end, the composition was less difficult.

"We were prepared for the fireworks, which started when we

finished the number. Mr. Sousa asked the man what he meant by quitting us cold, and added, 'Suppose I quit conducting in the middle of the piece?'

"Then came the astounding reply from the culprit, 'Mr. Sousa, if I practiced for fifty years I would not be able to play it, as it is impossible for a cornetist to finger it. As for conducting it, Mr. Sousa, it is just as easy to conduct in six sharps as in the key of C.'

"We expected a scathing rebuke, but nothing happened. Mr. Sousa just stood there, looking at the man. The Governor was noted for his fluent command of the English language, but for once it appeared he was at a loss for words. With a faint smile, he returned to his podium and proceeded with the program.

"A few days later he handed me the 'jinxed' composition and asked me to 'fix it up.' I transposed it to the key of C. Thus some of the brilliancy was retained, while the extremely difficult and impossible sections were eliminated. In its new format, *With Pleasure* became one of the favorite Sousa compositions."

Sousa was extremely lenient with a player who made an honest mistake. This was remarkable in a musician of Sousa's unquestioned musical stature. Toscanini often flew into a rage. Once, when some wrong notes were played by the trumpet during rehearsal, he rushed backstage and, in his uncontrolled anger, drove his fist through a plywood panel in a door. When something went wrong, Pryor gave vent to his anger by making the air blue with "cuss words." Kryl often held up an offending player, even during a concert, to ridicule. But Sousa bent over backward in his mild treatment of an offending player.

Rudolph Becker, who joined Sousa's first band in 1892 as baritone saxophonist and who played under Sousa for many years, says the great bandmaster "displayed little of the fiery temperament so often associated with creative talent. He rehearsed his musicians with great strictness but few fireworks. The closest he ever came to losing his temper was an occasional impatience to get started with rehearsals. At such times he would tap his baton sharply against the music rack, and say, 'Gentlemen, please! Let us get in tune before I die.'"

This even temper stayed with Sousa to the end. He didn't, like some, grow crotchety in his old age. Frank Sullivan, saxophonist with the Sousa band during the last six years of its existence, recalls that "one evening during a concert, Sousa cocked his sensitive ear to the

This even temper stayed with Sousa to the end.
He didn't grow crotchety in his old age.
BETTMANN ARCHIVE

sound of a sour note. Without a quiver of his baton, he swept his eyes over the eighty-odd musicians until they rested on the offending bandsman. Mr. Sousa didn't scowl; he just looked.

"It was five or six months before the same composition appeared again on the band's program, which was being presented in a different part of the continent. But one or two bars before the tricky passage, Sousa turned, raised his hand in the direction of the same player, and smiled. When the uneasy player completed the part without muffing it, Sousa bowed slightly from the waist in acknowledgment."

Similar instances of the same attitude occurred often, with slight variation. A cornet player persisted in playing F instead of F# in one of Sousa's marches. This went on for concert after concert, and still Sousa said nothing, although he grimaced whenever the wrong note was played. Finally the bandsmen began to be so amused that they would snicker whenever the cornetist pulled the boner, and the man eventually discovered that he was playing the wrong note. On the day that he corrected his mistake Sousa smiled in the direction of the long-offending musician, then placed his hand over his heart, and looked devoutly toward the ceiling. This was the only form of reprimand ever given.

Jack Richardson, the big player of the big sousaphone, one time missed the word to proceed to the next number on the program. This particular number had a soft opening, but Jack, thinking that the band was playing one of The Old Man's marches as an encore, plowed in fortissimo with his big sousaphone. Next day, when the band came to the same place in the program, Sousa first carefully raised his palm in Jack's direction before bringing in the rest of the band with his baton.

William Fletcher, who played clarinet from 1904 to 1906, says he saw Sousa disgruntled but once. "We were playing the *Carnival of Paris* overture by Svendsen without a rehearsal, at a sparsely attended matinee," Fletcher recalls. "Everything went well until a few measures from the end. Then a stand of clarinets 'plugged up a hole,' but, as usual, Mr. Sousa did not show any signs of irritation. About ten days later this same overture was programmed at Los Angeles, and the same thing occurred. This was too much. As The Old Man stepped down from the podium, and before he turned to face the audience, he was heard to say, 'Christ All Mighty! TWICE IN THE SAME PLACE!'"

Years later another exasperating situation caused Sousa to resort to strong language. This occurred during the last few years of the band's existence. Eddie Wall, solo clarinet in the band at the time, recalls: "The road program that season included Chadwick's highbrow *Tam O'Shanter,* and in the smaller towns it was customary to make a large cut and begin the number at letter H, where it opened with a little duet for oboes. Bus Russell, the librarian, announced the cut one day, before the curtain went up, but when this point in the program was reached and the number began, both oboe players were dreaming, with faraway looks, and sat holding their oboes on their

knees. After a few bars of oompah the clarinets played a short inter-
lude, and the music returned to the oboe duet. Still no sounds from
the oboes. Mr. Sousa, who up to this time had not raised his eyes
from the score, looked up; and, coming out with his favorite 'cuss
words,' said heatedly, 'Christ All Mighty! *Play something!*'"

Eddie Wall also tells of another fiasco which foreboded one of those
rare outbreaks by Sousa but which resolved itself before this became
necessary. "The overture to Tschaikowsky's seldom-played opera *The
Voyvode* was on the regular evening program one year while we were
on the road," says Eddie. "This number works up gradually through
a rapid allegro to a powerful climax, when a pistol is fired. Immediately, there follows a slow, solemn movement through to the end.

"After we had played it steadily for a couple of months, one night
things went wrong. Someone failed to come in properly; this un-
settled others, and matters grew steadily worse until the whole band
was hopelessly lost. Mr. Sousa seemed helpless to control the run-
away. When the time for the pistol shot came, there was no shot.
John Heney, the drummer, held his fire. Everyone started stalling
around, filling in and hoping for something to happen. Finally Jack
Richardson stopped playing, turned around to Johnny Heney in
back of him, and shouted, 'Let 'em have it, Johnny!' Johnny fired
the shot, and immediately everyone found his place in the slow
movement, and we all finished together."

Many newcomers to the band have testified to Sousa's thought-
fulness and consideration. Typical of many such stories is the one by
Carroll Carr, first clarinet with Sousa from 1922 to 1926. "The first
day I reported for rehearsal," Carr relates, "the band was playing
one of Sousa's famous marches. The piece contained a long and difficult cadenza for the first chair clarinet. I recall to this day how
nervous I was as I contemplated playing this passage under the eyes
of its composer.

"As that part of the score was reached, Mr. Sousa turned away
from the clarinet section and pretended to be straightening up his
music stand. This kind and thoughtful act erased my nervousness,
and from that time on I never felt any hesitancy in performing any
piece under the friendly conductor."

Composers found Mr. Sousa approachable. After more than a half
century Dr. James Francis Cooke remembered with pleasure his first
contact with Mr. Sousa. He says, "When I was thirteen years old, I

wrote two marches: the *High School March* and the *Princeton Tigers*. My publisher told me that Sousa was going to play them at Manhattan Beach. We lived in Brooklyn, a distance of nine miles from Manhattan Beach. I walked there and back. Mr. Sousa played my marches, and I went around and thanked him. He made me so important that day that I have never been so important since."

There was plenty of horseplay in the band, but Sousa didn't seem to mind—he even seemed to enjoy it. Gus Helmecke, bass drummer with Sousa for many years, once advised Sousa that a slight change should be made in a percussion part. As Gus was head of the section and an old-timer with the band, Sousa gave him the go-ahead. The piece was a piccolo solo, and at the next concert, as the soloist completed his opening cadenza, an answering "cuckoo" came from the percussion section. Gus had written in the part for an unsuspecting member of the section. Sousa barely managed to keep his face straight, but the soloist was visibly shaken.

Gus was a practical joker, and was continually pulling something. In 1921, when the band was playing in Little Rock, Ark., Gus invited several members of the band to be his guests at an "Ozark Dinner," which was supposed to be famous all over that part of the country. Gus had Bill Bell [bass tuba] help him stage the affair.

When the guests walked in and sat down, there was brought to each place a plate with a small mound of sauerkraut on it, and on top was mounted a hot dog with four toothpick legs. That was the famous Ozark Dinner.

One day, not long afterward, as the Sousa special train was passing through some Middle West farm land, the noise of the train startled a bunch of pigs, which suddenly jumped up and scattered in all directions. Without a moment's hesitation Eddie Heney, saxophonist, yelled: "There goes the flute section. What'll we ever do without them this afternoon?"

Al Knecht, tenor saxophone, 1905–15, used to tell about a certain horn player who was in the band with him during his early days. "This horn player," Al recalled, "had a wife who insisted on touring with the band. She wasn't good looking, wasn't pleasant to anyone, but came along just the same, her husband buying the railroad tickets for her each day. Finally one of the men in the band decided that the time had come to stop all the nonsense. He cornered the horn player one morning and insisted that for the good of the whole organization he should send his wife home, or leave her at the next town. Perplexed, the horn player stammered, 'Boy, I'd rather have her travel with me than have to kiss her goodbye.' "

Joe DeLuca, euphonium soloist, was the victim of several practical jokes, one of which Eddie Wall, solo clarinet, recalls. "At a matinee program at the Bozeman, Montana, high school auditorium, Sousa's *Showing Off Before Company* was played. A feature of the number was a euphonium solo, to be played by Joseph DeLuca. The solo was called *Beautiful Colorado,* in the cadenza of which Joe had introduced some 'chords,' or three notes played at the same time. These chords were a sort of specialty with Joe, and he was very proud of his ability to produce them.

"Before the concert, some of the boys had found, in a classroom, a small, yellow wooden duck on wheels, which they carefully brought on stage and concealed in the clarinet section. When Joe reached the cadenza, and was rocking back and forth, putting his whole heart into it, the duck was slyly wheeled into place next to his feet. Expecting applause at the conclusion of his solo, Joe was surprised to be greeted with loud laughter by the younger members of the audience. Noticing at last the cause of the merriment, Joe kicked the toy duck off the stage.

"After the concert, Joe immediately complained to Mr. Sousa, saying in his broken English, 'Pleesa, Mista Sous', I am insult.' Mr. Sousa finally was able to soothe DeLuca by issuing orders that in the future no jokes were to be played on Joe while he was performing."

Owen Kincaid and Eddie Heney, two saxophonists with Sousa in the late 1920's, collaborated in a couple of practical jokes that were the subject of investigation by some of the victims. Only a few years ago did Kincaid reveal the identity of the perpetrators. "Eddie Heney and I went out for a glass of beer," said Kincaid, "and we spied some smelly, dried fish. We bought some, and the next day before the concert we rubbed them all over the mouthpieces of 'Whoopie' Monroe, Jim Slantz and Joe DeLuca. When they picked up their instruments just before the concert, Whoopie was just plain disgusted, but Slantz, who never cleaned his mouthpiece anyway, never noticed that anything was wrong. DeLuca got so mad he nearly chewed the mouthpiece off his tin pipe.

"Sometime later, Eddie and I bought about a dozen books on French art. Quite awhile before the concert we placed a picture of a 'nekked' girl in everyone's book, including our own, to escape detection. As I remember, we were playing *La Voyvode*—anyway, it was some long, loud and lousy tune. We placed the picture at a fast turn, where the music was fast and the player had to flip the page quickly.

"Well, brother, this stopped the band! Poor old Paul Gerhardt nearly swallowed his oboe. Buck Weaver [clarinet] just plain laughed out loud. Charlie Wall [clarinet] had a far away look in his eyes. Johnny Dolan [solo cornet] took it as a matter of course, as if he had been expecting it. Billy Tong's [cornet] neck was a dark crimson, and Gabe Russ [bass tuba] just stopped playing and gazed fondly at the picture. We never did know what the audience thought, but The Old Man quickly grasped the situation and shouted, 'Begin at letter G,' and most of the band came in together and managed to finish without further mishap."

Nearly twenty-five years have elapsed since Sousa died in March 1932. He died "in the harness" in Reading, Pa., shortly before he was to direct the Reading High School Band, and the day before he was to direct the famous Ringgold Band, both as guest conductor.

It has been estimated that twelve to fifteen hundred different musicians played in the Sousa band during its existence. Many of these have passed on, "to join The Governor's Ensemble," but several hundred alumni now belong to the Sousa Band Fraternity Society, established in 1947 to perpetuate the Sousa memory. On the roster of the Society in 1953 was the name of Rudolph Becker, baritone saxophone with Sousa's original 1892 band and the last surviving member. In addition to the social function of bringing old-time Sousa men together for gab fests about the good old days, the Society has been carrying on a long series of Sousa memorial concerts all over the country.

Another memorial was established in 1952, when the Sousa family presented to the Library of Congress a priceless collection of original manuscripts of Sousa's compositions, together with his medals and a collection of batons. These latter include jeweled memorial batons and a well-worn, simple wood baton which Sousa used to call his "twenty-five-cent special."

Probably the most important memorial of all is the great Sousa library of band music, presented to the University of Illinois. This great collection, packed in forty-two trunks, arrived at the university in November, 1932, during the regime of Austin A. Harding, director of bands at the university and a long-time personal and professional friend of Sousa. A preliminary inventory of twenty-five of these trunks revealed 2890 pieces of music for bands. A partial breakdown is given below:

110	Sousa marches
37	grand marches
57	other marches
375	vocal solos
237	overtures
78	grand operas
164	light operas
204	waltzes
37	gavottes and old-time dances
15	choruses, sacred and operatic
43	instrumental solos
123	violin solos
91	potpourri
120	fantasias, caprices, scenes
193	suites and ballets
41	reminiscences
97	rhapsodies, tone poems
73	introductions, finales
275	songs and serenades
2370	total

Mark H. Hindsley, present director of bands, is of the opinion that when a careful inventory of all forty-two trunks is taken, there will probably be considerably more than three thousand complete arrangements for concert band, hundreds of them in manuscript as prepared for Sousa's Band. Crowded facilities at present make a proper inventory impossible, but a contemplated new band building will include space for the Sousa library, where it can be adequately catalogued and stored. When this is accomplished, the University of Illinois will have the most extensive library of band music in America.

With the music library will also be exhibited Sousa's music rack and his podium. The latter is of special interest. For many years it served the dual purpose of a trunk for the music rack as well as being a podium. Every musician who played with Sousa remembers this podium, about four feet square and covered first with a red carpet and in later years with a green carpet.

Originally it was somwhat higher than it is now. As Sousa grew older, he kept shaving down the height, until at last he had reduced it by four inches. This is about the only concession he ever made to his advancing age. This plain but celebrated podium has, therefore, been a kind of inverse gauge for measuring the musical stature of Sousa. As the podium grew lower and lower, the nation's admiration and affection for Sousa grew higher and higher.

Sixteen
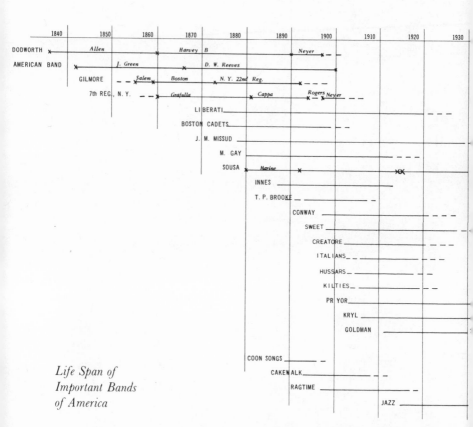

EPILOGUE

BY THE

GOLDMAN BAND

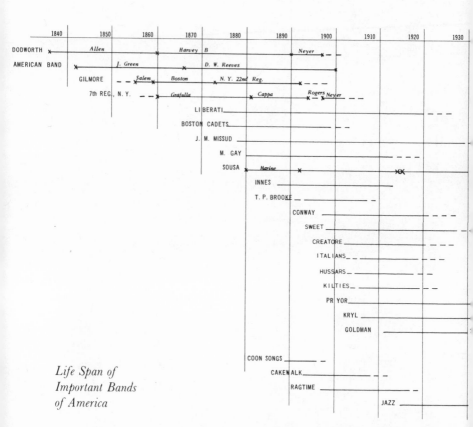

	1840	1850	1860	1870	1880	1890	1900	1910	1920	1930
DODWORTH	×	Allen		Harvey	B		Neyer × —			
AMERICAN BAND	×	J. Green		D. W. Reeves						
GILMORE		— — ×Salem×	Boston	× N. Y. 22nd Reg.		× — — —				
7th REG. N. Y.		— — ×	Grafulla	× Cappa	Rogers Neyer	× — × — — —				
LIBERATI								— — —		
BOSTON CADETS						— —				
J. M. MISSUD										
M. GAY						— — —				
SOUSA	× Marine	×			××					
INNES										
T. P. BROOKE	—	— —								
CONWAY					— — —					
SWEET										
CREATORE					— — —					
ITALIANS	— —			— — —						
HUSSARS	—									
KILTIES	—				— —					
PRYOR										
KRYL										
GOLDMAN										
COON SONGS		—								
CAKEWALK			— — —							
RAGTIME			— —							
JAZZ										

*Life Span of
Important Bands
of America*

*This graph was prepared to serve as a quick reference and it is not intended to
be a complete record of bands of the era. The 1910 peak of prestige and popularity of the concert band, often referred to in the text, is not fully reflected in
the graph. Simplification made it necessary to omit many bands which sprang
up shortly before 1910 and died shortly after.*

On June 22, 1953, the Goldman Band, under Dr. Edwin Franko Goldman, played an important concert in New York. Many notables were present, including New York Mayor Vincent Pelletterri and the famous modern composers and conductors Aaron Copland, Morton Gould, and Percy Grainger.

This concert marked the two-thousandth performance of the Goldman Band under the sponsorship of the Guggenheim family, and the forty-first anniversary of founding of the Goldman Band. It also happened to be the one-hundredth anniversary of Monsieur Louis Antoine Jullien's series of celebrated concerts, which "rang up the curtain" on the Golden Age of Bands of Music.

Without implying that Bands of Music are a thing of the past this concert by the Goldman Band furnished a fitting epilogue to the story on bands of America, and in a dramatic way "rang down the curtain." The famous business bands of Gilmore, Liberati, Brooke, Innes, Sousa, Creatore, Pryor, Conway, Kryl, and Sweet are no more. For over a half century they trouped across the continent, bringing great music to millions. Only in America, home of free enterprise, could such bands exist. They marked an era and fulfilled their destiny.

A new kind of concert band has taken their place, and the man who best typifies this new kind of band and marks this transition is Dr. Goldman. The Goldman Band survived the automobile, the phonograph, the movies, and the radio, powerful forces which crushed the famous bands of yesteryear. For three decades it has stood as America's foremost symbol of what a modern concert band should be.

Goldman was one of the few pupils of Jules Levy, celebrated cornet virtuoso. He once tried out for a position in Sousa's Band but was turned down only because there was no vacancy at the time. When he was seventeen years old he became a trumpeter with the Metropolitan Opera Orchestra, and for a number of years he played under the most famous opera conductors of the time.

In 1912 he formed his first band, known at that time as the New York Military Band. This was a sort of experiment of Goldman, in which he sought to demonstrate his idea of what a concert band could be if it were comprised of the finest musicians, devoted itself to regular rehearsals, and played only the very best in music.

For several years he supported the Goldman Band by public subscriptions and played regular summer concerts on the campus of Columbia University and on the Mall in Central Park. In 1924, Daniel and Murry Guggenheim and their wives underwrote the band's efforts, and since 1930 these concerts have been sponsored by the Daniel and Florence Guggenheim Foundation as the Guggenheim Memorial Concerts, a gracious gift by a music-loving family to the citizens of New York.

Although the Goldman Band is a local band, through radio it has been shared with the nation. Furthermore the personal influence of the great conductor of the Goldman Band has spread from coast to coast. For many years he championed various movements of which the aim was to raise the standards of musical performance by the concert band. He battled for original compositions, written by eminent composers, expressly for band performance. He advocated improvements in instrumentation of the concert band and in more adequate publication of band music.

In school band contests and festivals he officiated as judge and adjudicator all over America, giving generously of his time, criticizing shortcomings, and offering helpful suggestions for improving teaching methods.

In 1929 he called a meeting of prominent bandmasters, including Sousa, and the American Bandmasters Association was founded. Dr. Goldman was elected its first president, and after holding the office for three years he was elected honorary life president. Through this association of leading bandmasters many reforms have been achieved for the benefit of American bands.

Dr. Goldman composed approximately one hundred musical works. His march *On the Mall* is currently rated as the most played march next to Sousa's *The Stars and Stripes Forever.* Among his influential books are *The Foundation to Cornet Playing, The Goldman Band System,* and *Band Betterment.* His son, Richard Franko Goldman, for twenty years shared his father's labors in the band field. His book *The Band's Music* is a powerful statement of the Goldman doctrine on improved instrumentation and music for bands.

When Dr. Goldman died in February 1956, he was universally acknowledged the "Dean of American Bandmasters," holding a place in the annuals of American bands second only to that of John Philip Sousa, whom he revered and whom he once characterized as "the most popular and universally loved conductor who ever lived."

Index

Abt, Franz, 108
After the Ball, 157
Ahlborn, George, 254
Ahner, 88
Alexander, Russell, 173
Alexander Band, 124
All We, Like Sheep, Have Gone Astray, 71
Allentown Band (Pa.) 63, 81, 124, 149, 163, 169, 279
Amateur Journal, The, 82
American Band, 63, 80, 123, 129, 138, 139, 163
American Bandmasters Association, 263, 310
American Brass Band, 40
American Quadrille, 22, 24
Anvil Chorus, 60, 68, 73
Anvils, use of, 17, 68, 73, 75, 130
Appleton's magazine, 210, 211
Arban, Joseph Jean B. L., 110
Arbuckle, Matthew, 21, 22, 84, 85, 86, 89, 90, 92, 93, 95, 99, 108, 109–15, 286; cornet duel with Levy, 110–13
Asbury Park, 242, 281, 282, 283
ASCAP, 260
Ash, Paul, 288
Askins, Harry, 289

Austin, F., 127
Away with Melancholy, 33

Bagley, 108
Bagley, E. E., 166
Baker, Elden, 131, 140
Balatha, 88
Baldwin, J. Thomas, 69, 70, 98, 129, 163
Band contests, 77, 205–6
Banda Rosa, 186, 205, 212, 236
Bands: adult amateur, 169–77; brass, 41; brass and reed, 41: chautauqua, 244–50; Civil War, 51; after Civil War, 78–83; civilian versus military, 123–25; Gilmore's new idea for, 44–45, 83, 96, 97, 99, 101, 121–25, 150, 270; instrumentation trends in, 51, 71, 78, 81, 82, 104, 105, 125, 128–29, 131, 132, 192, 205–6; and orchestras, giant, 16, 17–18, 51, 60–63, 96, 102–3, 121, 265–67, 276–77; reed and brass, 78, 79, 105, 106, 107, 128, 129
Bands, business, beginning of, 150–51, 171–77, 187; Brooke, Thomas P., 133, 148, 184; Conway, Patrick, 242; Creatore, Giuseppe, 215, 216; Innes, Frederick N., 126–28, 179; Kryl,

Bands *(cont.)*
  Bohumir, 235–36; Liberati, Alessandro,
    125, 133, 177; Pryor, Arthur, 238, 239;
    Sousa, John Philip, 125–26, 134, 143,
    146, 147–50, 167; Sweet, Albert, 244–
    46
Barnetz, Captain Price L., 63
Barnum, P. T., 20, 23, 90, 109
Bartow, William, 279
Battle Hymn of the Republic, The, 46, 48, 50,
    65
Baull, 131
Bayer, Fred, 292–93
Baynes, William, 122
Becker, Rudolph, 148, 149, 299, 305
Beethoven, Jullien's playing of, 28, 29
Begnis, Giuseppe de, 19
Belgian Guides, 108
Bell, Bill, 303
Bellstedt, Herman, 163, 232, 235, 236
Bellstedt & Ballenberg Band, 163, 180, 186
Bent, B. C. (Ben), 89, 90, 92, 93, 94, 108,
    114, 116, 120, 121, 130, 179, 229
Bent, Thomas C., 179
Bent Bros. Military Band, 116
Bergmann, Carl, 88
Berlioz, Hector, 17, 61, 12, 14
Bernstein, 93
Berv, Isadore, 279, 280
Besson, 110
Bianco, Emilio, 280
Biese, Paul, 288
Birmingham *Post,* 199
Blakely, David, 119, 134, 145, 146, 147,
    149, 150, 151, 153, 160, 161, 189
Blauert, Otto, 149
Bode, Albert, 130, 131, 139, 286
Boese, Thomas, 56
Booth, Clarence, 298
Borrelli, James, 280, 292
Boston Band, 205
Boston Brass Band, 16, 38, 40–43, 122
Boston Brigade Band, 41, 44, 45, 97, 270
Boston Cadet Band, 69, 98, 116, 129, 163
Boston Conservatory founded, 56
Boston *Herald,* 203
Boston Music Hall, 45, 47, 53, 60

Boston Musical Instrument Company, 82
Boston Philharmonic, 57
Boston Symphony Orchestra, 88
Bottesini, 21
Boyer, James F., 112
Bracht, F., 93
Brehany, Louise, 261
Broatmann, 127
Brockton Band (Mass.), 16, 98, 124, 163
Bronson, Colonel Howard, 263
Brooke, Thomas Preston, 16, 17, 116–18,
    126, 133, 155, 169, 181, 184–86, 192,
    193, 194, 212, 224–28, 229, 236, 239,
    244, 252, 270, 289, 309; and Chicago
    Marine Band, 181, 184–86, 192, 193,
    194, 212, 224–28; as composer, 117;
    "Popular Music King," 17, 185; as
    trombone player, 117
Brooklyn Philharmonic Society, 86, 89, 103
Brown Brothers, Six, 252
Bruggman, 130
Bugle, E♭ keyed, 31–39
Bull, Ole, 18, 19, 66
Burlesque shows, 53
Buys, Dr. Peter, 291–92, 298–99

Cakewalk, 203, 204, 226, 287
Campbell, A. J., 177
Cannon, use of, 51, 68, 73, 75, 130
Cappa, Carlo Alberto, 16, 114, 119, 127,
    129, 144, 240
Carley, R. W., 63
Carlo, De, 93, 130
Carnival of Venice, 111, 230
Carr, Carroll, 302
Carter, T. M., 163
Carthage Light Guard Band (Mo.), 170
Cassassa, Charles H., 213, 222, 260, 261,
    278
Cassassa's Cornet Band, 213
Castle Garden, 21, 22, 24
Cavanagh, 130
Centennial Exposition, Philadelphia, 95–
    101, 157
Central Park, 79, 122, 309
Central Park Garden, 88, 90, 91

Chandler, Daniel H., 63
Charlestown, Mass., 40, 43, 44
Chautauqua bands, 244–50
Chiaffarelli, 222
Chiari, de, 130
Chicago festival, 72–75
Chicago Marine Band, 181, 184–86, 192, 193, 194, 212, 224–28
Chicago Philharmonic Society, 88
Chicago Symphony Orchestra, 157
Chicago *Tribune,* 75, 218–19, 225, 296
Church Company, John, 155
Cimera, Jaroslav (Jerry), 236
Cincinnati Philharmonic Orchestra, 88
Cincione, Philip, 273
Clappé, Arthur A., 183
Clarinet, bass, 78
Clarke, Edwin, 254, 257
Clarke, Ernest, 131, 134
Clarke, Herbert L., 120, 134–36, 139, 140, 141, 164, 165, 194, 201–02, 209, 211, 241, 252, 254, 259, 286, 291
Clarke, Tom, 179
Cleveland Gray's Band, 129
Cleveland *Leader,* 218
Coates, Thomas, 63, 80
Coleman, Harry, 148, 154, 155
Concerts, Gilmore's promenade, 45, 46, 47, 48, 50, 86, 109
Conrad, Herman, 131, 134, 183, 192
Conterno's Band, 180, 205
Conway, 127
Conway, Patrick, 16, 234, 242–44, 250, 260, 261, 270, 274, 278–81, 309; as cornet soloist, 244; Military Band School of, 281
Cooke, Dr. James Francis, 161, 286, 287, 302
Coon-Sanders, 288
Copland, Aaron, 309
Corey, Ralph, 200, 202, 254
Cornell Cadet Band, 242
Cornet, E♭, 32, 34, 35, 36, 82
Cornet, rotary-valve, 82
Corrado's Italian Band, 222
Courtois, Antoine, 110
Couturier, E. A., 142

Cox, John, 130, 148, 290
Creatore, Francesco, 222
Creatore, Giuseppe, 16, 17, 212–23, 232, 233, 236, 239, 244, 248, 270, 271–72, 274, 288, 289, 309; as trombone player, 213
Cusimano, Charles, 280

Darling Nellie Gray, 53
Davis, Arthur C., 280
Delany, 127
DeLuca, Joseph, 202, 232, 273, 279, 280, 297, 304
Detroit National Guard Band, 98, 99
Ditson, Oliver, 58
Ditson & Co., Oliver, 45, 58
Dodge Brothers Concert Band, 274
Dodworth, Allen, 41, 42, 78
Dodworth Band, 40, 41, 47, 50, 78, 79, 80, 83, 108, 109
Dodworth, Harvey, 33, 47, 50, 63, 78, 79, 80, 108, 128
Dodworth & Co., 45
Dodworth family, 41, 45, 78
Dodworth's Brass Band School, 42
Dolan, John, 279, 286, 305
Dolgorovsky, Princess, 93–94
Dominant magazine, 183
Donatelli, 222
Downing, D. L., 78, 79, 80, 114, 155, 244
Drum, bass, largest ever built, 23, 66–67, 181
Dublin *Mail,* 199
Dunbar, Ralph, 246
Duss Band, 229, 234
Dwight, John S., 25, 56, 57, 58, 68, 71
Dyhrenfurth, 88

Easton Band (Pa.), 63, 80
Ebert, Thomas, 142
Ebor cornos, 37, 78
Eichberg, Julius, 56, 57, 60, 68
El Capitan, 194, 263
Elgin Watch Factory Band, 129
Elkins, Eddie, 288
Ellington, Duke, 204
Emerson, Walter, 108, 114, 115, 116

Ernst, Alfred, 205
Etude, The, magazine, 286
Ewing's Zuave Band, 275

Fagotti, 127
Falcone, Mario, 280
Farmer, H. G., 18, 108
Fast, H. C., 142
Ferulla, 222, 234
5th Regiment Band (Mass.), 124
5th Regiment Band (Ohio), 177
Fireman's Quadrille, 27
1st Brigade Band (Colo.), 129
1st Brigade Band (Pa.), 124
1st Regiment Band (Cal.), 213
Fitchburg Band (Mass.), 129
Flagg, Eben, 41
Flagg's Brass Band, 40
Fletcher, William, 155, 301
Florio, Salvatore, 273
Foster, Stephen, 48, 53
Foster, William, 149
4th Regiment Band (Mo.), 238
Freudenvoll, Charles W., 104, 137, 138, 147, 150
Fries, Henry, 77
Fritz, Ed, 149
Fry, William H., 25–26
Fulgum, Ralph, 296
Fuller, Bob, 296
Funaro, Pasquale C., 202, 229, 273

Gallo, Stanislao, 221, 222
Gallo's Primary Italian Band, 222
Garde de Paris Band, 77
Garde Républicaine Band, 69, 71, 191–92, 205, 260
Gargiulo, 222, 234
Garing, A. J., 254
Garry Owen, 83, 267
Gay, Mace, 16, 98, 163
Gerhardt, Paul, 305
Germania Society, 20, 57, 223
Gerts, Frank, 272
Giannone, Erminio, 177, 273

Gilmore, Patrick S., 16, 21, 22, 30, 31–142, 147, 159, 164, 167, 200, 259, 261, 277, 309; and bands, new idea for, 44–45, 83, 96, 97, 99, 101, 121–25, 150, 270; and band versus orchestra, 132; as composer, 51, 85, 138; concerts by, promenade, 45, 46, 47, 48, 50, 86, 109; as cornet soloist, 34–35, 40, 85–86, 92; compared with Sousa, 159; and 22nd Regiment Band (N.Y.), 49, 76–101, 167, 179, 180
Gilmore Band Library Publishing Company, P. S., 142
Gilmore & Co., 54
Gilmore Garden, 90, 95, 102–3, 108
Gilmore, Graves and Co., 54
Gilmore & Russell, 43
Gladiator, The, 154
Gleason's Pictorial Drawing-Room Companion, 40, 41, 42
Glenville Brass Band (N.Y.), 82, 83
Godfrey, Dan, 77
Goldkette, Gene, 288
Goldman, Dr. Edwin Franko, 114, 263, 308–10; as composer, 310
Goldman, Richard Franko, 310
Goodman, Captain A., 63
Goodman's Band, 63
Gould, Morton, 309
Goulden, Howard, 292, 296
Grafulla, C. S., 79, 80, 108, 122, 155
Grainger, Percy, 309
Grand National Concert, New Orleans, 16, 49–53, 60
Green, Joseph, 40, 80
Greenleaf, James, 46
Gregory's Italian Band, 222
Grenadier Guards Band, 69, 71, 77, 105, 205
Grett, William, 183, 186
Grosshurt, Gus, 149
Guarante, Frank, 288
Guggenheim Memorial Concerts, 310
Gungl's Band, 223

Haines, Leroy, 241
Halgreen, Henry, 46

Hallett, Mal, 288
Handzlik, Leon, 279
Harding, Austin A., 305–6
Harper's Weekly, 128
Hartmann, John, 99, 111.
Hecker, Professor J., 129
Helleberg, August, 192, 232, 254, 280
Helmecke, Gus, 207, 263, 292, 303
Henegar, Russ, 159
Heney, Eddie, 303, 304
Heney, John, 302
Henning, W., 179
Henry, Hi, 112
Henschel, Georg, 88
Henton, H. Benne, 236, 279, 280
Herbert, Victor, 140–42, 164, 180
Hertz, Henri, 19, 95
Hess Grand Opera Company, C. D., 131
Higginson, Colonel Henry Lee, 88
High School Cadets, 154, 155, 166
Hindsley, Mark H., 306
Hinton, Colonel G. F., 190, 209
Hippodrome, Barnum's, 90, 109
History of the National Peace Jubilee and Grand Musical Festival, 54
Holton, Frank, 148
Holy, Holy, Holy! Lord God Almighty, 54
Hook, E. & G. G., 64, 65
Horner, Anton, 192
Howe, Julia Ward, 46
Hughes, 22, 23
Hughes, Rupert, 169
Hunky Dory, 203

"Ice Cold Cadets," 155
Immensaphone, 183, 184
Imperial Guards Band, Prussian, 77, 105
Innes, Frederick N., 16, 17, 96, 97, 98, 101, 116, 126–28, 133, 148, 169, 179–84, 186, 204, 229–35, 236, 239, 244, 248, 252, 270, 271, 274, 289, 309; and National School of Music, 271; and trill valve, 179–80; as trombone soloist, 97–98, 126, 179–80
Innes' Festival Band, 179, 180
Innes' Great Band, 127, 148

Instruction books, early, 42, 82
Instruments, keyed versus piston, 36, 37, 80; over-the-shoulder, 40, 41–42, 82; piston, 80
International Exhibition, Paris (1867), 77, 105
"Irish Orpheus," 16
Italian Bands, 187, 212–23, 289

Jabon, F., 148, 290
Jazz, 284, 287–89
Jeanie with the Light Brown Hair, 53
Jenkins Music Company, 204
Jingle Bells, 53
John Brown's Body, 46, 52
Jolson, Al, 27
Jones, Isham, 288
Jordon, Eben, 59, 69
Journal of Music, Dwight's, 25, 57, 58, 68
Jullien, Antoine, 15–30, 43, 58, 61, 84, 110, 122, 181, 217, 309; use of baton by, 28, 29

Kaiser Franz Grenadier Regiment Band, 69, 71, 77, 205
Kansas City Band, 129
Kansas City *Journal,* 217–18
Kegel, Carl, 93
Keller, Matthias, 66
Kendall, Edward (Ned), 31–39, 40
Kenecke, Emil, 240
Kilties Concert Band, 275
Kincaid, Owen, 304
Kirchner, Adolph, 181
Klinger, Martin, 163
Klose, 127
Knecht, Albert, 254, 255, 256, 257, 258, 259, 279, 303–4
Koch, Henry, 148, 290
Koenig, 21, 22, 110
Kroll and Reitzel, 79
Kryl, Bohumir, 16, 17, 164–65, 187, 225, 229, 230–33, 235, 236, 239, 244, 248, 270, 274, 276–78, 289, 299, 309; and

Kryl, Bohumir (cont.)
Bohemian Band, 276; as cornet soloist, 229, 230-32; and opera company, 277
Kryl, Josie, 277
Kryl, Marie, 277
Kuhn, John, 292

La Barre, Gene, 296
La Rocca, Nick, 287, 288
Lacalle, J., 139
Lasky, Jesse, 183
Lavalle, J., 179
Lavigne, 21
Lawton, Stanley, 254
Lazano, Pedro, 279, 280
Lefebre, E. A., 21, 84, 85, 86, 89, 93, 95, 99, 104, 130, 131, 139, 141
Letsch, F., 93, 94
Letsman, 93
Levy, Jules, 22, 90, 92, 93, 95, 97, 98, 99, 102, 108, 109-15, 200, 309; and American Military Band, 114; and cornet duel with Arbuckle, 110, 113; solo repertoire of, 111
Lewis, Ted, 284, 288
Liberati, Alessandro, 16, 17, 96, 98, 99, 101, 114-16, 125, 133, 134, 169, 177-79, 186, 190-91, 236, 238, 239, 244, 248, 252, 270, 272-74, 289, 309; as composer, 179, 273, 274; as cornet soloist, 114-16, 134, 273; and Grand Military Band, 177, 272; and World Renowned Liberati Band, The, 133
Liberty Bell, 155, 263
Lily Dale, 34
Lincoln (Neb.) Evening News, 230
Lind, Jenny, 20, 53, 89
Listen to the Mocking Bird, 53
London Daily Mail, 196-98
Lopez, Vincent, 288
Los Angeles Daily Times, 230-31
Los Angeles Examiner, 230, 232
Luedtka's Band, 222
Lyon, George, 63
Lyon, Marv, 149, 254, 290
Lyon & Healy, 63

MacDonald, Murdock, 275

Madison Square Garden, 109, 119, 136, 229
Maginel, F. A., 123
Manhattan Beach, 119, 131, 136, 159, 160, 161, 193, 303
Manhattan Beach, 155, 263
Mantia, Simone, 165, 200, 201, 202, 238, 240, 241, 258, 283
Manzi, Armando, 273
Mapleson Opera Company, 126, 127
Marching Along, 209, 290
"March King" title, 155, 165-66, 185
Marshall's Band, Topeka, Kan., 170
Mason, Arnold, 280
Mason, Lowell, 66
Mason & Hamlin Organ Co., 58
Maupin, William, 275
Maupin's Band, 275
May, Ollie, 282
Mead, Leon, 128-30, 169, 205
Meert, 127
Messinger, Robert, 148
Metropolitan Band, Chicago, 169
Metropolitan Band, Dayton, 129
Metropolitan Band, Detroit, 169
Meyers, Albertus, 279
Miel, 131
Military Bands in America (Mead), 128-30
Millhouse, Ross, 254
Minninger, William, 63
Minstrel shows, Negro, 53
Missud, Jean, 16, 123, 129, 155, 244
Mix, Emil, 254, 264
Modern Instrumentation and Orchestration, Berlioz, 61, 62
Mollenhauer, Emil, 205
Mollenhauer brothers, 21
Money Musk, 33, 39
Monroe, "Whoopie," 304
Morin, H., 179, 229
Morse, Francis, 33, 34
Moscow, Professor C. E., 63
Moscow's Band, 63
Mueller, Ernst, 139
Music, popular, appeal of, 146, 151, 157-58, 159, 260-61
Musical Courier, 139

Musical Protective Union, 86, 87
Musical World, 26
My Old Kentucky Home, 53

Nashville *American,* 182
Natiello, Ernesto, 222
National anthem, 65–66
National Emblem, The, 166
National Peace Jubilee, 16, 44, 54–69, 77, 130
Nearer, My God, to Thee, 54, 89, 278
Nearing, Turner, 275
Negro, Luke Del, 179, 192
New England Conservatory founded, 56
New Orleans, Grand National Concert, 16, 49–53, 60
New York *Courier and Enquirer,* 25, 28
New York *Herald,* 191
New York *Journal,* 216
New York Military Band, 309
New York Philharmonic, 88
New York *Sun,* 113
Neyer, Ernest, 79
9th Regiment Band (Pa.), 124
9th Regiment Band (N.Y.), 77, 79, 114
Nordica, Lillian, 104, 108, 126
Norton, Lillian. *See* Nordica, Lillian
Norrito, Joseph, 148, 254, 290
Nosses, Five, 252

Offenbach, Jacques, 96, 99, 100
Old Black Joe, 53
Oliver, King, 287
Omaha *Bee,* 274
Ophicleide, 36, 41, 181
"World's Largest," 23
Organ, Cabinet, 58; pipe, "world's largest," 64–65, 66
Orchestras, early symphonic, 88, 89
Ordway Brothers Music Store, 40

"Panic March," 163
Parepa-Rosa, Euphrosyne, 65, 67, 68, 94
Parks, summer amusement, list of, 234–35
Patti, Adelina, 53, 89
Patz, Gustav, 129
Paulus, 77
Pechin, Ernest, 279

Perfetto, John, 202, 254
Pew, Howard, 149, 151, 186, 212, 227
Philippine Constabulary Band, 205, 260
Philippini, Don, 220, 222, 234, 248, 288
Phinney, Frederick, 163, 234
Pittsburgh *Evening Chronicle,* 19
Poet and Peasant Overture, 53, 245
Polka, 22
Portland Band (Me.), 63
Power's Kilties, 275
President's Band of Mexico, 205
Presser Company, Theodore, 263
Pryor, Arthur, 16, 17, 133, 148, 155, 165, 187, 192, 194, 198–200, 202, 203–4, 210, 233, 237–42, 244, 250, 270, 274, 281–83, 289, 299, 309; and cakewalk and ragtime, 203–4; as composer and arranger, 198, 204, 239, 283; and profane language, 281–82; as recording pioneer, 239–40; as Trombone soloist, 198–200
Pryor, Arthur, Jr., 283
Pryor, Roger, 283
Pryor, Sam, 238
Pryor, Walter, 238

Quadrille, 22, 23

Raffayolo, Michael, 130, 131, 139, 200
Ragone, V., 179, 229
Ragtime, 203, 204, 225–26, 228, 287
Randall, Charles, 280
Raymond, Alice, 226
Reeves, D. W., 16, 63, 123, 129, 138, 139, 140, 150, 155, 163, 164, 173, 244; and American Band, 63, 80, 123, 129, 138, 139, 163; as composer, 155, 173
Rehrig, Harold, 279
Reichart, 21
Reitzel, Kroll and, 79
Reynolds, Everett R., 163, 189
Richardson, Jack, 301, 302
Ringgold Band, 81, 124, 163
Ringwall, Oscar, 177
Rise of Military Music, The, (Farmer), 108
Ritter, Frédéric L., 88
Ritze, 131
Rivela, 222
Rogers, Walter, 122, 240

Rolfe, B. A., 183

Root, Virginia, 253, 256

Rosa, Carl, 65

Rosander, Arthur, 295

Rosati, 234

Rose, Eugene, 210

Royal Artillery Band, 77

Rupp, 130

Russ, Gabe, 305

Russell, Clarence (Bus), 254, 297, 301, 302

Russell, Joseph M., 43

Russell & Tolman, 45

Ruzzi, 222

St. Louis Symphony Orchestra, 205

Salem Brass Band, 31, 39, 43, 44

Salem Cadet Band, 123, 129, 163

Salli, Di, 177

Samuels, E. A., 82

San Diego City Guard Band, 113

Santa Claus symphony, 25, 26

Saro, 77, 108

Satriano, 222

Saxhorns, 37, 42, 78, 82, 132

Saxonians, 223

Saxophones, 78

Saxtrombas, 37

Schaich, S., 149

Schensley, 296

Schuler, John, 202

Schultz, 109

Scotch Highlanders, 275

Seavy, Hod, 186, 192

2nd Regiment Band (Ill.), 121, 123

Seltzer, Frank, 140

Semper Fidelis, 145, 154, 166

Senna, Paul, 254

Seventh Air Varie (De Bériot), 85, 99, 111

7th Regiment Band (N.Y.), 79, 83, 108, 114, 122, 127, 129, 144

71th Regiment Band (N.Y.), 125

73rd Regiment Band (Austria), 77

Seymour, Charles, 89, 90, 163

Shaap E., 179, 229

Shannon, Thomas, 139

Shaw, J. F., 100

Shelburne Falls Military Band, 63, 82

Simon, Frank, 297

Simons, Gardelle, 200, 202, 229, 278, 280, 281

69th Regiment Band (N.Y.), 122

Slantz, Jim, 304

Smith, Bert, 241

Smith, Jerome, 34, 43

Smith, J. F. O., 82

Smith, Walter, 148, 240

Smoky Mokes, 203

Smyth, 77

Sorrentino, Eugenio, 212, 236, 239

Sousa, John Philip, 16, 17, 21, 30, 96, 99, 100, 101, 105, 125, 126, 134, 138, 143–48, 148–67, 186, 187, 189–209, 222, 238, 244, 251–68, 270, 274, 278, 284–307, 309, 310; band library of, 305–6; on band versus orchestra, 192; and chautauqua, dislike for, 248, 250; at Chicago World's Fair, 147, 157–59; command performances by, 194–96; as composer and arranger, 101, 125, 145, 154, 155, 157–58, 161–62, 195, 198, 203, 207, 261, 267, 298–99, 304; Gilmore compared with, 159; and instrumentation for bands, 191–92; and jazz, 287–89; marches of, five best street, 166; marches, publishers of, 154, 155, 263; marches revised by Helmecke, 263; "March King," 155, 185; musical instruments played by, 100, 261; origin of name of, 208–9; and phonograph, attack on, 210–11, 241, 286–87; and rehearsals, 149–50, 156–57; road band of, 159, 165, 166–67, 209, 259, 291; at St. Louis World's Fair, 203–6; at San Francisco Exposition, 260–61; showmanship of, 162–63, 255, 258, 261; style of, 262–63; and tempo, increase in, 144, 263–64; in U. S. Navy, 264–68

Sousa Band Fraternity Society, 305

Spaeth, Sigmund, 158, 162

Specht, Paul, 288

Specht's Georgians, 288

Staats, 148, 290

Stanley Opera Company, 148
Stars and Stripes Forever, The, origin of, 161–63
Steckelberg, 109
Stengler, August, 130, 140
Stockigt, 130
Stokowski, Leopold, 262
Stonewall Brigade Band, 63, 81, 84, 124
Strauss, Johann, 69, 70, 155, 208
Strauss, Richard, 193
Stross, 127
Stross, Richard, 286
Sullivan, Frank, 162, 166, 299–300
Sweet, Albert, 16, 17, 28, 187, 234, 244–50, 252, 270, 274–76, 289, 309; and White Hussars Band, 17, 244–50, 252, 274–76

Ta-ra-ra-boom-deay, 158
Terrace Garden, 88, 90
3rd Regiment Band (Neb.), 170
3rd U. S. Cavalry Band (St. Louis), 170
13th Regiment Band (N.Y.), 50, 78, 116, 128, 133, 148, 180, 181
Thomas, Theodore, 22, 53, 86, 88, 89, 90, 91, 108, 111, 122, 157, 158
Thunderer, The, 154, 166
Thursby, Emma, 86, 87, 89, 93, 103–4
Tobin, 127
Toledo City Band, 129
Tolman & Co., H., 52
Tommasino, Alfredo, 221, 222, 234
Tong, Billy, 305
Toscanini, 282, 299
Tour, Columbian, 132, 137–39, 147, 150
Tour, Gilmore's European, 104–8
Tour, Sousa's World, 209, 210, 211, 251–59
Tourjée, Eben, 56, 59, 63, 64, 68
Tours, Sousa's European, 189–209; of Thomas and Gilmore, 87, 88, 89
Trognitz, R. E., 113, 273
Trout, 127
Tuba, BB♭ bass, 78; largest ever made, 181–84, 185, 186
24th Volunteer Regiment Band (Mass.), 46, 47, 84

22nd Regiment Band (N.Y.), 49, 76–101, 167, 179, 180

Unger, 88
U. S. Marine Band, 69, 77, 80, 100, 105, 126, 129, 134, 143–48, 151, 260, 264, 265
Upham, Dr., 56, 57, 60
Upton, George P., 75
Urbani, F., 139
Uri, Matus, 130

Van der Stucken, 88
Variations, Proch's, 89, 103
Verdi's Italian Band, 222
Vereecken, Ben, 254
Vessella, Marco, 220, 222, 232, 234, 236, 239, 248
Veterans Corps Band, Baltimore, 170
Vohkins, 131

Wadsworth, F. W., 139
Wall, Charlie, 305
Wall, Eddie, 301, 302, 304
Wall, Edmund A., 254
Walrabe, 109
Waring, Fred, 28
Washington *Evening Star,* 147
Washington Park on the Delaware, 177–79
Washington *Post,* 43
Washington Post, The, 154, 166, 193, 194, 259
Weaver, Buck, 292, 305
Weber, Ernest, 131
Weber's Band, 205, 234
Weil, William, 163, 204, 233, 236
Weldon, Fred, 121, 123, 163, 164, 173, 234
Weston, Harry, 131
When Band (Indianapolis), 120, 164, 165
When Johnny Comes Marching Home, 52
Whirlwind (Levy), 111, 135
White, William Carter, 295
White Hussars, 17, 244–50, 252, 274–76
Whiteman, Paul, 288
Whittier, Harry, 131, 179, 200
Wieprecht, 61, 77, 78

Williams, 127
Williams, Ernest, 280
Willow Grove, 159, 177–78, 180, 186, 193, 202, 213, 214, 242, 252, 264, 278, 279
Wilson, 131
Wind-Band and Its Instruments, The, 183
Winter, Joseph, 81, 163
Wise, Joe, 179
Wood Up Quickstep, 32, 33, 34, 35, 36
World Peace Jubilee, 16, 49, 69–71
Wrecker's Daughter, The, 33, 39

Wright, E. G., 54
Wright, Gilmore & Co., 54
Wuille, 21

Zach, Max, 205
Zedeler, Nicoline, 253
Zerr, Anna, 23, 27
Zerrahn, Carl, 56, 57, 59, 61, 62, 68, 88
Zilm, 131
Zimmerman, 77
Zimmerman, Leo, 202, 240

77011